THE
TV GUIDE
TV BOOK

40 Years of the
all-time greatest:
TELEVISION
Facts, Fads, Hits,
and History

THE
TV GUIDE
TV BOOK

40 Years of the all-time greatest:
TELEVISION
Facts, Fads, Hits, and History

By Ed Weiner & the Editors of TV GUIDE

HarperPerennial
A Division of HarperCollinsPublishers

FIRST EDITION

Designed by Evangelist & Kreloff

Library of Congress Cataloging-in-Publication Data

The TV guide TV book / Ed Weiner and editors of
TV guide. —
    1st ed.
        p.   cm.
    ISBN 0-06-055325-1 / ISBN 0-06-096914-8 (pbk.)
    1. Television programs—United States—
Miscellanea. 2. Television programs—United
States—Quotations, maxims, etc. 3. United
States—Popular culture. I. Weiner, Ed. II. TV guide.
PN1992.9.T83 1992   92-52633
791.45'75'0973—dc20

92 93 94 95 96 ◆/RRD 10 9 8 7 6 5 4 3 2 1
92 93 94 95 96 ◆/RRD 10 9 8 7 6 5 4 3 2 1 (pbk.)

197 8275

For Hilda and Sam Weiner, whose purchase of a TV back in 1950 started an infant's lifelong obsession; and for Ginger Restemeyer, who has to put up with it now.

"It hasn't turned out as I expected."
—Dr. Vladimir Zworykin, the "father of television," 1967

CONTENTS

ACKNOWLEDGMENTS

Thanks must go to the following, who helped to provide, clarify, winnow, slice, dice, check and double-check, urge, advise, cajole, shepherd and soothe—all so that this modest volume might attain some of its immodest goals:

At *TV Guide:* Joe Robinowitz, Barry Golson, Roger Youman, Teresa Hagan, Peter Abel, Pat Murphy, Helene Curley and all those in Radnor's National Editorial and National Programming departments who cared enough to ask.

At HarperCollins: Craig Nelson and Jennifer Hull.

As well as: Superagent Lisa Bankoff at ICM, and Jennifer Shenk, whose last-minute and hurried hip-deep wading into the morass of information to find the truth amidst the myth and press-agentry was greatly appreciated.

And finally to Steven Jobs and Stephen Wozniak, creators of the Macintosh computer, and to Chester Carlson, father of the photocopying process, without whose inventions this book would not have been possible.

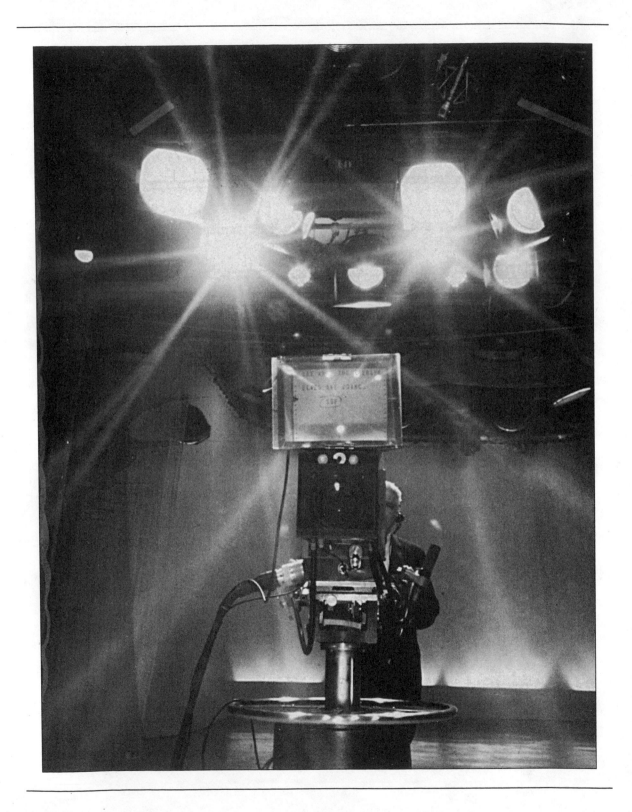

Introduction

While we were doing the research for this book—reading every page of the more than 2,000 issues published since Day One, wading through the room of floor-to-ceiling file cabinets stuffed to overflowing with familiar and unique photo images—one piece of information repeated itself and rose above the rest: There has never been anything like *TV Guide*. No other publication has ever dominated its area of concentration so completely and so successfully as this one has. Not *Sports Illustrated,* not *Popular Mechanics,* not *Cosmopolitan* or *Vogue* or the *National Enquirer* or *Time* or *Prevention,* not even *National Geographic.*

Here's the test that proves it: Name another mass-audience magazine about television, with local listings and feature articles, that can be found at the newsstand you frequent or the supermarket you shop at. You can't. There isn't one. And those slim, underdetailed Sunday-supplement listings booklets are distant cousins, poor relations, trying to get by on gilt by association.

For 40 years, without fail, *TV Guide* has been the world's most popular magazine about the world's most popular entertainment-and-information medium. The two were made for, and grew with and helped nurture, each other. Playing a delicate balancing game—like rolling across a high wire on a tricycle—*TV Guide* has been television's peppiest cheerleader, its most acute critic, and its chief Boswell. It is a difficult role that it has played with distinction.

Merely to skim the pages tells the whole story. Writers as diverse and opinionated as Margaret Mead, Joe McGinnis, S. J. Perelman, Arthur Schlesinger, Jr., Garrison Keillor, David Bradley, Katharine Hepburn, Dr. Ruth Westheimer, Isaac Asimov, Peter Bogdanovich, Stephen King, and President Gerald Ford have provided articles for *TV Guide.* Erich Segal and William F. Buckley, Jr., contributed short stories to it. Betty Friedan examined the woman's image on TV. Gloria Steinem told "Why I Consider *Cagney and Lacy* the best show on TV." Joyce Carol Oates wrote in praise of *Hill Street Blues.*

Along with its staple of personality profiles, *TV Guide* explored issues of the times—as they affected and were affected by television—in multipart series about black Americans involved in broadcasting and covered by it, feminism, the Vietnam War, gay rights, and coverage of politics; it once spent nearly an entire issue probing the relationship between TV and the troubles in Northern Ireland. It probed and dissected the creatures of its own particular environment: the networks, and who ran them; news operations, and how they decided what we would see and be told; ratings services, and what their numbers meant; the government, and how it ruled and shaped what went over the airwaves. And, from its early editions on, *TV Guide* understood that the TV we watched did not exist in a vacuum, and it strove always to place U.S. TV in its proper international context.

To complement its news and features, *TV Guide* felt it had an editorial obligation, and often just a burning need, to drop the reporter's objective mask in order to comment and opinionize—angrily, wryly, whimsically, wistfully—about what was happening on home screens and how they happened to happen: trends, errors, industry and management decisions, the involvement or apathy of the American viewing public. "As We See It" served that function. Usually no more than about 500 words per column, it was *TV Guide*'s intellectual and emotional outlet for nearly 30 years. At the time, the *TV Guide* editors who wrote it surely had no sense of longevity about these shoot-from-the-hip, lively, and seemingly perishable pieces—they merely gave vent to whatever *TV Guide* thought needed underscoring, excoriating, applauding, analyzing, or simply scratching one's head over that week. Seen now, though, the "As We See It" columns are nothing less than a wonderfully concise, well-written, and thoroughly thoughtful and consistent social history of television, unlike any other. To read them is to understand the context of TV viewing, and to appreciate the personal and private love/disappointment relationship we've all had with it since the first test pattern. We've included whole and partial "As We See It"s in this volume, along with the feature that succeeded them: the far more nuts-and-bolts, thumbs-up/thumbs-down "Cheers 'n' Jeers."

In words and photos, *TV Guide* quickly established itself as the magazine of record for television—if you wanted to know about it, and it was about TV, it probably appeared in *TV Guide*. Using that material, shepherding it, shaping it, we've created a book that is no standard A-to-Z history of the medium, nor is it an almanac or merely a book of facts and lists. It is, rather, a scrapbook of shreds and bits and pieces of shared experience, a book of memories harking back to a simpler time when everybody watched Uncle Miltie, and moving up to the present, with its scores of specialized channels, a fragmented audience, and, perhaps, a regrettable loss of sense of community.

A television screen is made up of thousands of small dots, pieces of information that, when illuminated and seen from a few steps back, form one single cohesive image: the TV picture. From the thousands of small pieces of information in these pages we hope the reader will step back and get the picture—and the sense of excitement and fun and the feel of what TV has meant to us all. To the writers, editors, and photographers whose intelligence, energy, and creativity illuminated and informed those pieces of shared experience over the 40-year history of *TV Guide*—and to the people, shows, and magical moments that are the story of TV—this book is dedicated.

TURNING ON, TUNING IN

To hear the more intemperate critics tell it, television is one of the most dangerous forces in American life.

In the '50s, it was claimed that TV would kill the art of conversation. We were also warned that TV would ruin everyone's eyesight, and told that so much sitting down (while watching TV, of course) augured ill for the National Lower Back.

Nowadays we hear that sex and violence on TV will destroy the moral fiber of the country, and that commercials in children's shows are turning youngsters into tiny consumers with distorted values. It seems like only yesterday (and it probably was) that FCC Commissioner Nicholas Johnson was saying that commercials for drugs (aspirin, stomach balm, other menaces) have made TV "the principal pusher to a junkie nation."

It must be a source of continual amazement to such critics to find, upon waking up each morning, that the Republic still stands. The critics may be surprised, but they won't be stopped: we learned recently that television stands accused of yet another crime.

Television, says a man we'll allow to remain nameless, is to blame for at least a part of the current energy crisis.

The man cites a Nielsen report that viewing has increased 16 minutes a day—almost 100 hours a year—in the average U.S. home. With the average TV set consuming as much as 350 watts an extra 100 hours a year in almost 65 million homes, *extra viewing alone* burns up more than 2 billion kilowatt-hours a year. Energy crisis? Blame television.

What to do? You *could* turn off your set and see if the Nation's woes magically disappear. But that is so unlikely that we don't recommend it at all—unless, of course, you're a myopic, noncommunicative drug addict with shattered morals, no furnace fuel and chronic lower-back pain.

June 2, 1973

1

Everywhere You Looked

Once TV sets became practically a part of the family, you could have them any way you wanted, take them anywhere you wished, find them designed in any cocka-mamie fashion you could imagine. A pleasant day in the country, staring at the TV, ignoring one another and the natural world, was made possible by early models that got power from your car's cigarette lighter. Portables came in various colors, shapes, materials, and levels of portability. The G.E. "Custom Design" became just another shish-kebob element on a living-room pole that also included a table, a light, and a planter. Philco's 1959 model had a nice flair, a big screen, and a clock, and RCA's "Hillsborough" model could be, as the publicity for it trumpeted, "converted from a console TV into a handsome living room table by a simple folding of the TV set out of sight into the recessed portion of the cabinet." But, of course, the high point of portability, luxury, and decadence was, as the woman here is doing, watching a March of Dimes telethon on your car television. In the back seat, of course.

We Will Control the Horizontal, We Will Control the Vertical

Local trouble cards from the 1950s

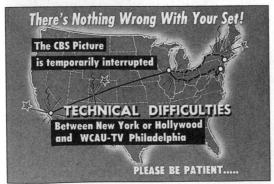

The Home Front

Does television keep children from reading? Does it affect their school grades? Their vocabularies? Does it make them listless? Aggressive?

Some answers to these questions are to be found in the latest report from Dr. Paul A. Witty of the School of Education at Northwestern University. Ever since 1949 Dr. Witty has been conducting continuing studies in Chicago area elementary schools on the effect of television on children. In the report on his 1965 survey, Dr. Witty cites his own findings and those of other authorities to support some conclusions that will interest parents.

Dr. Witty: "TV offers not an obstacle to reading; actually it can be a source of stimulation and incentive."

A Stanford University study: "On the basis of data at hand we cannot say that heavy television viewing, at any stage of the elementary school, significantly lowers school grades."

A number of studies show that children in TV homes have better vocabularies when entering school than children who have not been exposed to television. But, says Dr. Witty, "Our studies suggest that the initial gains in the vocabulary of young children will not persist unless there are efforts to sustain them."

A British study: "Even heavy viewing does not necessarily make children more aggressive or listless."

Perhaps the most surprising aspect of Dr. Witty's findings has been the evidence of growing sophistication in children's viewing tastes. In 1949 the favorites among the elementary school students he studied were *Hopalong Cassidy, Howdy Doody, Lone Ranger,* Milton Berle and Arthur Godfrey. In 1965 children in the same grades of the same schools picked as their favorites *Man from U.N.C.L.E., Bewitched, Shindig, The Addams Family, My Favorite Martian* and *Bonanza.*

August 6, 1966

"We're a tray family," a lovely lady told us recently. "My children don't know what it is to eat dinner at a table. Every evening we haul our trays up to the TV set, which is in our guest room, to eat. It's awful. Why don't you do something about it?"

"It's your problem," we pointed out, "and it's up to you to solve." Then we suggested that most homes have definite times for eating, and television is not permitted to interfere with meals.

"Hah," she said. "Now you tell me! It's too late. We'd never get away with turning off the set during dinner."

Perhaps, instead of "too late," she should have said, "too much trouble." It's never too late to make a new start in the right direction, if the new start is worth the effort. And getting the youngsters to eat dinner at a table should be worth the effort.

One easy solution for our problem-mother might be to have the set develop a mysterious ailment that would require a couple of weeks' study by a repairman. In the absence of television, the kiddies might be introduced to a dinner table. There they possibly could become interested in Dad's report of the day at the office, or even Mother's blow-by-blow of the afternoon's Scrabble game. They might even learn to take part in the table chatter and find out about conversation, which their ancestors enjoyed in place of television.

Don't get us wrong. We love television. But family life is pleasant, too, and one should not obviate the other. Indeed, TV can be an important part of family life. Just a part, though.

August 14, 1954

Cheers 'n' Jeers

CHEERS: And our Soap Opera Fan of the Week Award to NBA All-Star forward Charles Barkley of the Philadelphia 76ers. Barkley arrived late at the office for a Jan. 19 afternoon game with the Phoenix Suns—because he didn't want to miss the end of *All My Children*. Barkley later griped to reporters that "these [afternoon] games interfere with my soap operas."

—March 7, 1987

JEERS: To the profound lack of imagination evident in the casting of TV-movies. It seems every time one of these projects is developed, the cry goes out from Hollywood: "Get me Jane Seymour or Jaclyn Smith." Shades of Richard Chamberlain! Both Seymour and Smith are attractive and capable actresses, but isn't there anyone else who qualifies?

—May 7, 1988

JEERS: To those local TV stations that snare viewers by running almost no commercials at the start of movies. Then, once we're absorbed in the action, the stations pile on a surfeit of ads as the film is building to a climax. We prefer a more even-handed, less disruptive approach.

—July 9, 1988

JEERS: To network sports personnel who buttonhole athletes for interviews right at the finish line. We saw this at the Winter Olympics and during the U.S. Olympic trials. The pushy TV people jump on the competitors right after the race—literally before they can catch their breath. We believe that these athletes have nothing so earth-shattering to say that it can't wait 10 minutes. Hey, it's tough to be quotable when you're hyperventilating.

—August 27, 1988

Gam show host Mary Hart of the syndicated gossip gabber Entertainment Tonight.

JEERS: To the numerous cable and independent stations that unconscionably profit by filling time with half-hour commercials masquerading as real programming. What you're getting is a lengthy sales pitch for some product or service. Scheduling these loathsome "commercial films" not only confuses viewers, but it also exploits whatever trust they may have in how television operates.

—October 15, 1988

JEERS: To *Entertainment Tonight* for unequal illumination. The syndicated show has a special spotlight, positioned to shine on co-host Mary Hart's celebrated gams as she sits at the desk. For the flimsiest excuse, Hart also is made to sashay across the set so the camera can admire her outfit and figure. What's good for the goose is good for the gander. Co-host John Tesh looks like a healthy specimen. Why not put him in a kilt and get him to drop and give us 50 push-ups at the close of each show?

—January 14, 1989

JEERS: To an alarming method of mauling movies. HBO and other telecasters are now routinely using a computerized technique called "time compression" to shoehorn feature films into their schedules. The process speeds up a film, ostensibly in a way the eye cannot perceive, shaving off as much as 10 percent of the movie's running time. ABC recently compressed 23 minutes during its rebroadcast of the post-apocalypse movie "The Day After." As if the pace of the world wasn't hectic enough, now we have to get used to speeded-up movies.

—March 4, 1989

CHEERS: To cable's Nick at Nite for paying tribute—in a tongue-in-cheek fashion—to one of TV's forgotten figures. For three years, this unheralded actress was on every episode of *The*

Patty Duke Show, yet we never saw her face. The premise of the '60s show, you'll recall, involved Patty and Cathy, indentical cousins, both played by Duke. Whenever one was supposed to be talking to the other, this actress stepped into the frame to play the back of Patty Duke's head. She labored in anonymity. She does still. Despite efforts, Nick at Nite couldn't establish her identity after all these years had elapsed. So an actress was hired to stand in for the two-hour tribute and was filmed only from behind. Perfect.

—June 3, 1989

JEERS: To the American Express purchase-protection commercial in which a young boy feeds the new VCR his morn-

Identical cousins go head-to-back-of-head on The Patty Duke Show.

ing oatmeal. We got this note from one of our readers in Alabama: "Don't think that 2-year-olds don't pay attention to commercials—ours did. So far she has fed our VCR a cheese sandwich, three pork-chop bones, two jelly breads and the remote control three or four times. Besides the fact that we don't own an American Express card—we are now stuck with a well-fed and broken VCR not guaranteed by anyone."

—*August 5, 1989*

CHEERS: To USA Network and the fledgling World League of American Football for coming up with the niftiest technological gimmick of the year: "Helmet Cam." The brainchild of director Craig Janoff, Helmet Cam is a tiny TV camera (about the size of a pack of chewing gum) mounted in the quarterback's helmet just above his eye. Through it, viewers at home see what he sees—including the sky and the turf when the signal caller gets sacked. The pictures are unprecedented and truly amazing.

—*April 20, 1991*

JEERS: To San Francisco PBS affiliate KQED-TV, which has filed suit in California seeking permission to tape the state's first execution since 1967. The station feels that showing someone die in the gas chamber will prove once and for all how barbaric capital punishment is. Leaving aside for a second the fact that even the condemned have a right to their privacy, no one who agrees with KQED's point of view needs to see someone executed to feel capital punishment is wrong, and those who don't agree probably won't be swayed either. The real audience for a televised execution is going to be the kind of jaded people who rent those "Faces of Death" home videos and they'll just be watching for the cheap thrill of it. *That* is barbaric.

—*April 20, 1991*

JEERS: And an Overkill Award to the Turner Broadcasting System's newest bright idea, the Airport Channel. TV monitors mounted at the gates in major airports will regale travelers with newscasts culled from Turner's CNN and CNN Headline News. We're not opposed to TV in airports, but we do wonder where it will end. Turner is also ready to roll out the Checkout Channel, a similar service designed for supermarket-checkout lines. What's next? The Elevator Channel? The Restroom Channel?

—*May 11, 1991*

Quotes

"All I know about television is that I want to get into it as soon as possible—before Milton Berle uses up all my jokes.**"** —*Bob Hope, 1949*

"I don't think any less seriously about Chester than I did about King Lear in college.**"** —*Dennis Weaver, 1963*

"I have a cook at home, but I still like to dine out once in a while.**"** —*Movie-studio head Samuel Goldwyn, on the possibility of TV's killing movie-going, 1949*

"The idea of getting just anybody to act a commercial is silly. It takes just as much talent and experience—maybe more—to get across a sales message or a demonstration as it does to commit murder or to make love convincingly before the camera.**"** —*Betty Furness, 1950*

"I have encountered a number of gloomy prophecies which picture the next generation as rendered almost illiterate by the TV screen—but I am of the opposite persuasion. Extending our experience through one sense should supplement rather than curtail the experience of other senses.**"** —*J. Roscoe Miller, President, Northwestern University, 1950*

"I was in on the ground floor of radio and dropped out of it, like a big dope. Now I'm in on the ground floor of TV, and I'm not giving up my lease until the landlord evicts me.**"** —*Ed Sullivan, 1951*

"You just sit there next to the orchestra and look dumb. Your name is Dagmar.**"** —*Jerry Lester to Jennie Lewis before the June 14, 1950,* Broadway Open House *broadcast*

"I've got a clause in my contract that says I can't read any other clauses in it.**"** —*George Gobel, 1953*

"I feel myself being drawn to television like a man in a canoe heading towards Niagara Falls.**"** —*Robert Young, 1953*

❝It was a foregone conclusion that women would take over the entertainment field in television for the simple reason that women are, on the whole, so much more appealing than men. Women possess the qualities of warmth and sympathy which immediately draw their fellow human beings toward them. Men may be clever, but it is the women who are good.**❞** —*Ashley Montagu, author of* The Natural Superiority of Women, *1953*

❝After you've done live TV there is nothing left in the world that can scare you any longer. You've had it.**❞** —*Joan Caulfield, 1954*

❝To me, the electrician is the most important part of the show. If he doesn't turn the lights on, there's no show.**❞** —*George Burns, 1954*

❝It's good to know that if you ever have a flat tire anywhere, someone might recognize you and help.**❞** —*David Nelson, on how it feels to be a national celebrity, 1955*

❝I started at the bottom in this business and worked my way right into the sewer.**❞** —*Art Carney, 1955*

❝Go on the air, get off a half-hour later, and fill up the time in the middle.**❞** —*Johnny Carson explaining the format of his new show, 1955*

❝I'll probably come out on the stage, take one look at those three-eyed TV monsters and faint dead away. And then where am I going to find another medium to make my comeback?**❞** —*Judy Garland, concerning her TV performing debut, 1955*

❝If a bomb fell on this room tonight, Pinky Lee would be the biggest star in television.**❞** —*Milton Berle, to a group of top TV comedians, 1955*

❝Would you say that watching a TV cooking program is the same as sitting down to a good meal?**❞** —*Bishop Fulton J. Sheen, on whether watching a religious show on TV is the same as going to church, 1956*

❝If you don't have a girl on the show, you don't have to shave so often.**❞** —*Broderick Crawford, on why there would be no love interest for him in* Highway Patrol, *1956*

❝Medicine men used to come to my town when I was a boy. They'd come rattling down the street in a wagon and pull up in front of the courthouse steps. Then they'd lower the tailboard and a funny fellow would step out and crack a few jokes. But as soon as the crowd of gaping yokels had gathered, the wit would launch into his sales pitch for Mother Bloater's elixir. Television is a tailboard lowered into the living room.**❞**—*Fred Allen, in his last interview, 1956*

❝In general, I must say American TV has one distinct advantage over the British brand. Over here, if the show's no good, one can still look forward to enjoying the commercials.**❞** —*Noel Coward, 1956*

❝I think people like to see a big guy like me get beat up.**❞** —*Clint Walker's explanation for the success of* Cheyenne, *1956*

❝The English produce the best talkers. The first people who ran for TV there were the Oxford and the Cambridge boys. That kind of person doesn't often go in for

TV in America. I'd say the boosting of the second-rate is a first-rate occupation here." —*Alistair Cooke, 1957*

"Q. Do you feel a sense of guilt when you ravage an innocent person?"
"A. I imagine if I ravaged an innocent person I definitely would feel a sense of guilt. But I can't think of an innocent person that I have ravaged...." —*Mike Wallace, 1957*

"When I was twelve my father tricked me with a deck [of cards] and I lost a $5 bet to him. He made me work it out, too. I was out there mowing the lawn for weeks. But I got the $5 back from my nine-year-old daughter just the other day. Same trick." —*James Garner, 1957*

"At the end of one of our little stories, you see—a story in which a murderer apparently has gotten away nicely with his crime—I come on and give some small hint to the effect that the murderer didn't really get away with it at all. Let us call it a small tolerance. I do it simply as a necessary gesture to morality."
—*Alfred Hitchcock, 1957*

"I'm really having fun with television. I haven't had so much fun since my early days in the business when I had the latitude to experiment. With TV, it's like a cage has been opened—and I can fly again." —*Walt Disney, 1957*

"Part of a radio show I had was called the 'Triple B Ranch.' I had a real stupid character on the show, who greeted everybody with 'Howdy doody!' That's how we got the show's name."
—*Buffalo Bob Smith, 1957*

"The chief function of these concerts, as far as I'm concerned, is to debunk all this pap that kids won't accept or enjoy classical music unless you spoon-feed it to them completely covered with sugar candy. It's impossible for me to say, 'Dear children, this is your Uncle Lennie speaking,' and then tell them about Brother Violin, Sister Viola, Cousin Bassoon, Uncle Contrabassoon and all that. This approach to the instruments bores me to pieces." —*Leonard Bernstein, 1958*

"We've asked both kids' parents not to talk about the show at all when the boys are around. The minute they turn into kid actors, the show is dead." —*Bob Mosher, one of the writer/creators of* Leave It to Beaver, *referring to Jerry Mathers and Tony Dow, 1958*

"Acting is okay for kids—real keen. It really is. But when I grow up I want to be something *really* good, a court lawyer who tries murders and stuff like that."
—*Jerry Mathers, 1958*

"Lassie bought it. Let's face it—Lassie buys everything." —*Lassie's trainer/owner Rudd Weatherwax, discussing his 160-acre ranch, 1958*

"As for the future, just remember this: There'll always be quiz shows."
—*Jack Barry, 1958*

"Before the movies and TV, people saw their favorites on the stage once in—how often? Two or three years. As a host, I'm on for a few minutes, but it's every week; and I sometimes feel even that's too often to look at the same mug. But this is our fifth season. The show is as popular as ever, I think I've got it figured right, and that I'll be around for a long, long

time.**99** —*Ronald Reagan, referring to* General Electric Theater, *1958*

66Until the mail started coming in, everybody on the lot expected someone like Cubby O'Brien to steal the show. Annette was the last person anybody at Disney's or at ABC would have picked. She had a nice smile and a sweet personality, and that was all. She lacked the talent for the elaborate routines all those kids on the first team were chosen for. She was hired just to make it an even 24 Mouseketeers. And yet the letters showed the one most people were interested in was Annette.**99** —*Unnamed Disney executive, 1959*

66Well, I'd say it's pretty good, considering it's for nothing.**99** —*Bing Crosby, on what he thought of TV, 1959*

66The simple truth is that good TV is good business. I'd rather hold the

attention of 8,000,000 people than bore 28,000,000. A sponsor can't expect commercials to do a job for him if the rest of his program offends the intelligence or good taste of the audience, but a lot of advertisers overlook that principle of merchandising. Fellows have told me they never watch the junk they sponsor. For the life of me I can't understand such lack of pride in anything identified with a company.**99** —*Joyce Hall, head of Hallmark Card Company and sponsor of the* Hallmark Hall of Fame, *1961*

66Sorry, we're not casting any young leading men today.**99** —*Unknown casting director who, without looking up, only heard Suzanne Pleshette's voice, 1962*

66You just can't do social significance on television. The medium will never have an Ibsen.**99** —*Rod Serling, 1962*

66People can't remember it. The first time I ever emceed my own show from Florida, with all my friends in New York watching, my major guests called me 'Mirth,' 'Herb' and 'Mark.' I've even been called 'Mew.' And one lady called me 'Worm.'**99** —*Merv Griffin, on his name, 1962*

66The funny thing is, I don't think I've ever been really drunk in my whole life.**99** —*Hal Smith, who played Otis, Mayberry's town drunk, on* The Andy Griffith Show, *1962*

66There's a lack of love on television. I like to deal with good human emotions, not distorted emotions. When something moves me to tears on stage, I know it's good. I like to think there are people who would like to stay home and cry—not laugh all the time or watch

some kid who hates his mother.**99**
—*Jack Webb, 1963*

66The finest display of Levi's we have
ever seen.**99** — *Spokesman for Levi Strauss
& Co., jeans manufacturers, speaking
of Donna Douglas's wardrobe in* The
Beverly Hillbillies, *1963*

66I will says this about McGavin. He is
going to be a very disappointed man on
the first Easter after his death.**99**
— *Burt Reynolds about Darren McGavin,
his* Riverboat *costar, 1963*

66If I can't get her live, she's out.**99**
—*Jerry Lewis, concerning the conditions
under which he would consider interview-
ing Queen Elizabeth for* The Jerry Lewis
Show, *1963*

66I have great faith in the public's ability
to arrive at a proper judgment of values.
I think there will always be a place for
a wholesome, happy approach to life to
balance the dramatic 'serious problem'
type of show. Occasionally critics have
complained that everyone on our show
is a nice person. I don't quite understand this type of complaint. Most
people are pretty nice. Harriet, David
and Rick are nice people, so are most of
our friends.**99** — *Ozzie Nelson, 1963*

66The theater is the actor's medium.
Movies are the director's medium.
Television is nobody's medium.**99** —*Lee
J. Cobb, 1963*

66We must be philosophical about this.
As we all know, TV is a great juggernaut
and we're all nuts and bolts attached to
it. Sometimes the nuts and bolts fall
off.**99** — *Alfred Hitchcock, on the cancel-
lation of his show after ten years, 1965*

66Who, me? Go down in a real submarine?
Never. My God, I get claustrophobia.**99**
—*Richard Basehart, star of* Voyage to the
Bottom of the Sea, *1965*

66I can't believe my luck in being on a
successful series. But right there, in that
character, are things I've spent my life
fighting—lack of coordination, lack of
ease, and the image of a dumb,
untalkative giant that people think of
when they see someone my size. I try
to keep my feelings out of the role.
Sometimes I slip. I think of Lurch as
a humanist. An individualist. A sort
of Thoreau. Strong, but intentionally
restricting his strength. Independent,
but very sensitive to human dignity.**99**
—*Ted Cassidy, Lurch on* The Addams
Family, *1965*

66If this series goes five years, I will be
only thirty-three and rich. Then I can
stop and do something I'd enjoy more. I
want to be a schoolteacher. That would
be a real challenge.**99** —*Bill Cosby, starring in* I Spy, *1965*

66Wouldn't it be a great world if all the
people dressed up like Bozos?**99** — *Larry
Harmon, owner and licenser of the TV
rights for* Bozo the Clown, *1966*

❝If I ever do a science-fiction show, I'm going to put pointed ears on him and use him.**❞** —*Gene Roddenberry, after having cast Leonard Nimoy in an episode of* The Lieutenant, *1967*

❝I did what his mother would have done. I bit him back.**❞** —*Marlin Perkins, on how he behaved when a lion cub bit him, on-air, 1967*

❝... marginally psychotic ... **❞** —*Robert Vaughn, describing* The Man from U.N.C.L.E.'s *Napoleon Solo, 1968*

❝The big issue in *Gidget* was my bellybutton. I could never show it. All the other girls bounced around in skimpy bikinis. Gidget's bathing suit always had to cover her bellybutton. Gidget was only half a person—all fantasy and no kissing. It was a reflection of the destructive morality of the '50s and '60s, which is when I was brought up. Everybody thought that men were out to get you—especially if you showed your bellybutton. And men, in turn, thought they had to get you. When young people get married thinking like that—and so many of them did—it has to mean trouble.**❞** — *Sally Field, 1973*

❝I didn't want to play a nun. You're not allowed to kiss or show your bellybutton.**❞** — *Sally Field, about her first thoughts regarding* The Flying Nun, *1968*

❝It will be interesting to see what viewers think the symbols are. I will say this: There are, within it, answers to every single question that can be posed, but one can't expect an answer on a plate saying, 'Here you are; you don't have to think; it's all yours; don't use your brain.'**❞** — *Patrick McGoohan, about* The Prisoner, *1968*

❝Ed Sullivan has introduced me as Jack Carson, John Crater, John Kerr and Carson McCullers. Now I have my contracts with him made out 'To Whom It May Concern.'**❞** —*Comedian Jack Carter, 1968*

❝When I go—and I'm going soon, believe me—there won't be anyone to take my place. The networks wouldn't stand for it. They just can't accept a broadcaster who is not a shill for a product or a team. Believe me, if they had any idea of how big I was going to get, they wouldn't have let me do it either. But now I'm too big. I mean too much to their image. I snuck up on them. I simply put my legal training together with standard reportorial techniques and eschewed the entrapment of play-by-play announcing, and suddenly I emerged as a unique and, I fear, irreplaceable, figure in broadcast journalism.**❞** —*Howard Cosell, 1968*

❝Good-bye, kids.**❞** —*the only words ever spoken by Clarabell (at the time, Lew Anderson), on the final* Howdy Doody Show, *1960*

❝People aren't just surprised that I write scripts. They're surprised I can even write my name.**❞** —*Michael Landon, 1969*

❝It's like being in love with a very loud and powerful lady who was once innocent but now drinks too much.**❞** —*Burr Tilstrom, about his love/hate affair with television, 1970*

❝I liked him, but it was a cold relationship. Bears aren't like dogs and horses. Ben didn't know me from a bag of doughnuts.**❞** —*Dennis Weaver, discussing his costar on* Gentle Ben, *1970*

❝Archie Bunker is one of the most indigenous American types. He is a funny yet tragic figure. James Baldwin says—and I am paraphrasing—'The American white man is trapped by his own cultural history. He doesn't know what to do about it.' No character fits this 'trapped American' better than Archie Bunker. Archie's dilemma is coping with a world that is changing in front of him. He doesn't know what to do, except lose his temper, mouth his poisons, look elsewhere to fix the blame for his own discomfort. He isn't a totally evil man. He wouldn't burn a cross. He's shrewd. But he won't get to the root of his problem, because the root of his problems is himself, and he doesn't know it. That is the dilemma of Archie Bunker.**❞** — *Carroll O'Connor, 1971*

❝She has the best tummy in the business. She has sensational armpits with no extra wrinkles or puffiness. She doesn't have particularly long legs, but she has a long, sinuous body, so when you see her navel and five inches below it, everyone gets nervous. They wonder what happened.**❞** — *TV costume designer Bob Mackie speaking of Cher, 1975*

❝To be honest, bitches are more fun. They don't make nice ladies very interesting in Hollywood. Good girls are put on pedestals where they can't move. If they do move, usually they fall off and become victims.**❞** — *Morgan Fairchild, 1981*

❝*TV Guide*: If you were in charge of TV programs, what changes would you make?**❞**
❝Miss Piggy: Ah, let *moi* see. First, I would put on no more than six shows that were exactly the same in any one week. It is very confusing when you cannot remember whether it is the two girls in Minneapolis who are sharing the apartment with the boy or the three girls in Cincinnati who are really boys dressed up like girls. Second, when a show became very popular, I would not have the stars go off to other shows and open restaurants. Third, I think there are altogether too many action shows where the best parts are given to automobiles. And finally, when there is something really good on, the other channels should run something you don't care about, like 'The History of Socks.'**❞** —*1981*

❝If Hugh woke up on Christmas Day and found a pile of manure under the tree, he'd wonder where they were hiding his pony.**❞** —*Joe Garagiola about Hugh Downs, 1982*

❝ ... [*The American*] *Sportsman,* now in its fifth season, hooks an estimated 18,000,000 viewers weekly, which goes to show that if you give the people what they want—a dead elephant—they will turn out.**❞** —*Melvin Durslag, 1969*

TV Secrets

• Fess Parker was a policeman in an early episode of *Dragnet,* and played his entire scene kneeling on the floor—to avoid towering over Jack Webb and Ben Alexander.

• How much did a contestant have left, after taxes, at the various stages of *The $64,000 Question?* Assuming a wife and two children, a gross annual income of $5,000, and the standard 10 percent tax deduction, here's the rundown:

PRIZE	AFTER TAXES
$ 1,000	$ 820
$ 2,000	$ 1,640
$ 4,000	$ 3,246
$ 8,000	$ 6,324
$ 16,000	$ 11,956
$ 32,000	$ 21,220
$ 64,000	$ 34,460

• The Automobile Legal Association said television's worst driver was Batman. On just one program, according to the organization, he made U-turns on a busy street, crashed through safety barriers, crossed road-divider markings, and failed to signal a single turn.

Holy fuel injection! The Batmobile.

• Robert Clary, who played LeBeau, a French prisoner of war, in *Hogan's Heroes,* had himself, during World War II, been kept in the Ottmuth, Blechhamer, Gross-Rosen, and Buchenwald concentration camps. His prison number, tattooed on the upper part of his left forearm, was A-5714. Meanwhile, John Banner, who played Sergeant Schultz on *Hogan's Heroes,* was an Austrian Jew who was driven out of Europe when the Nazis took over Austria, and whose entire family was wiped out.

• *My Three Sons* began as a proposed series for the Lennon Sisters.

• Barbara Eden, when cast as the dumb blonde in TV's *How to Marry a Millionaire,* modeled her performance on her pet poodle, whose emotions, she says, were also "all on the surface."

• Gentle Ben hated to run, so most of his running was performed by a stand-in named Buck.

• Liberace's first stage name was Buster Keys.

• Martin Landau turned down the role of Spock on *Star Trek*—which then went to his friend, Leonard Nimoy—to take his role in *Mission: Impossible.* When Landau left the show, his replacement was— Leonard Nimoy. Then, when Nimoy left *Mission: Impossible,* it was decided not to replace him, but instead to have guest stars for various parts. The first guest star: William Shatner.

● CBS turned down the pilot for *The Muppet Show*. According to producer Bernie Brillstein, the network's marketing-research department said that any show with a frog as the host wouldn't work.

● Peter Jennings is a high-school dropout.

● In Japan, Emmanuel Lewis, of *Webster,* is considered a deity. That's because GIs

Superman (George Reeves) springs into action — with the help of a diving board.

in postwar Japan handed out thousands of copies of a doll that Japanese families took into their homes and turned into a symbol of good fortune. That doll looks exactly like Emmanuel Lewis, and many of the Japanese felt that Lewis was this doll come to life.

● When John Tesh did the news in Nashville on station WSMV in the 1970s, the weatherman was Pat Sajak—and the person anchoring the news for the competition was Oprah Winfrey.

● An Emmy is made of pewter with gold plating and worth $150.

● After his near-fatal auto accident on January 24, 1961, Mel Blanc did the voices of Barney Rubble, Dino, and other assorted characters for the first 65 episodes of *The Flintstones* flat on his back, with the microphone hanging over his bed.

● To give it just that certain, that exotic, that unreproducible *je ne sais quoi,* this is the trade secret of how the Universal Studios wardrobe magicians took brand-new raincoats and turned them into the rumpled, lived-in (and, apparently, slept-in) coats worn by Lieutenant Columbo:
> *Sandpaper*—to scuff the cuffs.
> *Bleach*—to soften the coat's too-new color.
> *Fabric softener*—to pulverize any stiffness out of the fabric.
> *Mineral oil*—blotched on to produce tacky grease stains.
> *Dirt*—rubbed in to produce grubby highlights.

Multiple washings, followed by hanging the coat to dry, with wet paper towels stuffed in the pockets—for extra bagginess.

● Tom Brokaw did not watch television until he was sixteen years old.

● According to a 1991 survey, 54 percent of Americans know that Judge Wapner runs *The People's Court* but only 9 percent know that Justice William Rehnquist heads the Supreme Court.

Icons

Icons

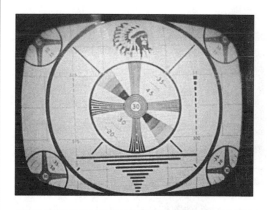

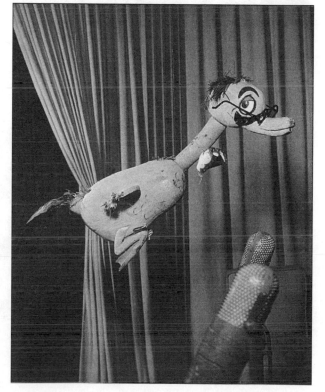

PEOPLE

Faces: Bishop Fulton J. Sheen (top left) wants you on Life Is Worth Living; underneath the hairdo- and makeup-protecting scarf is Betty Furness (top right); Donna Douglas is under wraps in one of The Twilight Zone's scariest episodes, "Beauty Is in the Eye of the Beholder" (bottom left); and Laura Palmer (Sheryl Lee) smiled innocently but walked with fire (and Bob) in Twin Peaks (opposite).

Before the Fall

The Fall Preview Issue has always been the fattest, most eagerly awaited edition of *TV Guide* each year since its first appearance in 1953.

Just before the 1954 Fall Preview Issue came out, somebody at *TV Guide* decided to take a copy of the upcoming issue's cover around to famous TV celebrities and have them photographed apparently reading the magazine with great interest. Whatever promotional value these photos were put to is lost in the misty past—they were never published in *TV Guide*.

The folks doing the staring are: Betty White, who was starring at the time in the syndicated series, *Life with Elizabeth;* Ed Sullivan; Danny Thomas, starring in *Make Room for Daddy* on ABC; Roy Rogers and Dale Evans, stars of *The Roy Rogers Show* on NBC; *Dragnet*'s Jack Webb; and a certain future President of the United States.

What will you watch tonight?

Will it be something you've liked for the past year or two or that new show scheduled at the same time? One is a known quantity. You feel the characters are old friends. You enjoy the stories. It's one of your favorite television programs.

The other one might be good— might be bad. You've read a little about it and you know the general plot from the listing details. It could be entertaining, but there's also the chance that you might be wasting a half hour or an hour.

May we presume to advise you?

Watch the new show. Maybe it'll be the last time you will, but watch the new show. Give it a chance. And if you're worried about missing an episode of your favorite—forget it. You can count on seeing it next summer, when the reruns bloom again.

We urge readers to sample the new shows early in the season in the hope that you'll keep going back to the best of them. If you do, those fellows at the rating services who study tea leaves, crystal balls and electronic gadgets to find out which shows are popular may get the word and pass it along to the sponsors. The sponsors then will be heartened and will stop listening to hints that their new show ought to be dropped right away before disaster sets in. *Father Knows Best* once came close to extinction in just

that manner. It was a near thing.

There have been other times when a new program has been a slow starter. At first no one tuned to it. Then a few people. Finally, thanks to word-of-mouth advertising, more viewers tuned in. Unfortunately, by that time the show had been canceled and a Western scheduled in its place.

So please take a look at the new programs early this season. The show you save may be a good one.

—*September 23, 1961*

On The Map...
Somewhere

Each week we visit families in their homes—only we never leave our homes. Those other houses and apartments belong to some of our favorite people, whom we've never really met, but whom we know better than some of the people we actually do know.

With eyes closed, and pulling on memories of decades, we could probably describe the places our favorite TV characters live: where the sofa is, the TV, the kitchen, the bedroom. From occasional shots during the shows, we even know what the places look like on the outside. We might even think we know how to get there. But do we know the addresses? What follows are the addresses where some of our favorite TV families live (even if the show's been off the air for 15 years, we know they still live there). Do you know who belongs where? The answers are at the bottom of the page.

1. 1030 East Tremont Avenue, Apartment 3B, Bronx, New York

2. 623 East 68th Street, Apartment 4A, New York, New York

3. 607 South Maple Street, Springfield, U.S.A.

4. 328 Chauncey Street, Brooklyn, New York

5. 211 Pine Street, Mayfield, U.S.A.

6. 518 Crestview Drive, Beverly Hills, California

7. 1313 Mockingbird Lane, Mockingbird Heights

8. 704 Houser Street, Queens, New York

9. Silverstone

10. 165 Eaton Place, London, England

11. 119 North Weatherly Street, Apartment D, Minneapolis, Minnesota

12. 627 Elm Street, Hillsdale, California

13. 698 Sycamore Road, San Pueblo, California

14. 1049 Park Avenue, Apartment 1102, New York, New York

ANSWERS: 1. Home of Molly and *The Goldbergs.* 2. Home of Lucy and Ricky Ricardo on *I Love Lucy.* 3. Home of the Andersons on *Father Knows Best.* 4. Home of Ralph and Alice Kramden on *The Honeymooners.* 5. Home of the Cleavers on *Leave It to Beaver.* 6. Home of the Clampetts on *The Beverly Hillbillies.* 7. Home of *The Munsters.* 8. Home of the Bunkers on *All in the Family.* 9. John Beresford Tipton's estate in *The Millionaire.* 10. Home of the Bellamy family and servants on *Upstairs, Downstairs.* 11. Home of Mary Richards on *The Mary Tyler Moore Show.* 12. Home of Dennis Mitchell on *Dennis the Menace.* 13. Home of *The Partridge Family.* 14. Home of Felix Unger and Oscar Madison on *The Odd Couple.*

With This Ring, I Try to Up My Ratings

The conventional wisdom, TV-style, has always been: when a show is in trouble or needs a boost, either (1) take the show to Europe for a few episodes, or (2) get somebody married.

Marriage is always good for shaking up a show's structure, and the wedding episodes themselves nearly always draw big ratings. But usually they are just ephemeral jolts, and the ratings, if they were heading south, continue in that direction soon after. And sometimes, as in the case of Rhoda's wedding—which was devised by producers who thought they needed to change the one-note/one-joke nature of the character and series because people were getting tired of it (although it was doing fine in the ratings)—wedded bliss destroys the balance and hastens shows' ends.

Here, then, are some of the most-watched and best-remembered (and highly publicized) fictional weddings on TV.

Nancy Remington (Patricia Benoit) to Robinson Peepers (Wally Cox), May 30, 1954, on *Mr. Peepers*.

Babs Riley (Lugene Sanders) to Don Marshall (Marty Milner), January 20, 1956, on *The Life of Riley*.

Kathy "Clancey" Daly O'Hara (Marjorie Lord) accepts the proposal of Danny Williams (Danny Thomas), April 25, 1957, on *The Danny Thomas Show.* The wedding will occur after the season, during summer reruns; the couple will take up residence on CBS.

Martha Hale (Abby Dalton) to Chick Hennesey (Jackie Cooper), May 7, 1962, on *Hennesey*.

Katrin "Katy" Holstrum (Inger Stevens) to U.S. Congressman Glen Morley (William Windom), November 1, 1965, on *The Farmer's Daughter*.

Agent 99 (Barbara Feldon) to Agent 86 (Don Adams), November 16, 1968, on *Get Smart*.

Jeannie (Barbara Eden) to Major Tony Nelson (Larry Hagman), after living together for four years, December 2, 1969, on *I Dream of Jeannie*.

Rhoda Morgenstern (Valerie Harper) to Joe Gerard (David Groh), October 28, 1974, on *Rhoda*.

Janet Blake (Pamela Hensley) to Dr. Steve Kiley (James Brolin), October 21, 1975, on *Marcus Welby, M.D.*

Sandra Sue Abbott (Betty Buckley) to Tom Bradford (Dick Van Patten), November 9, 1977, on *Eight Is Enough*.

Lucy Ewing (Charlene Tilton) to Mitch

Cooper (Leigh McCloskey), January 23, 1981, on *Dallas*.

Laura Baldwin (Genie Francis) to Luke Spencer (Tony Geary), November 16 and 17, 1981, on *General Hospital*.

Sue Ellen Ewing (Linda Gray) to J. R. Ewing (Larry Hagman), a remarriage, December 3, 1982, on *Dallas*.

Soon-Lee (Rosalind Chao) to Max Klinger (Jamie Farr), February 28, 1983, on *M*A*S*H*.

Victoria Gioberti (Jamie Rose) to Nick Hogan (Roy Thinnes), March 11, 1983, on *Falcon Crest*.

Krystle Grant (Linda Evans) to Blake Carrington (John Forsythe), officially, December 28, 1983, on *Dynasty*.

Emily Haywood (Marion Ross) to Captain Merrill Stubing (Gavin MacLeod), May 24, 1986, on *The Love Boat*.

Ann Marie Romano (Bonnie Franklin) to Samuel Clemens Royer (Howard Hesseman), May 16, 1983, on *One Day at a Time*.

Thelma Frye (Anna Maria Horsford) to Reverend Reuben Gregory (Clifton Davis), February 3, 1990, on *Amen*.

Woodrow "Woody" Boyd (Woody Harrelson) to Kelly Gaines (Jackie Swanson), May 15, 1992, on *Cheers*.

Fussin' and Feudin'

Like a hunter stalking its prey, follow the tracks of an ego and you'll soon come upon a feud standing at the end of them.

Television—especially live television —had its share of often childish and spiteful ego conflicts and vendettas played out in view of the public, in newspaper gossip columns and on-air.

It's not surprising. Television was —and, to a certain extent, still is—the most personal, most tension-filled, most tightwire-ish of all mass media. It's you there on the screen, where the audience can see and hear you being you; often they think that the fictional you—the character you're playing—is the real you. The pressure of putting together a show—a show that has your name on it, one that is shaped by you to mirror what you consider the most attractive aspects of your own personality—under extreme, often near-impossible time and budgetary conditions, makes you edgy and protective and defensive against even the smallest critiques . . . or the most threatening ratings challenges. The *Godfather* ethic—"It's not personal, it's just business"—doesn't cut it on TV. It *is* personal. That's why TV works, and people watch it. And feuds begin.

Feuds battled in plain sight are such attention-getters that sometimes phony feuds are staged—like the classic one between Jack Benny and Fred Allen, or the lesser one between comic Sam Levenson and playwright/caustic wit George S. Kaufman on the early-1950s panel show *This Is Show Business*. These bring all eyes around to performers and shows that want to or could use the jolt of publicity, or that simply want to have a little bit of toying fun with the columnists and audiences.

Then there are the real ones. . . .

Ed Sullivan seems to be indicating he owns this TV—which was true: on Sunday nights he owned almost every TV.

Ed Sullivan seemed to string one feud after another, and they were doozies. The added aspect to them was that Sullivan had his own column in which to wage his wars. Sullivan went toe to sensitive toe with newsprint rival Walter Winchell, whose old column and writing style at the New York *Graphic* were taken over by Sullivan when Winchell jumped to the *Daily Mirror.* Sullivan had tiffs with Jack Paar, Arthur Godfrey, and comedian Jackie Mason (whose on-air hand gesture toward Sullivan when his act was cut short was interpreted by Sullivan as obscene). Sullivan was feuded against by Frank Sinatra in 1955 over whether Sinatra did or did not refuse to appear on Sullivan's *Toast of the Town;* Sinatra went so far as to take out an ad in a show-business trade paper, addressed directly to Sullivan, and calling him "sick, sick, sick."

But Sullivan's most heated, vitriolic, and public skirmish was with Steve Allen, who came on during the summer of 1956 on NBC with his own Sunday-night variety show opposite Sullivan's. Though Sullivan ultimately won the ratings set-to, sending Allen retreating to Mondays after three years, the two pummeled each other over who was stealing whose guests and other equally important issues of the day. Allen's show had Elvis Presley on before Sullivan's did, and beat Sullivan in the ratings because of it, which did little to endear the two hosts to each other. Sullivan's revenge was to book Presley for three appearances that very next Monday morning, after the ratings came out, use the Presley appearances to trounce Allen, and be the one most remembered as the Elvis showcaser.

Sullivan and Allen even took their feud to the pages of *TV Guide,* where they faced off in side-by-side columns in the October 20, 1956, issue. Allen, though not accusing Sullivan directly, pointed the finger at the Sullivan production staff for pirating his scheduled guests and stealing his show's idea to do a James Dean tribute to coincide with the premiere of the Dean movie *Giant.*

"First of all, I want to say I truly regret that this particular issue has been turned into a matter of personalities," Allen wrote, "and that the matter has been clouded with irrelevant details." He went on to explain his chronology of the James Dean affair, and concluded: "If, by chance, Ed was completely innocent in all this . . . then I hereby offer him a full public apology. On the other hand, if Ed booked 'Giant' and the Winslows [Dean's aunt and uncle] knowing full well that we were counting on these items, then I think someone owes me an apology."

Sullivan's companion counterpoint was far more direct and cutting. In it, he called Allen "a Johnny-come-lately to the Sunday night network arena," dismissed other Allen contentions of guest-stealing ("It is hardly plausible that our show, which in its ninth year can claim to have originated most of the techniques of television variety presentation, needs to 'steal' anything from the Allen program which just started operating opposite our show on Sunday nights this year"), said Allen's statements indicated "that what he wanted was some cheap publicity," and concluded: "From now on, I just wouldn't trust Allen. It's as simple as that."

The feud churned on, and when, during the summer of 1957, Allen's producer, Jules Green, claimed Sullivan "cheated the public" by announcing Harry Belafonte for his show when Belafonte never appeared, Sullivan retorted, "I have no comment on either of those two punks [Allen and Green]."

It finally got to the point where *TV Guide,* in its "As We See It" editorial column of August 31, 1957, felt the need to take both men to task. "The feud between Ed Sullivan and Steve Allen," the editorial began, "has reached a point where it no longer makes good publicity, good television or good sense. . . . Viewers are bored by the whole mishmash. Sponsors are tired of having the audience twist dials from one show to the other—especially, as one survey showed, during commercials. It would be better all 'round if both men confined their competition to turning out the best possible entertainment—instead of the nastiest possible statements to the press."

Ventriloquist Paul Winchell feuded with ventriloquist Jimmy Nelson, with accusations flying back and forth over who was using whose material.

Jackie Gleason and Milton Berle went at it for a while; Gleason was angered that some of his best writers had been hired away by Berle, and also that Berle was using Gleason's trademark line, "And awaaay we go!"

Red Skelton accused Sid Caesar of stealing his pantomime routines, which led to a mini-feud.

Bud Abbott and Lou Costello feuded with Dean Martin and Jerry Lewis—both teams being alternating (and much compared) hosts on the *Colgate Comedy Hour* in the early 1950s—mostly over old-timer–versus–newcomer professional jealousies.

Arthur Godfrey had publicized verbal run-ins with Dorothy Kilgallen and others of the press, calling critic John Crosby a "fatuous ass" and Ed Sullivan a "dope."

Jack Paar, as emotional, high-strung, and unobstructedly human a personality as TV has had, had publicized flare-ups with Walter Winchell, Ed Sullivan, Dorothy Kilgallen (she knocked his support of Fidel Castro; he ridiculed her

Jack Paar may look blithely unconcerned here, but his feuds were legendary and vitriolic. We kid you not.

looks and the way she spoke—"She must use Novocain lipstick"), and his own network, NBC. He walked off his show in an emotional reaction to the network's censoring of a joke about a water closet.

What might appear to some to be a feud, and to others merely a continual battle of wills, went on between Carroll O'Connor and Norman Lear, respective star and producer of *All in the Family.* Mostly it was over control and direction of the show and interpretation of the Archie Bunker character. Money, too, was a big

All parties—producer Norman Lear in the foreground, Carroll O'Connor and Jean Stapleton as Archie and Edith Bunker in the background—take a break from the tensions on the set of All in the Family.

The body language says it all in this 1976 shot: Harry Reasoner and Barbara Walters were simpatico . . . not.

issue, as were Lear's veto of O'Connor's doing beer commercials and of cutting the show's rehearsal-to-shooting schedule back from five days to four. O'Connor effected a "sick-out" or two to get what he wanted, although Lear apparently won out most of the time.

There was little love lost between Barbara Walters and Harry Reasoner. Reasoner fumed when Walters became his cohost on the ABC nightly news. He didn't want to share his position, her lack of solid news credentials irked him, and her million-dollar salary didn't help, either. The chill was evident, and stayed that way until Reasoner returned to CBS and *60 Minutes.*

The 1980s saw a series of smallish head-buttings that made biggish head-lines: Bryant Gumbel warred with David Letterman for four years over the late-night-show host's stunts and statements; and then a leaked Gumbel memo criticizing many aspects and people of the *Today* show led to a distinct chilliness between Gumbel and memo-targeted weatherman Willard Scott; dueling egos pretty much capsized the hit series *Moonlighting,* with star Cybill Shepherd fighting with executive producer Glenn Gordon Caron—who left the show—and costar Bruce Willis; Johnny Carson tuned out Joan Rivers, when he felt it was disloyal of her to accept an offer by the fledgling Fox network to do a late-night show opposite him; and John Ritter and Joyce DeWitt refused to speak to or appear on the same soundstage with *Three's Company* costar

Suzanne Somers after she missed two taping days—a back injury, she said; a "convenient illness," the producers said—when her reported demands for an exorbitant raise (from $30,000 an episode to $150,000 per) and 10 percent of the profits were rejected. The show went on without her, except for about a minute at the end of each show, at which time she would be seen talking to the cast on the telephone; these segments were taped with her isolated from the others in a remote section of the studio.

The biggest, most public, most dwelled-upon feud of the early 1990s was the one between Delta Burke and the cast and staff of the CBS sitcom hit *Designing Women*. (Roseanne Barr seemed to be at the center of all the other feuds, including one with Arsenio Hall and several with her producers and writers.) After Burke criticized producers Linda Bloodworth-Thomason and Harry Thomason in an Orlando *Sentinel* interview, the Thomasons responded, and the cross-fire escalated, with volleys of accusations and snide remarks, and wound-licking over personal slights (including Burke's alleged lack of sympathy after Bloodworth-Thomason's father's death and attacks on Burke's growing weight). Cast members took sides, and Burke was soon off the show.

Time ran out rather quickly on the happy days of Moonlighting, *as Cybill Shepherd and Bruce Willis (seen here in the show's 1985 pilot) became the center of fights and falling-outs.*

ABC

33

It's All Relative

Buff Cobb Wallace, former wife and TV partner of Mike Wallace, was the grand-daughter of humorist Irvin S. Cobb.

Tim Considine is the son of movie producer John Considine and Carmen Pantages, of the theater-owning Pantages family; his uncle was newspaper columnist Bob Considine.

Richard Boone was a distant nephew of Daniel Boone.

David Janssen's mother was Bernice Dalton, an ex–Ziegfeld star.

Jack Kelly is stage star Nancy Kelly's brother.

Old Ebony, Chuck Connors' horse in *The Rifleman,* was the grandson of 1925 Kentucky Derby winner Flying Ebony.

Cesar Romero was the grandson of the Cuban patriot José Martí.

Among the happy Reiner family listening to father Carl reading the dictionary, of all things, is future actor/writer/director and Meathead, Rob Reiner.

Making room for daddy Danny Thomas, in a rare moment of repose before exchanging belly laughs for belly flops, is the Thomas brood, with his elder daughter second in line on the springboard: Marlo Thomas.

Leslie Nielsen was the nephew of character actor Jean Hersholt.

Meredith Baxter-Birney is the daughter of *Hazel*'s Whitney Blake.

Linda Kaye, Betty Jo in *Petticoat Junction,* was the daughter of the show's producer, Paul Henning.

William Windom, who played a congressman from Minnesota in *The Farmer's Daughter,* was the great-grandson of William Windom, a congressman from Minnesota.

Patrick MacNee was David Niven's cousin.

Peter Jennings' father, Charles Jennings, was a vice-president of the Canadian

Long before Bewitched, *Elizabeth Montgomery cut her acting teeth on father Robert's TV dramatic show, and in 1951 they appeared together for the first time in "Top Secret," seen here (with Margaret Phillips, left), in which she played—what else?—his character's daughter.*

Broadcasting Company, and at one time "The Golden Voice of Canadian Radio"— head announcer on six of the eight Canadian-network radio shows then on the air.

Mike Connors and Cher are distant cousins.

Georganne LaPiere, who played the role of Heather Grant on *General Hospital,* is Cher's half-sister.

Tony Roberts is the son of Ken Roberts, announcer on the CBS daytime soap opera *Love of Life,* and the cousin of character actor Everett Sloane.

TV newsman Chris Wallace is not only the son of Mike Wallace, but also the stepson of William Leonard, former president of CBS News.

Rachel Dennison, who played a character named Doralee in the TV series *9 to 5,* played the same part her sister, Dolly Parton, played in the movie original.

John James, Jeff Colby in *Dynasty,* is the son of New York radio personality Herb Oscar Anderson.

Tracy Nelson is Rick Nelson's daughter, Ozzie and Harriett's granddaughter.

Lorenzo Lamas is the son of actors Fernando Lamas and Arlene Dahl.

Charles Haid is Merv Griffin's cousin.

Perry King is the grandson of legendary editor Maxwell Perkins.

Susie Garrett of *Punky Brewster* is the sister of Marla Gibbs.

Carlos Montalban, the actor who for 15 years played "El Exigente" on Savarin coffee commercials, is the older brother of Ricardo Montalban.

Dynasty's Catherine Oxenberg is the daughter of Princess Elizabeth of Yugoslavia.

Philip McKeon, who played Linda Lavin's son in *Alice,* is the brother of Nancy McKeon, Jo in *The Facts of Life.*

Katey Sagal is the sister of twins Liz and Jean Sagal, who starred in NBC's *Double Trouble.*

The Aurness brothers—who grew up to be James Arness (left) and Peter Graves—at age 16 and 13, respectively, on the dock at their summer home in Ox Lake, Minnesota, in 1939.

*Posing for a 1950 Father's Day publicity shot are
Edgar Bergen's two children: Charlie McCarthy on
the left, and four-year-old future Murphy Brown,
Candice Patricia, knocking on wood.*

Joanna Kerns, the star of ABC's *Growing
Pains,* is the sister of ABC sportscaster
and 1964 Olympic gold-medal-winning
swimmer Donna de Varona.

Jack Coleman of *Dynasty* is the great-
great-great-great-great-great-grandson of
Benjamin Franklin on his mother's side.

Camilla More, who played Gillian
Forrester on NBC's *Days of Our Lives,*
is a descendant of the 16th-century
statesman and writer Sir Thomas More.

Timothy Daly of *Wings* is the brother of
Tyne Daly, and both are the children of
James Daly.

Carroll O'Connor is the cousin of the *New
York Times* TV critic John J. O'Connor.

Holly Robinson of *21 Jump Street* is the
daughter of Matt Robinson, who played
the part of Gordon for years on *Sesame
Street.*

Michael d'Abo, father of *The Wonder
Years* star Olivia d'Abo, was lead singer
for the 1960s rock group Manfred Mann,
and co-wrote "Build Me Up Buttercup," a
hit for the Foundations.

Melanie Wilson, Jennifer the stewardess
on *Perfect Strangers,* is the daughter of
Dick Wilson, better known for 25 years
as Mr. Whipple of "Please don't squeeze
the Charmin" fame.

Carrie Mitchum, Donna on *The Bold and
the Beautiful,* is the granddaughter of
Robert Mitchum.

Rain Pryor, T.J. on *Head of the Class,* is
Richard Pryor's daughter.

Ben Stiller, of MTV's *The Ben Stiller
Show,* is the son of Jerry Stiller and Anne
Meara.

Dean Stockwell's father, Harry, was the
voice of Prince Charming in Disney's
Snow White.

Tori Spelling, Donna Martin in *Beverly
Hills 90210,* is the daughter of the show's
producer, Aaron Spelling.

Antony Alda, shady Johnny Corelli on
Days of Our Lives, is actor Alan Alda's
half-brother.

MILBURN McCARTY ASSOCIATES

*You'd think one Schultzy would be enough, but Ann
B. Davis of* The Bob Cummings Show *and later*
The Brady Bunch *is on the left, while twin sister and
non–show business type Harriet is on the right.*

The Beauty Queen Route

Edie Adams

Edie Adams—Miss Television, 1950

Susan Anton—Miss California, 1969

Jacqueline Beer (*77 Sunset Strip*)— Miss France in the 1954 Miss Universe contest

Lindsay Bloom (Velda on *Mike Hammer*) —Miss Omaha; Miss Arizona; Miss U.S.A., 1973

Delta Burke—Miss Florida, 1974 (won the talent competition at the Miss America pageant)

Angie Dickinson—one of six "T-Venuses" chosen to appear on NBC's *Colgate Comedy Hour* in 1953–54 season

Donna Dixon—Miss Virginia U.S.A., 1975

Donna Douglas—Miss New Orleans, 1957; Miss Baton Rouge, 1958

Mary Frann—America's Junior Miss, 1961

Phyllis George—Miss America, 1971

Deidre Hall—Junior Orange Bowl Queen, 1960 (she was 12 at the time)

Jenilee Harrison (*Three's Company, Dallas*)—Miss Young America

Mary Hart—Miss South Dakota, 1970

Shirley Jones—Miss Pittsburgh, 1952

Gunilla Knutson ("Take it all off" shaving-cream commercial)—Miss Sweden, 1961

Cloris Leachman—Miss Chicago, 1946; Miss America finalist

Lee Ann Meriwether—Miss San Francisco; Miss California; Miss America, 1955

Bess Myerson—Miss America, 1945.

Deborah Norville—Georgia's Junior Miss, 1976

Dian Parkinson (*The Price Is Right*)— Miss World-U.S.A.

Jeannine Riley (*Petticoat Junction*)— Blossom Day Queen, Madera, California

Diane Sawyer—America's Junior Miss, 1963

Deborah Shelton (Mandy Winger in *Dallas*)—Miss U.S.A., 1970

Cybill Shepherd—Miss Teenage Memphis, 1966; Model of the Year, 1968

Cynthia Sikes (*St. Elsewhere*)—Miss Kansas, 1972

Nancy Stafford—Miss Florida, 1977.

Shannon Tweed (*Falcon Crest*)— Playboy Playmate of the Year, 1982

Karen Valentine—Miss Teenage Santa Rosa; Miss Sonoma County

Shawn Weatherly—Miss Universe, 1980

Lee Meriwether, Miss America, 1955—the first to be crowned on TV—went on to star in Barnaby Jones *and was one of several actresses to play Catwoman on* Batman.

Heart Throbs

Television may be a cool medium, as Marshall McLuhan pointed out. But a considerable amount of heat and general body warmth has been generated by a platoon of photogenic, sexy (though wholesomely so), come-hither, and slightly plastic/bland stars in roles that, if their producers didn't exploit this audience/animal attraction from the start, they sure hopped onto it quick. Sex sells. And, as many of these lip-smacking TV desserts produced viewer warmth by playing characters who played it cool, maybe McLuhan was right on the money.

DICK ZIMMERMAN

Kate Jackson, Farrah Fawcett-Majors, and Jaclyn Smith were the girls next door—if you happened to own real estate next to a detective agency with gorgeous ex-cop operatives who didn't believe in bras, as was the case in Charlie's Angels.

Shakespearean-trained Diana Rigg epitomized the cool chic sexuality of late-1960s London as jumpsuited or leathered Mrs. Emma Peel in The Avengers.

James Dean and Naomi Riordan seem to be having a terrible time in a bare room in "A Long Time 'Til Dawn," the November 11, 1953, production of the Kraft Television Theatre.

The teen of the 1990s found soulmates and dream dates in the smart and realistic surprise hit, Beverly Hills 90210. Here, left to right, are Ian Ziering, Jennie Garth, Luke Perry, Gabrielle Carteris, Shannen Doherty, Douglas Emerson, Jason Priestley, Tori Spelling, and Brian Austin Green.

Annette Funicello's talent, among other things, developed during her Walt Disney years, where she became the center of adolescent male attention on The Mickey Mouse Club. *Here, at 14, she's with Tim Considine in the 1956 "The Further Adventures of Spin and Marty."*

Richard Chamberlain (Dr. Kildare), sexpot dancer/entertainer Joey Heatherton, and Nick Adams take a break from being teen idols in a 1963 posed candid shot.

John Stamos's boyish yet sultry dark good looks made him a must-watch 1980s hunk on shows like Full House.

One of these men was not considered a sex object in 1964. You would be correct in assuming it was Leo G. Carroll (right) as Mr. Waverly; David McCallum as Illya Kuryakin (left) and Robert Vaughn as Napoleon Solo were the hot items on The Man from U.N.C.L.E.

The Marilyn Watch

Other than Garbo, no performer was ever more sought after for a TV appearance than Marilyn Monroe. Every time somebody had a project that was perfect for her, every time she apparently nearly almost agreed to perhaps try to find time to think about playing a part on TV, press agents went into overdrive and it made news. Unfortunately, that's all it made—the shows were never produced; in retrospect, some were silly, but the prospect of others was intriguing. *TV Guide* stood the Marilyn Watch, following the pursuit in its pages, mostly in the "New York—" and "Hollywood Teletype" industry gossip columns.

What follows is a chronology of items, showing the lure she had for TV producers—even beyond the grave.

"[NBC] has made Marilyn Monroe a firm offer to play 'The Brothers Karamazov' as a three-hour, three-parter." *—August 27, 1955*

"NBC and Marilyn Monroe are at least talking about her doing the controversial classic, 'Lysistrata,' which is scheduled, with or without Miss Monroe, for *Producers' Showcase*."*—February 18, 1956*

"There will be no Marilyn Monroe on TV this year. 'Lysistrata,' in which she was to have starred on *Producers' Showcase* Jan. 7, has been canceled in favor of 'Pal Joey,' starring José Ferrer." *—November 17, 1956*

"NBC still has ambitious plans to do 'Lysistrata' as a spectacular, now tentatively scheduled for November with both Marilyn Monroe and Katharine Hepburn hopefully pencilled in as the leads. John Huston is to produce and direct." *—January 19, 1957*

"Marilyn Monroe may be one of the stars in three one-act plays by Tennessee Williams set for *Du Pont Show of the Month* next spring."*—September 14, 1957*

"With the producer of almost every TV spectacular trying to sign Marilyn Monroe, NBC's Martin Agronsky thinks he has pulled the coup of the season. He'll interview Marilyn and her husband, playwright Arthur Miller, on an upcoming *Look Here!* show." *—October 12, 1957 [Monroe had been interviewed by Edward R. Murrow on* Person to Person *in 1955.]*

"Marilyn Monroe, who has shrugged off television, now reportedly saying 'maybe' to producer Robert Saudek for an *Omnibus* appearance in the fall—perhaps in something written by her husband, Arthur Miller." *—June 14, 1958*

"Late word is that Marilyn Monroe's available for the Ford series if the right property is found." *—July 11, 1959*

"Marilyn Monroe is expected to make her long-awaited TV acting debut as Sadie Thompson in Somerset Maugham's 'Rain,' an NBC special this spring. Her fee, which she'll turn over to Actors Studio, is termed the highest ever paid a star, which means

In one of the rare times she did make it onto TV, Marilyn Monroe waits in the Connecticut home of business associate Milton Greene to be interviewed by Edward R. Murrow on a 1955 Person to Person.

it tops Sir Laurence Olivier's $100,000 for *The Moon and Sixpence,* Elvis Presley's $125,000 for Frank Sinatra's special last year." —*January 28, 1961*

"Rod (*The Twilight Zone*) Serling will adapt W. Somerset Maugham's 'Rain' to TV for Marilyn Monroe, Fredric March and Florence Eldridge (Mrs. March)." —*February 25, 1961*

"Marilyn Monroe hasn't been able to postpone a Hollywood movie commitment, so chances are now remote for her to star in 'Rain,' that projected NBC special next season. She was to have taped the show this spring for televising in the fall." —*May 20, 1961*

"Marilyn Monroe's deal to star in 'Rain' is on again. She's expected to tape the 90-minute NBC special in July for presentation in early fall, probably in the

time period following the first *Bob Hope Show.*" —*June 17, 1961*

[August 5, 1962—Marilyn Monroe found dead of barbiturate overdose in her Hollywood home.]

"Official Films is preparing a half-hour special, 'The Marilyn Monroe Story,' to be aired in December." —*October 27, 1962*

"Julie London on Feb. 13 stars in an *Eleventh Hour,* 'Like a Diamond in the Sky.' The story will have overtones of the life the late Marilyn Monroe." —*February 2, 1963*

"Mike [Wallace] will narrate 'Marilyn Monroe,' a documentary set for March 24 on ABC." —*March 16, 1963*

"Director John Huston will narrate the *ABC Stage 67* Nov. 30 documentary on 'The Life and Legend of Marilyn Monroe.'" —*October 22, 1966*

Till Death Do Us Part

Characters die on TV all the time. In fact, sometimes it seems as if we've lost more people in the TV wars than in all the world wars.

But that's fiction. Unfortunately, sometimes it's the performers themselves who die—for real—during or between seasons, throwing the shows they appear in into a tizzy, and requiring some quick and fancy replacement footwork on the part of producers.

Here are some of those sad moments, the comings and goings of familiar performers, and how the people who make TV handled the situations. And, as in life, the subject of their deaths was usually avoided—they just disappeared.

Joseph Kearns, who played Mr. Wilson on *Dennis the Menace,* died during the 1961–62 season and was replaced by Gale Gordon, who played his brother.

After only four episodes were filmed, Diana Hyland, the mother of the Bradford brood in *Eight Is Enough,* died. When the series returned in the fall 1977 season, Betty Buckley was brought in to replace Hyland as the new wife of widowed Tom Bradford (Dick Van Patten).

Freddie Prinze, star of the NBC hit sitcom *Chico and the Man* (which premiered September 13, 1974), committed suicide in 1977 at age 22.

After only a few episodes were in the can, Peter Duel, star of the Western *Alias Smith and Jones,* shot himself to death on December 31, 1971. His role was quickly recast, with Roger Davis taking over.

On March 3, 1966, Alice Pearce, who

William Frawley—vaudevillian, movie actor, I Love Lucy *veteran—made his last regular series TV appearance as "Bub" O'Casey in* My Three Sons. *This 1960 first-season shot shows (clockwise from top) Frawley with the Douglas clan: Don Grady (Robbie), Fred MacMurray (Steve), Stanley Livingston (Chip), and Tim Considine (Mike).*

played Gladys Kravitz on *Bewitched,* died of cancer. Her role as Gladys was taken over by Sandra Gould until the show's demise in 1972.

During the 1968 season, Bea Benadaret died, leaving *Petticoat Junction* without its mother figure, Kate Bradley. *Lassie's* June Lockhart came in as the town doctor until the show went off the air at the end of the 1969–70 season.

On *Phyllis,* 87-year-old Mother Dexter (Judith Lowry) married 92-year-old Arthur Lanson (Burt Mustin) in December 1976. Not long after, both actors were dead.

After production of the 1977–78 season, Will Geer—Grandpa Walton on *The Waltons*—died.

After appearing on *What's My Line?* the night of November 7, 1965, Dorothy Kilgallen went home, wrote her next day's column, and died of an unintentional alcohol-barbiturate poisoning. Her spot as a permanent panelist—which she held for 16 consecutive seasons was never filled; only guest panelists sat there until the show's run ended on September 3, 1967.

Richard Hart, the star of *Ellery Queen,* died after the December 28, 1950, show at age 35. The next week's episode went on as if nothing had happened, with a new Ellery—Lee Bowman—in the role.

George Cleveland, "Gramps" of *Lassie,* died in 1957 during the summer after his third year in the role. He was replaced by George Chandler as Uncle Petrie Martin for the 1958–59 season.

During the 1960–61 season of *Wagon Train,* Ward Bond died, and was replaced by John McIntire.

Nicholas Colasanto as Ernie "Coach" Pantusso with some of the cast of Cheers *(clockwise from right): Rhea Perlman, Ted Danson, Shelley Long, and George Wendt.*

On July 11, 1965, Ray Collins—Lieutenant Tragg of *Perry Mason*—died. The policeman foil for Perry was played for the last season of the show by Richard Anderson as Lieutenant Drum.

When actress Barbara Colby was murdered in Los Angeles, she had just completed the third episode of *Phyllis* in the role of Julie. Liz Torres took over the same role a short time later.

When Michael Conrad died after three and a half seasons of *Hill Street Blues,* he was replaced by Robert Prosky, playing Sergeant Stanislaus Jablonski.

When Jim Davis, Jock Ewing on *Dallas,* died in 1981, the producers couldn't do anything immediately about the death of Jock on the series, because they were in the midst of dealing with the death of Kristin in the Ewing swimming pool. So

Legendary Western film director John Ford and star Ward Bond prepare a scene for "The Colter Craven Story," a Wagon Train *episode that aired on November 23, 1960. This would be their last collaboration; Bond died soon after.*

they made up a story of how Jock had to go to South America on a special mission for the government, kept him alive with phone calls to Southfork until the time was right, then had him go down in a plane, at which time he was missing and presumed dead.

When Nicholas Colasanto, who played Coach the bartender on *Cheers,* died in 1985, he was replaced by Woody Harrelson as Woody, who was a junior version of Coach. And no wonder: since the Coach-type character worked well in the mix of personalities on the show, the writers wrote it so that Woody had taken a mail-order bartending course from Coach and had turned up in Boston to meet him personally. The writers wrote in Coach's death, and Woody's hiring.

When Redd Foxx reported to work on *The Royal Family* on October 11, 1991, he thought he had a touch of something; he wasn't feeling well. During a run-through for the series' eighth episode, he collapsed and died at age 68. The series continued that season without him, his death was worked into the narrative, and he was not replaced, although Jackée was added to the cast, playing his and Della Reese's daughter.

Happy Holiday

The job of network publicity departments is to get their shows and stars seen and mentioned in the press as often and as glowingly as possible. These attempts have taken many forms, from press releases and informational packets to what we have on these pages: holiday- or event-linked photos featuring programs and talent that would make an editor (especially a tired one, with some space to fill) want to put them in the paper. Stunt shots and pneumatic beauties never hurt a photo's chances.

The selection here is from the *TV Guide* photo files, and never made it into the magazine.

Joining in New Year's festivities (seems like some party) are, left to right, Polka Dottie, El Squeako Mouse, Rootie Kazootie, and Gala Poochie. The photo also announced Rootie's new Saturday-morning ABC-network TV show beginning on January 3, 1953.

ALBERT FREEMAN

Paul Winchell and Jerry Mahoney usher the new year in with a bit of typical imagery, even though one of them is a diapered dummy.

Cleo, the thinking-out-loud basset hound of The People's Choice, seems to have really tied one on. But, then, she always looked that way.

The cast of The Bob Cummings Show—left to right, Dwayne Hickman, Bob Cummings, Rosemary DeCamp, and Ann B. Davis—do actually a pretty meager job of decking their hall with holiday cheer. But it's the thought that counts.

Comedian Ken Murray, as Father Time, poses with Darla Hood, once famous for being a member of the "Our Gang" troupe and later his leading lady on CBS's Ken Murray Show.

Hard to believe but true—yes, that's 60 Minutes' tough, hard-nosed interviewer, Mike Wallace, doing a jig in honor of Saint Patrick's Day in his earlier days as one half of the CBS-TV afternoon show Mike and Buff; his Emerald Isle dancing partner is his then wife, Buff Cobb.

TV Guide Picks the 20 Top Television Personalities of the 1980s

1. Bill Cosby—"By any measure, he's the most successful entertainer in history."

2. Larry Hagman—"He played the smiling cobra with such campy finesse that millions of viewers found themselves hooked, in 1980, on what became TV's greatest cliffhanger: Who Shot J.R.?"

3. Oprah Winfrey—". . . likable, down-to-earth warmth enabled an overweight black woman to explode into a phenomenon of the '80s."

4. Ronald Reagan—"The first made-for-TV president."

5. Joan Collins—"Long before Leona Helmsley and Tammy Faye Bakker, there was Alexis Morell Carrington Colby Dexter Rowan. . . ."

6. Ted Koppel—"He brought to television an unparalleled depth of coverage that was both slick and informative."

7. Vanna White—"The TV camera has a way of getting to the truth, and Vanna came across as what she is: sweet, clean-cut, unaffected."

8. David Letterman—"His sardonic sensibility and off-center charm became an in-the-know cultural beacon in the non-stop blather of TV talk shows."

9. Michael J. Fox—"Fox himself deserves much of the credit for turning *Family Ties'* glib, conservative Alex P. Keaton into a charmingly sly yet surprisingly vulnerable character."

10. Tom Selleck—"Selleck was TV's dominant male sex symbol of the '80s."

11. The California Raisins—"Never had dried fruit been so much fun."

12. Sam Donaldson—"What Howard Cosell was to TV sports in the '70s, Sam Donaldson has been to TV news in the '80s: aggressive, abrasive, obnoxious—and loud."

13. John Madden—"As CBS's Emmy-winning football analyst . . . he thinks he's the luckiest guy alive."

14. Hulk Hogan—"Professional wrestling came of age—big time—in the '80s. And with it came the full-blown prominence of the sport's master of the universe."

15. Don Johnson—"As undercover cop Sonny Crockett on NBC's *Miami Vice,* Don Johnson redefined cool in the '80s."

16. Roseanne Barr—"Was there any regular female performer on network television bigger than roly-poly Roseanne Barr this decade?"

17. Dan Rather—"Inquiring minds often wanted to know more about what the *CBS Evening News* anchorman was saying and wearing than what he was reporting."

18. Morton Downey, Jr.—"He was the Sultan of Shock TV."

19. ALF—"The wisecracking alien from the planet Melmac crashed through the garage roof of the Tanner family on an NBC sitcom in 1986, and suddenly Miss Piggy seemed passé."

20. Pee-wee Herman—"One of the more unlikely stars to emerge this decade."

December 9, 1989

Loved Him, Hated Her

When, in 1989, *TV Guide* polled TV producers, directors, writers, actors, crews, designers, hair and makeup specialists, publicists, drivers, gofers, and others who come in contact with TV stars, it came up with this list of the most-liked and least-liked stars.

THE GOOD GUYS	THE BAD GUYS
Carol Burnett	Valerie Bertinelli
Ted Danson	Fred Dryer
Linda Evans	Faye Dunaway
John Forsythe	Redd Foxx
Marla Gibbs	Kate Jackson
Mariette Hartley	Brian Keith
Katherine Helmond	Jane Seymour
Angela Lansbury	Robert Urich
Judith Light	Ken Wahl
Bob Newhart	Raquel Welch
Christopher Reeve	
Lee Remick	
Tom Selleck	
Jaclyn Smith	
Robert Wagner	
Betty White	

BAD GUYS LIFETIME ACHIEVEMENT AWARDS

Robin Givens
Bryant Gumbel
Shelley Long
Cybill Shepherd
Bruce Willis

SHOWS

The Andersons of Father Knows Best: *left to right, Bud (Billy Gray), Kitten (Lauren Chapin), Jim (Robert Young),*
Margaret (Jane Wyatt), and Betty (Elinor Donahue).

The American Family

Fads and phases may come and go on television—all Westerns, which then disappear to make room for all doctors, followed by a clean sweep and the insertion of all sit-coms, and then enough lawyers to start an ambulance-chasing relay team.

But through it all, the one constant, important, unyielding element of TV fiction is the family—nuclear, extended, fractured, makeshift, dysfunctional, whatever. The center of the home-screen universe is the family. The cowboys wanted to find a piece of land, settle down, and start one—the Cartwrights had one, Matt and Kitty may have thought of having one, and we assumed that Roy and Dale had the same one on-screen that they had off it, but it was pretty ambiguous. Detectives and cops regretted how they let theirs deteriorate and drift away, which is why they boozed and broad-ed their way to penitence. Doctors and lawyers thought of one (they usually had family photos in silver frames on their desks), but had to spend too much time away at work to make for a happy one.

Then, of course, the families on-screen were watched by families at home—nuclear, extended, fractured, makeshift, dysfunctional, whatever—and some were Nielsen families, who in turn were watched by other people.

When our families watched those families, we identified with them (although they solved their problems in 30 minutes minus commercials, whereas we had to go to group therapy for 50 minutes twice a week). Or we pitied them, and they made us feel better. Or we laughed at them, and they made us feel we were all family. Except their house was always neater, they had better-looking food in their refrigerators, and their back and front doors were never locked, which means they lived in a better neighborhood than we did.

From *Mama*'s Hansens to Fox's Simpsons, TV has always showcased the keystone to the grand structure of life in this part of the planet: the American family.

Along about 300 B.C. a Greek playwright named Menander observed, "Marriage, if one will face the truth, is an evil, but a necessary evil."

This morsel of wisdom went unchallenged for about 2200 years. Then came television, and Menander was amended to read: "Marriage, if one will face the truth, is an evil, but in television it's an unnecessary evil."

Which is why there are no husbands in *Here's Lucy, Julia, The Ghost and Mrs. Muir, The Big Valley* and *The Doris Day Show*. And which is also why there are no wives for the No. 1 characters in *Mayberry, R.F.D., My Three Sons, Bonanza, Lancer,*

Daktari, Will Sonnett and *The Beverly Hillbillies*. The central figures of all these shows *once* were married, of course, a fact which serves to legitimize the children; but the spouses have conveniently passed on to leave the field clear for middle-aged romance whenever the spirit moves the writers.

This plethora of widows and widowers—really, it's enough to make an old-fashioned, self-respecting census-taker bust right out laughing—offers a strangely distorted version of the average American home. Indeed, we may have millions of youngsters in this country feeling put upon because they've got to tolerate both a mother *and* a father while the kids on TV have only one *or* the other.

Actually we suppose the present popularity of truncated families is an improvement over what we used to have—bumbling husbands constantly being straightened out by clever wives. It got so that for a while "husband" and "stupid" were synonymous.

Would it ever be possible to get back to the normal family relationship of *Father Knows Best?*

Or have we progressed too much for that?

October 19, 1968

The Cleavers of Leave It to Beaver: *left to right, Ward (Hugh Beaumont), June (Barbara Billingsley), Wally (Tony Dow), and Theodore "The Beaver" (Jerry Mathers).*

The Stones of The Donna Reed Show: *top to bottom, Dr. Alex (Carl Betz), Donna (Donna Reed), Mary (Shelley Fabares), and Jeff (Paul Petersen).*

The Coneheads of Saturday Night Live: *left to right, Jane Curtin, Dan Aykroyd, and Laraine Newman.*

The Waltons: *clockwise from top, John Boy (Richard Thomas), Grandpa Zeb (Will Geer), Grandma Esther (Ellen Corby), Olivia (Michael Learned), Erin (Mary Elizabeth McDonough), Mary Ellen (Judy Norton-Taylor), Jason (Jon Walmsley), Elizabeth (Kami Cotler), John (Ralph Waite), Ben (Eric Scott) and Jim-Bob (David W. Harper).*

The Huxtables of The Cosby Show: *back row, left to right, Sondra (Sabrina Le Beauf), Vanessa (Tempestt Bledsoe), Theo (Malcolm-Jamal Warner); bottom row, left to right, Denise (Lisa Bonet), Dr. Cliff (Bill Cosby), Rudy (Keshia Knight Pulliam), Clair (Phylicia Rashad).*

The Ewings of Dallas: *back row, Pam (Victoria Principal), Bobby (Patrick Duffy), Jock (Jim Davis), Sue Ellen (Linda Gray), J.R. (Larry Hagman); seated, Lucy (Charlene Tilton) and Miss Ellie (Barbara Bel Geddes).*

The Conners of Roseanne: *clockwise, from top, Becky (Lecy Goranson), Dan (John Goodman), D.J. (Michael Fishman), Roseanne (Roseanne Barr Arnold), and Darlene (Sara Gilbert).*

The Bundys of Married . . . with Children: *back row, right to left, Kelly (Christina Applegate), Bud (David Faustino); front row, right to left, Al (Ed O'Neill) and Peggy (Katey Sagal).*

The Taylors of The Andy Griffith Show: *Opie (Ronny Howard) and Sheriff Andy (Andy Griffith), among TV's first wave of widowers with children.*

The Simpsons: *back row, left to right, Homer, Marge; front row, left to right, Lisa, Bart, and Maggie.*

The Cartwrights of Bonanza: *left to right, Hoss (Dan Blocker), Ben (Lorne Greene), Adam (Pernell Roberts), and Little Joe (Michael Landon).*

The Hands That Rocked the Cradle

Kid shows—afternoons with Popeye, weekends with The Little Rascals or Looney Tunes—nearly always had a human host, and more often than not that host had a puppet, marionette, or dummy—elaborately custom-made, lumpily and cheaply hand-crafted, or plain old store-bought—somewhere at hand. And, occasionally, literally on hand. Some puppeteer/hosts broke the local barrier and made it nationally; others stayed close to home, and became to their young viewers colorful babysitters, primary ethicists, best friends, local legends . . . and the happiest of memories.

Lest it be forgotten, the very first Emmy ever awarded went to a puppeteer—20-year-old Los Angeles ventriloquist Shirley Dinsdale (her dummy/companion was named Judy Splinters)—as Outstanding Personality in Television in 1949.

COLUMBIA/CRONENWETH

Rin Tin Tin—not hard of hearing—in this 1958 photo is fitted with a radio receiver, permitting his trainer to give "Rintie" instructions during long shots as far as 300 yards from the camera.

RENI PHOTOS

Yes, that's Kermit, practically a tadpole, sitting atop Paul Arnold on Footlight Theater, *on WRC-TV, Washington. Behind and below Arnold were the just-starting-out Jim Henson and Jane Neble, experimenting with the first Muppets. Here, Kermit plays Nanki Poo in a production of* The Mikado.

Tricky, anarchic Froggy the Gremlin was the constant undoing of Andy Devine and Midnight the Cat on the nationally televised Andy's Gang, sponsored by Buster Brown, seen in this 1955 photo.

Rootie Kazootie—Howdy Doody's slightly formidable competition— went out nationally from ABC's New York studios, along with human sidekicks Todd Russell and daffy policeman Mr. Deedle Doodle.

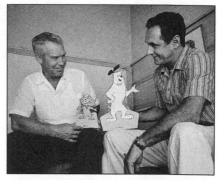

Bill Hanna (left) and Joe Barbera at the start of their TV-cartoon dynasty, with two of the reasons: Ruff and Reddy.

Captain Kangaroo (Bob Keeshan) joins Mrs. Eleanor Roosevelt in a publicity shot (date unknown) promoting UNICEF, the United Nations International Children's Emergency Fund.

"Miss Frances" (Dr. Frances R. Harwich) rings Ding Dong School—the first educationally oriented network program for preschoolers—into session in this 1952 photo.

Dr. Mort Neimark had his brief brush with fame as host of Chicago's Smile Club on WBKB-TV. With the happy dentist are Okay on the right, and Dekay, with the frown.

A plastic sheet placed over the screen and crayons to draw on it were the gimmicks and fun—and the parental nightmare (when kids without the plastic went ahead and drew on the screen anyway)—of Winky Dink and You, with host Jack Barry.

Soupy Sales started out in Detroit before he hit it big, went national, and became the very unsquare root of pie. From the start, all the elements were there, including the furry arms of White Fang (pictured) and Black Tooth, as well as hand-puppets Pookie and Hippy.

Gas gets ready to pop a balloon as Don Herbert prepares to pop a science-project question on Mr. Wizard.

Shari Lewis, one of puppet-dom's most successful women ventriloquists, with Charley Horse (left) and Lamb Chop (right).

"Get moose and squirrel"—and the funny bone of a nation. Jay Ward's creations— Rocket J. Squirrel, Natasha Fatale (both voices by June Foray), Boris Badenov (Paul Frees), and Bullwinkle J. Moose (Bill Scott) of The Bullwinkle Show.

The Making of a Star

After wearing out two Ollies during the years of *Kukla, Fran and Ollie,* puppeteer Burr Tillstrom let *TV Guide* in on the making of Oliver J. (Jethro) Dragon III, 1956 model:

"Tillstrom found the new version quite a problem. The jaws (sawed from a warped pear crate and hinged with scrap leather), the face (yellow satin) and the chin (chamois) were easy. But his spotted skin was a puzzler until Tillstrom remembered a phony ocelot coat Imogene Coca wore on *Your Show of Shows.* He bought the coat.

"Ollie's hair was even tougher. It was made of Mongolian wolf, and China's Bamboo Curtain probably would have kept him bald had a friend not re-discovered a lady puppet Tillstrom gave him many years ago. She had a wolf-hair boa, which Burr reclaimed and fashioned into dragon hair.

"From kid gloves came eyes and a tooth. Lashes and brows are clipped wool felt. His innards, however, really set Ollie apart from the rest of history's dragons. They're real gold cloth."

October 13, 1956

Burr Tillstrom, the usually unseen man behind the hands, joins in this 1952 pose with Kukla (left), Fran (Allison), and Oliver J. "Ollie" Dragon.

Playing Games

Game shows, among the oldest, most popular, and cheapest-to-produce programs on television, have tended to come in a handful of distinct forms. There were:

Panel Shows: These tended to be variations on, and elaborations of, parlor games. There was never much money involved; the fun was in watching urbane and witty panelists (whatever became of that species?) react and interact to guess a secret, dispense proper advice, offer criticism, or wrangle with the language. Shows like *What's My Line?, I've Got a Secret, To Tell the Truth, Masquerade Party,* and *Pantomime Quiz* fall into this category. Variants—shows basically played for laughs, and giving the comic/host a showcase for his wit—would include *You Bet Your Life, Do You Trust Your Wife?,* and *Who Do You Trust?,* among others.

Quiz Shows: Players for these were usually non–show-business types, picked from the audience or selected through an audition/screening process. A certain amount of skill or knowledge was required, and sizable cash amounts or expensive prizes were the reward. Players would have to: remember where things were hidden (*Concentration*), connect the dots to guess a famous face (*Dotto*), decode a phrase based on the uncovering of hidden letters (*Wheel of Fortune*), provide the correct questions to provided statements (*Jeopardy!*), guess a word based on clues of related words (*Password*), estimate the retail price of an item (*The Price Is Right*), and so on.

TV game shows' biggest money-winners, in a 1957 photo: (left to right) Michael Della Rocca (The $64,000 Question, $64,000 Challenge), Robert Strom (The $64,000 Question), Charles Van Doren (Twenty-One), Thomas Kane, Dr. Joyce Brothers, and Peter Freuchen (all three on both The $64,000 Question *and* Challenge*).*

Big Payoff Shows: These were quiz shows that dangled huge amounts of money in front of contestants, if they could answer terrifically difficult questions of esoteric knowledge. They were played to the high-drama hilt, complete with drum rolls and isolation booths. Also, unfortunately, a few in the 1950s were rigged, which nearly deep-sixed the quiz-show genre entirely. Prime examples of the Big Payoff shows were *The $64,000 Question* and *Twenty-One.*

Stunt Shows: In these, contestants could win moderate amounts of money, or appliances, or merely the thanks of a grateful nation, by enduring indignities or pressure-packed party-game situations. *Beat the Clock* and *Truth or Consequences* were chief examples; *The Gong Show* was a mutation.

Agony Shows: These programs let the national viewing audience be witness to often pathetic, painful, and embarrassing tales of woe and deprivation told by several poor souls, one of whom would be voted the "winner" among the afflicted and would win often rather inappropriate prizes. There is no better example of these than *Queen for a Day.*

RON SLENZAK

Three panelists vied for cash prizes—and a certain amount of pride, especially if one was a five-time-undefeated champion—by guessing the correct questions to match given answers on the classic, long-running Jeopardy! *Art Fleming hosted the original daytime version during the 1960s and 1970s; Alex Trebek, seen here, headed the syndicated version starting in 1984.*

Game shows made celebrities and even heroes of their winners, and made careers and fortunes for their emcees—the best, most likable, and most trusted of whom (like Bob Barker, Bud Collyer, Bill Cullen, Monty Hall, and Jack Bailey) went from one show to the next, stringing together years of full employment as that most elusive of TV personalities: host. And the

Pat Sajak was the host, Vanna White (about whose all-American good looks much was made) was the letter-turner, in the guess-the-words game show that was the most popular syndicated show in America, Wheel of Fortune. *The first* Wheel of Fortune, *not related, was an early-1950s audience-participation series that rewarded people for their good deeds and was hosted by Todd Russell.*

same went for favorite models, product-pointers, letter-turners, and elbow-grabbers like *Let's Make a Deal*'s Carol Merrill and *Wheel of Fortune*'s Vanna White.

Whereas today it would seem almost inconceivable for, say, Dan Rather or Ted Koppel to be a game-show host, in the early days of TV there was no such barrier. Walter Cronkite (*It's News to Me*), John Daly (*What's My Line?*), and Mike Wallace (or Myron Wallace, as he was known when he hosted *Majority Rules* from Chicago in 1949–50) all were game-show hosts.

For as long as there is television and people with playful minds and a gambling streak, there will be game shows, morning, noon, and night, on network, cable, and syndication.

"Suppose you have four contestants and you give each of them $1000. Now you introduce a small boy and his dog, and ask them how *little* money they would take to shoot the dog in front of the boy. . . . Now, of course, we wouldn't shoot any dog in front of anybody. We would modify this into—well, just something distasteful, say jumping into ice-cold water with their clothes on. The show was a parody but it had one good element. The bidding went downward.

"I used to think *Greed* was the ultimate in game shows. No more. The ultimate? It would be one in which the contestant dies on the air. I swear it's conceivable!" —*Chuck Barris, speaking of an idea for a game show,* Greed, *and other things, 1975*

"On paper, it doesn't sound like much, but she has become a very important part of the show. She should get a lot of credit for that. But, of course, if you put 'letter turner' on your 1040 Form, it sounds a little strange. But then, so does 'gameshow host.'" —*Pat Sajak, about Vanna White, 1985*

One of these three women was who she said she was. The others were impostors, who would be questioned by panelists trying to determine who the real one was, on To Tell The Truth. *The host was Bud Collyer.*

Charles Van Doren, one of the key figures in the game-show scandals, in one of his Twenty-One appearances that riveted the nation. Jack Barry was the host.

Ubiquitous host Bud Collyer stands amid the rubble of a stunt that occurred on a Beat the Clock Crockery Night in 1953.

EUGENE COEAL

Hollywood Squares *was a funny game of tic-tac-toe, with X's and O's awarded when contestants correctly agreed or disagreed with responses to questions given by celebrities who often lied, frequently joked. Peter Marshall hosted; Paul Lynde became a huge celebrity by providing hilarious answers in the center square.*

As the mystery guest signed in, regular panelists Arlene Francis, Dorothy Kilgallen, and Bennett Cerf would try to guess his or her identity and occupation on the near-legendary What's My Line?, *with host John Charles Daly.*

Long before The Dating Game, The Love Connection, *and even* Studs, *there was* Blind Date, *hosted by Arlene Francis (then Melvyn Douglas and later Jan Murray), which had college men or servicemen on one side of a barrier, female models on the other, querying each other via a special telephone hookup. Winners went on a date.*

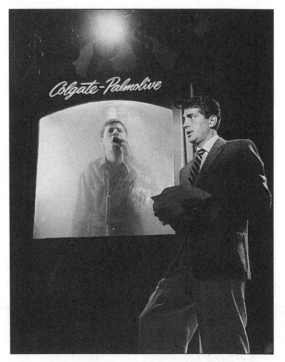

Dean Martin and Jerry Lewis spoof the big-giveaway quiz shows of the 1950s in a skit on the Colgate Comedy Hour.

In this 1955 Truth or Consequences *stunt, a blindfolded and earmuffed contestant was told he was going to bathe in a prominent Hollywood home, and if he could guess which one, he would win a freezer. He was driven around Hollywood, returned to the corner of Sunset and Vine, and led into a room with a bathtub; a truck derrick lifted the room, and he found himself the object of amused pedestrians.*

NBC/HERB BALL

Host Jack Bailey stands with the Queen for a Day, *who is surrounded by models wearing the wardrobe presented to her.*

NBC/ELMER W. HOLLOWAY

Shot before continuously rolling film cameras, and with the show scripted to a large degree in order to let host Groucho Marx prepare his ad-libs, the silliness of You Bet Your Life *gave Groucho a second career, a whole new audience, and a big bank account.*

"...With the News"

No question about it, we're getting the news faster and faster. If only it'd come better and better.

—December 17, 1966

"There *is* good journalism on television, more than critics give it credit for. And I have a suggestion. Long ago when Murrow was active at CBS News, he did not see why broadcasters should not turn about and examine what newspapers do. The result was a radio series called *CBS Views the Press*. There has been nothing quite like it since. That is too bad. It would be healthy if there were again today, in this business of criticism, a two-way street."

—Edward Bliss, Jr., in a "Commentary," July 15, 1978

Whenever television deals with subject matter slightly more involved than custard pie–throwing, comedy-drama or straight news reporting, there is a tendency to sugar-coat, to find ways of presenting material in two-syllable words, amply illustrated. One gains the impression from such programs that the producer said to himself: "I understand this stuff, but the average viewer is much less intelligent than I am. So if I want to keep my audience at all, I'd better reduce it to kindergarten level."

Ed Murrow seems to operate on a different premise. His two TV offerings, *See It Now* and *Person to Person,* give the viewer credit for having some brains of his own. Murrow talks *to* his audience, not *down* to it. He does not apologize for presenting, say, Sen. Margaret Chase

Dave Garroway faces the early morning on Today; *then Garroway meets the onlookers—mostly out-of-towners—who came to see and be seen through the big plate-glass window wall of the ground-floor Rockefeller Center studio.*

Smith to discuss Russian politics and living conditions. He did not attempt to translate into simple concepts Dr. J. Robert Oppenheimer's rather scholarly Atomic Age concept. Murrow's programs don't do the thinking for the audience—they make the audience think.

For respecting his viewers; for bring ing them informative shows, Ed Murrow deserves his high place among the important figures in television.

—*February 5, 1955*

Yes, there certainly *is* a place on television for frank, unrehearsed interviews of people in the public eye. Every so often we see such an interview—one that pinpoints weaknesses as well as the strength of the person being interviewed, one that is not entirely devoted to plugging a movie, or a book or a pct project.

We had hopes that *The Mike Wallace Interview* would be such a program. Instead, Wallace is so eager to be sensational, so concerned with showmanship, that his program loses the significance that might be forthcoming from a more sincere reportorial effort.

The clocks above his head took a licking but kept on ticking as John Cameron Swayze read the latest updates on NBC's Camel News Caravan *in the early 1950s.*

Wallace's first guest was Gloria Swanson, who had a pitch—an alleged cancer cure. His second was a Ku Klux Klan mogul who had a pitch—segregation. Then came Mickey Cohen, a gangster who had a pitch—criticism of Los Angeles city officials.

If Wallace were an experienced reporter he hardly would have glossed over Gloria Swanson's endorsement of a so-called cancer cure that is not accepted by recognized authorities on that disease. Nor would he deliberately have drawn from Miss Swanson the exact address to which unfortunate cancer sufferers might write for "information" on the "cure" and—understood, though not mentioned—perhaps send a contribution.

A reporter would not have skipped from charge to charge with a Klan chieftain, permitting him to deny everything; a reporter would have kept digging. Nor would a reporter put a gangster on television to assault respectable officials, and then wish him luck.

Wallace's show is sensational and controversial. But please bear in mind

Edward R. Murrow and two of his "boys"—Eric Sevareid (seated) and Charles Collingwood—wait out the returns during the 1952 election coverage on CBS.

that it's a *show.* It is not responsible reporting—although it should be.

June 29, 1957

Commentators who know what to say are *usually* competent. Commentators who know when to shut up are *always* competent.

That seems to be the opinion of readers who tell us they start climbing the walls when, during network coverage of, say, an Apollo mission, the network commentators blithely talk on over the voices of the astronauts and Mission Control officers.

"They seem to have reached the conclusion that their asinine comments are more appreciated than the astronauts' conversations," one furious Cape Canaveral, Fla., reader wrote us. "I sug-

Once called "the most trusted man in America," CBS's news-anchor giant Walter Cronkite in a familiar pose—at the news desk, covering breaking stories.

gest," he continued rather unkindly, "that these harbingers of doom be locked together in a space capsule and allowed to talk each other to death."

Similar sentiments were voiced by readers during last year's political conventions when the networks decided on and off that general background and behind-the-scenes political activity were more important than what was happening on the convention floor—or that the floor was more interesting than what the speaker on the rostrum was saying.

And, of course, there are certain sports commentators, like the baseball lads who give the life history of a player every time he comes to bat, and who feel compelled to gabble on and on describing what the viewer can see for himself. And the football commentators who never let you hear the bands.

Silence is a wonderful thing, especially with a medium that is supposed to be visual. As that noble old Roman Publilius Syrus said: "I have often regretted my speech, never my silence."

Which is good advice for TV com-

Former code clerk and Soviet defector Igor Gouzenko, in hiding in Canada, gives his first interview, on television, to Drew Pearson (date unknown).

mentators—and for all of us, for that matter. There's just too darned much noise in this world.

July 5, 1969

In the event the fact has escaped his attention until now, Speaker Sam Rayburn should be informed of an Associated Press report that the last session of the Supreme Soviet, Russia's parliamentary body, was televised.

This couldn't happen in America, where regular sessions of Congress and its committee meetings are closed to television cameras. Only for an occasional Presidential message, or a talk by a foreign diplomat, are Americans permitted a televised glimpse of their Representatives at work.

Quite aside from the value to our people, and to our Government, of giving us a direct look at Congress in action, Congressional telecasts would have a direct bearing on our propaganda war with the Soviets.

It would be much easier, much more effective, to permit the telecasts than to explain to the world why they are not permitted.

March 24, 1956

CHEERS: To the expansion this week of the half-hour *MacNeil/Lehrer Report* into the *MacNeil/Lehrer Newshour.* This should add breadth to its customary depth good news for news buffs.

—September 3, 1983

CHEERS: To *60 Minutes.* Morley Safer's segment on the apparent inconsistencies during the trial and sentencing of Lenell Geter was instrumental in winning the convicted robber at least temporary freedom—and showed off the CBS pro-

gram at its crusading best.

—February 4, 1984

JEERS: To NBC's Roger Mudd, for his overly adversarial interview with Sen. Gary Hart on "Super Tuesday." "Will you do your Teddy Kennedy imitation for me now?" Mudd asked Hart. How about doing your Edward R. Murrow imitation for us, Roger?

—April 14, 1984

CHEERS: To C-SPAN and Cable News Network, for providing a public service by televising the political conventions gavel-to-gavel; and to ABC, CBS and NBC, for providing a public service by

The man who replaced Cronkite—feisty, hardworking, controversial reporter Dan Rather became his network's standard-bearer in 1981—and remained just as feisty, hardworking, and controversial.

If American news has a homespun, eloquent poet laureate, it is Charles Kuralt of CBS, whose "On the Road" reports captured the essences of the American experience, and whose Sunday-morning news program became a soothing, enlightening habit.

not doing so. Most viewers ended up with far more choice than they had in the past when gavel-to-gavel was *de rigueur* for the networks. Now, the only losers are those political junkies *without* cable.

—September 1, 1984

CHEERS: To Deborah Norville, the fresh-faced new anchorwoman on *NBC News at Sunrise*. At the ungodly hour of 6:30 A.M., Norville manages to be cheerful and intelligent, delivering the news without being either treacly or abrasive. We hope to see more of her.

—March 7, 1987

JEERS: To those local-station "news updates" that aren't updates at all, but rather thirty-second or one-minute promos for the station's latenight newscast. Instead of giving us useful headline information, these pale imitations of the networks' news breaks bombard viewers with empty phrases: "Big fight at City Hall today!" "Will skies clear for the weekend?" "A tight one for [the local baseball team]—did they pull it out?" Come on, guys, give us a break. In fact, give us a news break and save the commercials.

—June 13, 1987

CHEERS: To the heightened political interest of the American public. A poll by the University of Maryland Survey Research Center indicates that the audience for C-SPAN, the public-affairs network, has increased by more than 40 percent in the past three years. While the Iran-contra hearings and the Senate examination of Judge Robert Bork for the Supreme Court vacancy may have been partially responsible, viewers do seem to care more about staying informed.

—February 27, 1988

Canadian-born Peter Jennings, whose first stint at anchoring the ABC news during the 1960s was a bust, came back in the 1980s after being a foreign correspondent, winning over large segments of the viewership with his crisp, informed delivery.

JEERS: To the evening newscasts on ABC, CBS and NBC for habitually ending their shows with soft features about flying-saucer builders, dogsled races, and the like. Granted, most of the news is bad, and these stories give anchormen an opportunity to sign off with a wry chuckle. But this fluff would be easier to take if these same news organizations weren't continually moaning that 22 minutes isn't enough time to explore the really important stories. There's a surfeit of entertainment on TV. We can take our news straight, thank you.

—March 5, 1988

JEERS: To the network news divisions for not being more responsive to viewers. Print publications contain letters to the editor columns. It's about time televi-

sion news provided a similar service.

—April 23, 1988

CHEERS: To Cable News Network, for its extraordinary coverage of the Persian Gulf war. From the outset of hostilities on Jan. 16, CNN's round-the-clock reporting has set the tone for how this conflict is being chronicled. Among the more memorable moments from the war's first days . . .

On the first night of the fighting, CNN's Bernard Shaw, John Holliman and Peter Arnett provided electrifying reports—from their room in Baghdad's Al Rashid Hotel—as Allied planes flew bombing missions against the Iraqi capital.

A day later (following a crackdown on journalists by Iraqi censors), Shaw and Holliman made their way to Jordan and eventually home—bringing with them

Tom Brokaw—seen here with cohost Jane Pauley on the Today *show—became New York–based coanchor (with Roger Mudd in Washington) of the* NBC Nightly News, *then sole anchor in 1983.*

extraordinary footage of that first night's bombing.

Meanwhile, Arnett elected to stay behind. Back in 1966, when he worked for the Associated Press, Arnett won a Pulitzer Prize for his reporting from Vietnam. At press time, he was the only U.S. television journalist still working in Baghdad.

The next night, Iraq launched its first Scud missiles against Israel, and CNN was back with continuous updates from Tel Aviv, Jerusalem, Washington and Saudi Arabia. In the process, a mass TV audience got its first up-close view of what CNN military analyst James Blackwell called "the fog of war"—the uncertainty that goes hand-in-hand with any military operation. That night we all came to real-

In 1979, the Iran hostage crisis spawned a regular late-night ABC update on the situation; Nightline soon became a permanent fixture, and its anchor, Ted Koppel, a respected hard-hitting interviewer.

ize we were in for a long haul: the war with Iraq wasn't going to be a miniseries.

—February 9, 1991

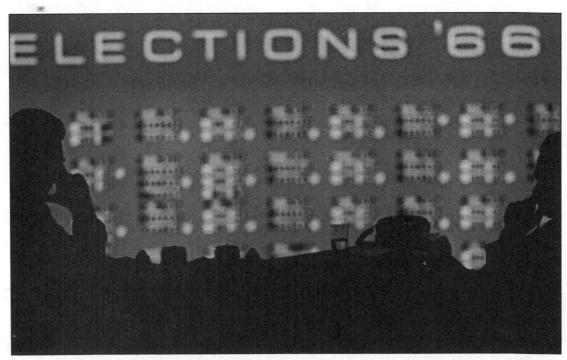

The powerhouse NBC news team of Chet Huntley and David Brinkley, brought together in 1956, anchored much of their network's coverage of major events, including here the 1966 off-year elections.

Ghosts of "Shock Theaters" Past

Three things converged in middle-to-late-1950s TV: the rise in power of American teenagers as a consumer demographic and a social force to be reckoned with; their fascination with and amusement at horror movies, and the cheaper and dumber and scarier the better; and the freeing up and sale to local TV stations by the Hollywood film studios of large numbers of post-1948 movies from their archives. Among these movie packages were dozens of low-budget werewolf and mad-scientist and invading-Martian epics.

One by one—in TV, imitation is the sincerest form of innovation—local stations began airing these movies on weekend nights, wrapped within a show variously called "Shock Theater" or "Monster Movies" or any number of combinations that had the words "ghost," "ghoul," "grave," "crypt," or other out-of-this-world terms in them.

These shows needed hosts, and often the station ID announcer, the weekend weatherman, or a particularly hammy and handy crew member would get done up in semi-horrify-

Miss Tarantula Ghoul, rising from a coffin on her KPTV, Portland, Oregon, show.

ing but mostly silly makeup and costume, affect a Bela Lugosi accent, and have a lot of unscripted fun, cracking up themselves and the cameraman. Frequently, during moments of high action or ultimate fright in the movies, the scene on-screen would suddenly cut to the studio, where the host would be seen somehow participating in or commenting on the film—cowering under a table, throwing an object at the movie monster, or providing similar ditzy, delightful interludes.

These hosts became local legends, had huge followings, and could cause near-riots at personal appearances.

Here, snapped for *TV Guide*—with a few in before-and-after shots—are a bunch of these hosts, back from the grave.

Greg Dunn/ "Gregore" on KMTV, Omaha.

Harvey Brunswick/ "Gregory Grave," host of Shock *on KMBC-TV, Kansas City, Missouri.*

Ray Sparenberg/"Selwyn," the host of Horror Late Show *on WISH-TV, Indianapolis.*

Dolores Denny/ "Marilyn the Witch," host of The Witching Hour *on KCMO-TV, Kansas City, Missouri.*

ANDERSON PHOTO CO.

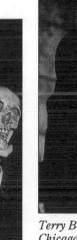

BILL KOFENDER

Tom Dougall/ "Mr. X," the host of Shock Theater *on WXYZ-TV, Detroit.*

MICKEY PALLAS

Terry Bennett, host of Shock Theatre *on WBKB-TV, Chicago.*

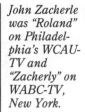

John Zacherle was "Roland" on Philadelphia's WCAU-TV and "Zacherly" on WABC-TV, New York.

Tom Leahy (left) and Lee Parsons/"The Host" and "Rodney" on Nightmare over KAKE-TV, Wichita.

The Future Was Then

Director George Lucas once said of his first *Star Wars* film that "the future should look used." On TV, it has nearly always looked practically borrowed, found in a dumpster, or at least bought on sale at a thrift shop. And, often, those are exactly the ways the costumes and props were accumulated for some shows. It was only after Lucas's movie in 1977, and, perhaps, Stanley Kubrick's *2001: A Space Odyssey* before it, became hits that the networks felt safe that futuristic and sci-fi shows weren't merely the domain of a cadre of nerdy cultists; hence, the producers were able to put some real set, prop, and special-effects money into these shows. Today, the cost to produce just

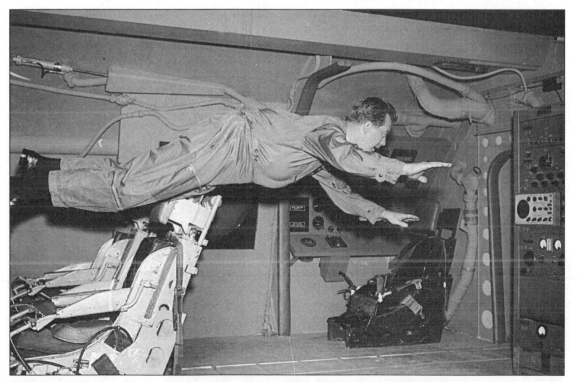

William Lundigan, weightless due to suspension wires, floats during the premiere episode, September 30, 1959,
of Men into Space.

one episode of *Star Trek: The Next Generation* could probably have covered a year's budget on *Space Patrol,* with big raises for all the actors thrown in for good measure.

But, way beyond the question of dollars, more to the point than the threadbare look and feel of them, these were the most optimistic, most hopeful shows on the air. Sitcoms told us there were things in life worth laughing at, including ourselves; detective shows said there were people making things safe for us now, and cowboy shows showed us who made things safe for us then. But the space and sci-fi shows told us there would be a tomorrow—and a generally pretty good one, if you didn't mind battling (and, of course, defeating) Romulans every now and then—and to a generation born with atomic war always dangling by a slim thread over its head, this was no small message. For some, these shows nearly became illustrated doctrines of quasi-religious belief.

The future may have looked used, but on TV it never was and never will be used up.

Today's television set is a first stage, a mere suggestion of what tomorrow's home communications centers will be.

Sooner or later, some authorities believe, most American homes will receive their programs by cable—a wire into their homes—rather than over the air. More important, two-way communication could make possible such additional services as burglar-alarm systems, shopping at home, computer access, facsimile newspapers and magazines, and many more.

Home video tape systems already are on sale and they include cameras for making tape to be played back over ordinary television sets as well as the capability of recording programs off the air. But the greatest potential is believed to be in movies, plays, and other programs in cartridge form which viewers would either buy or rent.

There is only one dark cloud in this sunny picture of what is on the way—very soon—in home communications: How on earth do our all-too-few creative people keep up with the demand for more and more information and entertainment? How can they fill 50 to 100 channels? How can they produce new entertainment to make buying or renting a video cartridge worthwhile?

It's like owning a Rolls-Royce and not being able to get enough gas to make it run.

July 18, 1970

Frankie Thomas, the title character in the early-1950s sci-fi kids' show Tom Corbett, Space Cadet *(based on Robert Heinlein's novel,* Space Cadet*), gets a helping hand four centuries in the future from Dr. Joan Dale (Margaret Garland).*

NBC

TWENTIETH CENTURY–FOX

The most enduring, age-defying science-fantasy series of all time, Gene Roddenberry's Star Trek, *in either its original or* Next Generation *incarnation, gives class to the form. Kirk, "Bones," and Spock (William Shatner, DeForest Kelley, and Leonard Nimoy) gave way to a new bridge and sick bay: (standing, rear) Lieutenant Worf (Michael Dorn), Wesley Crusher (Wil Wheaton), and Lieutenant Commander Data (Brent Spiner); (below, left to right) Commander William Riker (Jonathan Frakes), Lieutenant Geordi La Forge (LeVar Burton), Captain Jean-Luc Picard (Patrick Stewart), Dr. Beverly Crusher (Gates McFadden), and Counselor Deanna Troi (Marina Sirtis).*

GENE TRINDL

June Lockhart and Guy Williams dangle, as did their characters Maureen and Professor John Robinson, who, with their family, crew, a curmudgeon, and a robot, were Lost in Space *for the 1965–67 seasons.*

The happy heroes of the Space Patrol—*who used the Brainograph to undo evildoers—were led by Commander Buzz Corey (Ed Kemmer, seated right); the rest of the crew were (left to right, standing) heroic Major Robbie Robertson (Ken Mayer), good-girl Carol Karlyle (Virginia Hewitt), bad-girl-turned-good-girl Tonga (Nina Bara), and (seated, left) comedy relief Cadet Happy (Lyn Osborn). The* Terra IV, *a 30-foot traveling model of their ship, made personal appearances around the U.S.*

David Hedison, looking as though he's going to pick up his sub and go home, wades in the tank holding models of the ship he pretended to be an officer on in Voyage to the Bottom of the Sea, *which starred Richard Basehart.*

Shows That Never Were

Some of them never got past the talking stage. Others were trial balloons, a way in which producers could place an item in *TV Guide* and see if anybody with power would jump up and down at the prospect, and come forward with gobs of money. More than a few actually made it to the pilot stage. (And, at the very least—which, in these cases, is also the very most—were shown during summer-rerun periods as fill-in programming.) Some even had a place on a network fall or second-season schedule before they were prematurely yanked.

But none of these shows or ideas for shows—each filtered from production offices and press agents up to the pages of *TV Guide*—ever became a series any of us ever had a chance to see.

With some of them, it is easy to figure out why—you can't even imagine how anyone would think such an idea could ever make it. Others seem to have held great promise, but probably fell apart in the casting or execution. Some we actually regret never having had a chance to see.

The vaults of film studios, the basements of networks, are piled high with the filmed evidence or the scripts for the shows that never were. Even as early as 1953, the casualty rate was staggering. During the first six months of that year, 250 new film shows were announced in Hollywood. Of those, 152 never survived beyond the initial ballyhoo. Forty-six reached the pilot-film stage before being dropped. Nineteen managed to live through 3 to 13 films. This was not an atypical year.

Here are some of what you might have viewed instead of what network or advertising executives thought you wanted to watch. Most, at least in concept, aren't any worse, and some sound a universe better than what went on the air . . . and, just as quickly, off it. Big names had little effect; originality played little part.

- *Safari*, a pilot based on the movie *The African Queen*, starring Glynis Johns and James Coburn. It was seen as the March 27, 1962, episode of *The Dick Powell Show*.

- *Horatio Alger*, starring Wally Cox, produced by José Ferrer. —*Early 1950s*

- *Police Hall of Fame*, produced by Bob Hope; each show would dramatize an outstanding police case and present a trophy to the officer involved. —*1953*

- A CBS series about a seven-year-old boy and his older brother, called *The Shrimp*, and featuring Richard Eyer, Sammy Ogg, Ken Peters, and Mary Shipp, set for the 1953–54 season. [This sounds like an early run at what became *Leave It to Beaver* in 1957.]

• Allyn Joslyn and Frances Gifford in a situation comedy called *My Wife, Poor Wretch.* —*1953*

• "There's a rumor that Peter Lorre and *New Yorker* cartoonist Charles Addams are nightmaring up a horror TV series." —*August 7, 1953* [*The Addams Family*, without Lorre, arrived September 18, 1964.]

• "Freddie Bartholomew, who apparently has grown up, has been cast as P. G. Wodehouse's 'Jeeves' in an upcoming Wodehouse film series." — *November 13, 1953*
    "CBS bought rights to P. G. Wodehouse stories as possible spectaculars next fall." —*June 29, 1957*
    "George Sanders, whose *Oliver Chantry* test film failed to sell as a series, is now being sought for a new one, *Jeeves*, based on the famed P. G. Wodehouse character." —*November 29, 1958*

• "CBS mapping an adult science fiction series, to be based on stories of Ray Bradbury." —*November 20, 1953* [Such a project would not occur, and then not on the networks but on cable, for another three decades.]

• "Humphrey Bogart has been quoted as saying he will produce and star with his wife, Lauren Bacall, in their own film series sometime next year." —*November 20, 1953*

• "Peter Lorre and Francis L. Sullivan are joining forces to do a new telefilm series based on Dashiell Hammett's most famous mystery story, 'The Maltese Falcon.'" —*January 29, 1954*

• "Tom Ewell, long signed to an NBC contract, finally gets a show. He's been set to play Mr. Blandings (the one who built the dream house) in a network series to be produced by Worthington Miner." —*April 16, 1954*
    "Maggie Hayes and Steve Dunne set to costar in *The Blandings,* half-hour television film series based on 'Mr. Blandings Builds His Dream House' and tentatively scheduled for NBC next season." —*March 21, 1959*

• "Mae West's upcoming film series will be based on travesties of famous romances. First victims will be Priscilla and John Alden, then Cleopatra, Camille, Du Barry, Fatima and Lady Hamilton." —*April 23, 1954*

• "Mickey Rooney Enterprises has signed Sabu to make a series of TV films in India. Title: 'The Magic Lamp.'" —*July 17, 1954*

• CBS once started to put together a show called *Meet the Hoboes,* featuring a panel of three hoboes and a banker, with a hobo as moderator. A quick tryout proved it to be an incredibly bad show. —*1954*

• *The Education of H*Y*M*A*N K*A*P*L*A*N,* based on the Leonard Q. Ross (Leo Rosten) books, starring Broadway and Yiddish stage actor/comedian Menasha Skulnik. —*1955*

• "Test film of the long-planned *Mr. Belvedere* series goes into production here this week with Hans Conried in title role." —*July 25, 1959* [*Mr. Belvedere* finally aired on ABC on March 15, 1985, with Christopher Hewett in the lead.]

• "Orson Welles' deal with CBS is a whopper: six 90-minute film shows, costing $500,000 each. Kicker is, later they'll be released to theaters as features. He'll do 'Trilby' as one show; a modern-dress version of Shakespeare's 'Twelfth Night,' made on the Riviera, as another." —*July 30, 1955*

● "Frank Sinatra and NBC are more than half-serious about a proposed half-hour weekly dramatic show in which Sinatra would play himself in his own home town." —*August 6, 1955*

● "Allen Jones, singing star of many Hollywood musicals, is working on a TV film series about an opera singer who disappears and turns Greyhound bus driver." —*August 6, 1955*

● "With the movie version of Paddy Chayefsky's 'Marty' a hot contender for Academy Award honors, NBC is cooking up a weekly TV series based on the 'Marty' characters." —*October 15, 1955*

"Screen Gems has given the title role in the planned TV series version of 'Marty' to Tom Bosley." —*December 5, 1964*

● "Frank Sinatra is mulling a TV series, *International House,* in which he is cast as the proprietor of a European hotel. It's a whodunit." —*November 12, 1955*

● "A new weekly program is in the works, titled *Presidential Sweepstakes,* in which 'fabulous prizes' will be awarded the first 10 home viewers who accurately forecast the Presidential and Vice Presidential nominees of both parties. Which network will carry the show has not been determined." —*November 26, 1955*

● "Mickey Rooney . . . will do a new series, *Lucky the Leprechaun . . .*" —*January 28, 1956*

*Rod Steiger and Nancy Marchand in "*Marty*" on* Goodyear Television Playhouse.

● Ralph Bellamy in *Guns of Destiny*—not a Western, but dramatizations of the backgrounds of famous firearms in history. —*1956*

● "Either Burl Ives or Francis L. Sullivan to play the title role when the *Nero Wolfe* telefilm detective series starts rolling." —*June 2, 1956*

"CBS has assigned Gordon Duff to produce an audition film on *Nero Wolfe,* with Robert Middleton the probable star." —*December 27, 1958*

"William Shatner up for the role of Archie in CBS's *Nero Wolfe* next fall. Kurt Kasznar has the title role in the show, to be produced on film by Gordon Duff in New York." —*March 28, 1959*

"Nero Wolfe—the gourmet sleuth who raises orchids in the detective novels of Rex Stout—will be the protagonist in a TV-

Though most of his TV projects ended up as much in the air as the papers in this 1956 publicity photo, Orson Welles did make occasional TV appearances, like this one, with Betty Grable, in a Ford Star Jubilee *production of "Twentieth Century."*

movie being filmed in New York for next season on ABC. Adapted by Frank Gilroy, the movie is also the pilot for a series. Cast as Wolfe is Thayer David. Also featured are Tom Mason, Anne Baxter and Brooke Adams." —*April 30, 1977*

[*Nero Wolfe* had a half-season run on NBC beginning January 16, 1981, with William Conrad as Wolfe and Lee Horsley as Archie Goodwin.]

● "Robert Young and Eugene Rodney, long-time partners in *Father Knows Best,* are readying a test film for a projected new series, *Saints of the Snow.* It will be based on Switzerland's famed hospice of St. Bernard." —*November 3, 1956*

● "Jan Clayton, who will soon complete enough *Lassie* films to last through next January, plans to go into a new series of her own based on a Bowery mission girl who also doubles as a nightclub singer." —*December 1, 1956*

- *My Man Sing*, about a girl who inherits a Chinese butler from her rich uncle. —*1957*

- "Paddy Chayefsky writing a new series for TV based on case histories culled from the files of the American Psychiatric Association. No starting date set." —*January 26, 1957*

- "There is a possibility Elvis Presley will turn out 26 Tennessee-localed TV films to keep his name burning brightly while in the Army." —*March 9, 1957*

- "ABC has optioned *Personalysis* as a possible entry next season. It's described as the first panel show dealing with psychology." —*March 16, 1957*

- "Anthony Quinn will finance, produce and star in three episodes of a planned series called *Gallery*, based on the stories behind famous paintings." —*April 6, 1957*

- "Errol Flynn will star in the new *Cavalry Patrol* film series, originally intended for Dewey Martin." —*April 13, 1957*

- *Three Musketeers*, featuring comedians Henny Youngman, Phil Foster, and Joey Adams. —*1957*

- "Orson Welles and producer Nat Wolff have plans for an experimental series of 13 half-hour films, each to cost no more than $5000, in which Welles would use a bare stage and only a handful of props. Object: To prove that a versatile actor can hold an audience against the competition of expensive network shows." —*August 24, 1957*

- "New TV show, *DLO* (for Dead Letter Office) is being planned by producer Harriet Parsons as an anthology-dramatic series based on the files of the U.S. Post Office." —*August 24, 1957*

- "Title of Mickey Rooney's proposed new series for CBS is *Personal and Private*, in which he'd play a private detective." —*January 4, 1958*

- "There's a test film being prepared for Ethel Merman in which she'd play a trouping singer constantly in a state of outrage against the lawlessness of the Old West." —*March 29, 1958*

- "Producer Alex Gottlieb will shoot a test film in April for a series, *Zsa Zsa in Paris*." —*March 29, 1958*

- "Jane Wyman wants to [do] a situation comedy series, *Cleary Penryn*, in which she would play a hotel chambermaid." —*May 3, 1958*

- "ABC pumped close to $100,000 into an Orson Welles test film, made in Rome and touted as the network's surprise series for next season. It now has been dumped. Says one official: 'It was so bad it should be aired as a quiz show called *What Is It?*'" —*July 12, 1958*

- "CBS planning a full-hour Western, with two new features—it's to be a live show and will have a female star. Titled *Sheriff's Wife*, it will detail the lives of the women behind the men who helped settle the West." —*July 26, 1958*

- "Zsa Zsa Gabor may wind up with her own 'Jack Paar' show on NBC, 10:30 to midnight on Saturdays. Plan is to give her a six-week trial on KRCA, the network's local outlet there, then expand it coast-to-coast." —*September 13, 1958*

- "A projected new series based on the Bergman-Boyer picture, 'Gaslight,' has James Mason, now out of *The Third Man* series, penciled in for the lead." —*October 18, 1958*

● "CBS is blueprinting a situation-comedy series dealing with 'the fastest brain in the West.' Tentative title: *Egghead.*" —*January 17, 1959*

● "Footballer Frank Gifford emerges as the lead in Warner Brothers' new hour-long series, *Public Enemy.*" —*May 3, 1958*

"Frank Gifford, New York Giants halfback, up for the lead in *War Against Crime,* a projected ABC fall series." —*March 21, 1959*

"Frank (*Medic, Lineup*) La Tourette will turn out a CBS series, *Turnpike,* to star long-time New York Giants football star Frank Gifford." —*February 13, 1960*

● "Constance Bennett now goes into the projected *Mother Is the Governor of Texas* series, originally planned for Helen Traubel." —*May 2, 1959*

Peter Lorre and TV had little luck together, but he did play opposite Jack Palance in the Playhouse 90 *version of F. Scott Fitzgerald's* The Last Tycoon.

● "A test film will be made early next month for a new series titled *Arabian Knights,* to star Yvonne De Carlo as Scheherazade." —*August 22, 1959*

● "The Andrews sisters planning *The Collectors,* a series without singing in which they'd star as bill collectors." —*October 24, 1959*

● "Bette Davis' *Wagon Train* episode, in which she plays Madame Elizabeth McQueeny, is the audition film for a new hour-long series, *Madame's Palace,* in which Miss Davis hopes to star next season." —*October 31, 1959*

● "*Hometown,* new series in the planning stage here, would feature stars in a series of guided tours through their own home towns." —*December 12, 1959*

● "Jackie Gleason may do 'Death of a Salesman' as a CBS special." —*February 13, 1960*

● "A sequel to *Superman,* titled *The Adventures of Superboy,* is being planned as a 26-episode series. Producers are searching for a young lead." —*February 27, 1960*

"Test film for a *Superboy* series has been completed, with John Rockwell in the lead." —*May 6, 1961*

[A syndicated Superboy show would not get off the ground for nearly three decades.]

● "Thornton Wilder's "Our Town," twice televised as a special, is now to be tested as a half-hour series." —*December 17, 1960*

● "In the test film for the proposed *Some Like It Hot* series Jack Lemmon and Tony Curtis, reprising their movie roles, will visit a plastic surgeon to change their faces. Then they'll turn over their roles to Vic Damone and Dick Patterson, who'll star in the series." —*April 8, 1961*

● "MGM plans a half-hour TV series, *Zero One*, to be produced in London, which will deal with plane crashes." —*October 7, 1961*

● "David Westheimer, author of the currently best-selling 'Von Ryan's Express,' an adventure novel about an escape from a prisoner-of-war camp in Italy, will develop a 30-minute comedy series for NBC. The project is *Campo 44*—about a prisoner-of-war camp in Italy."—*June 20, 1964* [This may have evolved into *Hogan's Heroes*, about a German prisoner-of-war camp, which premiered on September 17, 1965.]

● "... *Take Me to Your Leader* stars Will Hutchins (*Sugarfoot*), and leans on unusual visual effects and running characters, who are a couple of traveling salesmen from Venus." —*January 25, 1964*

● "CBS has made a deal with Art Linkletter to keep *We Pay Your Bills*, a game show, ready for use as a substitute for the first new CBS series to be canceled. The show—in which a guest contestant brings in an unusual bill and celebrity panelists try to figure out what it is for—will run once a week as a 15-minute segment on *House Party* until it is needed on the evening front."—*September 12, 1964*

● "Pilot for a series starring Bette Davis as an interior decorator has gone into production here." —*January 12, 1964*

● "Metro-Goldwyn-Mayer has now filmed a total of eight pilots for new series. The latest, for CBS, is *Happily Ever After*, a comedy in which Oscar-winner (for 'Elmer Gantry') and musical-comedy star Shirley Jones stars as a mind-reading housewife." —*January 9, 1965* [Is it coincidence that *Bewitched* had become a hit on ABC starting the previous September?]

● "Pat Boone signed to do a pilot with 20th Century-Fox several months ago, and the studio has now come up with the show: it is *My Island Family*, a comedy about the efforts of a young American engineer to build a modern water-supply system on a remote South Pacific island." —*January 16, 1965*

● "Last spring CBS's enthusiasm for a Tarzan TV series faltered because of obvious problems of locating the stories in Africa. But now producer Sy Weintraub has put writer Clair Huffaker to work on the pilot script for *Tarzan on Venus*." —*January 23, 1965*

● "Producer Jay Ward and Sid Caesar are planning a half-hour comedy series called *Prince Fred*. Sid would play a midwestern dentist who inherits a European kingdom." —*July 3, 1965*

● Screen Gems shot a pilot for *The Mouse That Roared*, starring Sid Caesar. —*1965*

● "Bill Dana has been given a go-ahead by CBS on his comedy series *Biggs and Small*, two characters who might turn up anywhere in time and place in various episodes—examples: at Custer's Last Stand and as blacksmiths to Paul Revere's horse." —*September 4, 1965*

● "Goodson-Todman has six new shows pending with NBC for the '67–'68 season. One of them, called *Uncle Helen*, would have Ray Walston playing a circus clown and the clown's own sister." —*August 13, 1966*

● "Orson Welles may become star of his own TV musical-variety show on NBC. He's formed a partnership with Greg Garrison, Dean Martin's producer, and they're making a pilot for NBC." —*October 12, 1968*

● "20th Century-Fox and NBC ... are producing *The Bear and I,* starring Joe Flynn, Soupy Sales and a bear who talks. . . . " —*January 8, 1972*

● "MGM has a TV-series version of 'The Sunshine Boys' in preparation for NBC. Neil Simon, who wrote the original play and then adapted it for the movies, is writing and directing the pilot." —*October 9, 1976*

● ". . . a pilot called *The Plant Family,* a comedy about an eccentric family who want to open a wax museum in their home." —*April 8, 1978*

● "Producers Sam Denoff and Joe Byrne have created 'The Jogger,' a half-hour situation-comedy pilot that they hope will be picked up for CBS's fall schedule. The main character is a man who runs in New York City's Central Park every day." —*January 20, 1979*

● "Flip Wilson is making a TV series comeback in 'The Cheap Detective,' a pilot based on the Columbia Pictures theatrical film that starred Peter Falk as a cut-rate private eye." —*November 10, 1979*

● "Todd Sussman is the star of 'Ethel Is an Elephant,' a Columbia Pictures Television pilot said to be 'about a guy who lives in New York, adopts an elephant and brings her home to live in a loft.' Playing Ethel is 'a male elephant we're bringing in from Oregon. And we have to photograph him in such a way that the audience won't know he's not an Ethel.' It's for CBS." —*March 29, 1980*

● "David Steinberg and Burt Reynolds have teamed up to coproduce 'The Fourth Network,' a 90-minute, late-night comedy special that's the pilot for a projected series next season on ABC. The comedic premise is an imaginary TV network whose executives hire a motley crew of performers to come up with programming for the midnight-to-7-A.M. time period. —*July 4, 1981*

● "Darren McGavin and Roddy McDowall costar in Walt Disney Productions' CBS pilot, 'Small and Frye.' A Disney source said that the series 'chronicles the whimsical adventures of two private investigators, one of whom has the ability to shrink to a 6-inch height.'" —*April 3, 1982*

● *Dr. Ruth's House,* a sitcom starring sex therapist Dr. Ruth Westheimer as a psychology professor who owns an off-campus rooming house and who is romantically involved with the dean. —*1990*

TV Guide Picks the 20 Top Television Shows of the 1980s

1. *The Cosby Show*
2. *Dallas*
3. *Hill Street Blues*
4. *Dynasty*
5. *Brideshead Revisited*
6. *Nightline*
7. *Cheers*
8. *Moonlighting*
9. *Miami Vice*
10. *The Day After*
11. *Wheel of Fortune*

12. *Lonesome Dove*
13. *L.A. Law*
14. *The Winds of War/War and Remembrance*
15. *Saturday Night Live*
16. *The Golden Girls*
17. Tabloid TV (*A Current Affair, Inside Edition, Hard Copy,* etc.)
18. *The Thorn Birds*
19. *The Wonder Years*
20. *St. Elsewhere*

December 9, 1989

AN ACTOR'S LIFE FOR ME

Tony Curtis was familiar and a star when he played the poet/ shepherd David in General Electric Theater's production of "The Stone" back in 1959. But the guy standing over his shoulder would actually soon become quite familiar to all TV watchers—and to Lorne Greene. It's Pernell Roberts, later Adam on Bonanza.

Before They Got Big: What the Stars Did Before They Became Stars

While waiting for that first big break . . .

● Dennis Weaver sold vacuum cleaners door to door, tricycles and ladies' hosiery; he was also a janitor and worked for a florist. When the director called to tell him he'd won the part of Chester on *Gunsmoke,* he was out delivering flowers.

The man with the puppets and the familiar grin on Albany, New York's UHF station, WCDA-TV, Channel 41, back in 1956 is none other than Ted Knight, later to become the endearing egomaniacal buffoon Ted Baxter on The Mary Tyler Moore Show.

● Arthur Godfrey was a factory worker, short-order cook, hotel night manager, taxi driver, and, finally, a cemetery-plot salesman.

● Fran Allison was an elementary-school teacher.

● Darren McGavin, who studied art at the College of the Pacific and designed sets at MGM, made ends meet by crafting leather handbags. He also was a stevedore, a truck driver, and a garbage shoveler.

● *Cheyenne*'s Clint Walker was a Hollywood nightclub bouncer.

● Director John Frankenheimer was offered a job at NBC's Hollywood studios—as a parking-lot attendant at $27.50 a week.

● Bob Denver was an athletic coach and a history-and-arithmetic teacher at the Corpus Christi Children's School in Pacific Palisades, California. He also worked a second job at the Post Office during Christmas rush.

● When Warren Oates was a struggling actor in New York in the 1950s, he not only checked hats at the "21" club, but also got a job at $5.60 an hour as "test pilot" for *Beat the Clock*. Stunts were tried out on him to make sure they were safe for the real contestants and to get an estimate of the time it took to perform them. He got the position because the previous job-holder got a part in a play. *His* name was James Dean.

● Jerry Van Dyke worked in a pizza joint and sold Bibles.

● Harvey Korman sold siding door to door.

● Fred Gwynne was an advertising copywriter assigned to the Ford Motor Company account at the J. Walter Thompson agency in New York.

● Don Adams did cartographic and engineering drawing. Says Adams: "If some of the bridges in Washington, D.C., bulge, I'm responsible."

Playing hotheaded, trigger-happy Rex Burley, convicted on eight counts of burglary in a 1952 Dragnet (Friday and Smith were working out of Robbery), is a young Martin Milner, who would soon be on the other end of the service revolver, working for Jack Webb as Officer Pete Malloy on Adam-12.

● Edgar Buchanan was a dentist.

● Robert Conrad drove a milk truck in Chicago.

● Jack Warden was a lifeguard at the indoor pool at the Park Sheraton Hotel in New York City and a bouncer in a dance hall.

● Leonard Nimoy was a soda jerk, a newspaper carrier, a vacuum-cleaner salesman, a vending-machine serviceman, a pet-shop employee, and a cab driver.

● Greg Morris had the 4:00 P.M.-to-midnight shift at a Hollywood liquor store.

● Michael Landon heated up glue in a ribbon factory and ran a machine that sealed

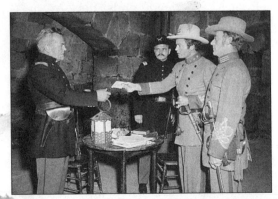

Though he was little known in 1956 (in fact, the credits on this photo merely lump him in with another "unident." actor), the actor second from the right would become the future's most persnickety doctor—that's DeForest Kelley (Dr. McCoy on Star Trek) as a Southern envoy in "The Fall of Fort Sumter" on You Are There.

hot cans of Campbell's Tomato Soup.

● Jack Scalia worked in a Campbell's Soup factory in Sacramento, mixing 8,000 to 10,000 pounds a day of Chunky Beef Soup in vats.

● Ed McMahon was a boardwalk pitchman selling vegetable slicers and other items in Atlantic City.

● Fess Parker was a janitor.

● Peter Graves drove a cab and painted house numbers on Los Angeles curbs.

● Bill Daily of *The Bob Newhart Show* worked part-time as a tailor in a tuxedo-rental agency in Chicago.

● John Saxon was a photographer's model for young men's swim trunks.

● Dick Cavett typed labels for a Wall Street firm and was a department-store detective.

● Valerie Harper worked as a telephone canvasser and a hat-check girl.

● Jack Klugman sold his blood for $5 a pint while sharing a room in New York with another aspiring actor, Charles Bronson, who had been a coal miner.

● Carroll O'Connor substitute-taught in the New York public-school system.

● Peter Falk was an efficiency expert for

Baby-faced Jack Lemmon wonders which Turner Twin has the proper permanent in his capacity as host of Toni Twin Time, *a CBS variety show that alternated Wednesdays with* What's My Line?

Jim Henson and Rowlf get ready in 1964 for their first big national exposure on ABC's The Jimmy Dean Show.

the State of Connecticut Budget Bureau.

● Rob Reiner was the youngest writer on *The Smothers Brothers Show.*

● Meredith Baxter was an usher, a file clerk, and a checker in a cafeteria.

● Lee Majors was a recreation director for the Los Angeles Department of Parks and Recreation at North Hollywood Park. (To be on the safe side, even after he got the role in *The Big Valley,* he kept his name on the Parks inactive list for two years, just in case acting fell through.)

● Adrienne Barbeau was a go-go dancer in New Jersey.

● Wayne Rogers was a busboy and a lifeguard, and shared an apartment in New York for a couple of years with another aspiring actor, Peter Falk, who at one

time was an efficiency expert for the State of Connecticut Budget Bureau.

● Claude Akins was a limestone salesman.

● Rue McClanahan was a waitress, took shorthand, and sold blouses.

● Max Gail of *Barney Miller* was a prison guard in San Francisco's Juvenile Hall and a piano player at the Hyatt House hotel.

● *Barney Miller*'s Ron Glass worked for an answering service.

● Isabel Sanford was a keypunch operator for the New York Welfare Department.

● Kevin Dobson worked for the Long Island Rail Road, as a trainman, a brakeman, and, finally, a conductor.

● Victoria Principal was a talent agent.

● James Garner was a carpet-layer.

Giving Howard Duff the eye in the 1953 pilot for the unsold Johnny Nighthawk *series is Angela Lansbury. Sexy, she wrote.*

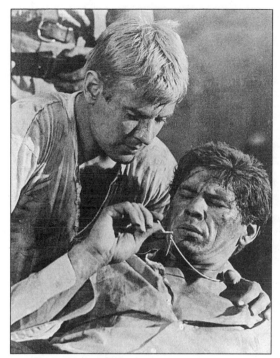

When you get to be a big star, it's the other actors who do the death scenes. But Charles Bronson wasn't a star yet in 1958, and so he died in Will Hutchins' arms on Sugarfoot.

- Bill Bixby was a lifeguard.

- David Doyle of *Charlie's Angels* packed false teeth for shipping.

- Vic Tayback was a Kelly Girl temp.

- Gregory Harrison was a doorman for a nightclub.

- Patrick Duffy was a carpenter.

- Ken Kercheval sold cemetery plots and encyclopedias, was an airlines reservation clerk, and was a dynamiter, blasting trap rock for a new sewer line under Manhattan.

- Ted Koppel was a copy boy at radio station WMCA in New York.

- Markie Post wrote questions for *Family Feud.*

- Bob Vila was a Peace Corps volunteer in Panama and a stagehand in Stuttgart, West Germany.

- John Ratzenberger was an assistant to a tree surgeon in London.

- Roseanne Barr was a cocktail waitress in Colorado.

- Steve Kanaly (Ray Krebbs in *Dallas*) managed a skeet- and trap-shooting club.

- Peter Coyote plucked chickens.

- Before she got a recurring role as Douglas Brackman's father's lover—and Douglas's as well—Bette Ford was, for

Clint Walker as Cheyenne *(in the show of the same name) looks as amazed as we do—underneath that makeup and buckskin is Michael Landon.*

What Bilko's doing in a classroom here in You'll Never Get Rich, *we'll never know. Maybe he's at Yale—at any rate, that's where the guy seated next to him—a very young Dick Cavett—got his schooling.*

five years, one of the most popular and successful matadors in Mexico.

● Marsha Warfield was an operator for a telephone-answering service.

● Kelsey Grammer unloaded fishing boats in Rhode Island, painted roofs in Florida and was a waiter in New York.

● Stephen Furst, Dr. Elliot Axelrod on *St. Elsewhere,* was a Los Angeles pizza-delivery man.

● MTV's Downtown Julie Brown worked the assembly line at a Sony television factory in Bridgend, Wales.

● Craig Nelson was a logger and a janitor.

● David Leisure, before getting a part on *Empty Nest* and becoming Joe Isuzu in those car commercials, was so poor he was forced to live out of his car—which was not an Isuzu.

● Jenny Jones, the host of her own talk/comedy show, was a backup singer for Wayne Newton.

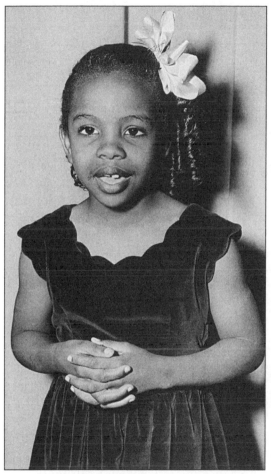

Captured here in her 1952 appearance on Ted Mack's The Original Amateur Hour *is little eight-year-old Gladys Maria Knight, sans her Pips.*

Back in 1953, he was Rod Brown, the captain of the rocket ship Beta in the "interplanetary space drama" Rocket Rangers *Saturday mornings on CBS. Fifteen years later, Cliff Robertson had a Best Actor Oscar. Funny business.*

The second young military nurse on the left was just starting out, and hadn't yet learned to scream for the Halloween slasher films or contend with the neuroses of Richard Lewis in Anything But Love. *That's Jamie Lee Curtis.*

How They Got Started

Unlike Lana Turner, not everybody gets discovered at the soda counter at Schwab's Drugstore. But some come darn close to that. Luck, serendipity, fate, being in the right place at the right time—these have played a great part in the way many actors and actresses have become actors and actresses, or become interested in theater, TV, and movie careers at all. Here are a few well-known TV names, and the ways they got their first big breaks.

● After failing to make the 1948 U.S. Olympic team in the decathlon, Dennis Weaver was the understudy for college friend Lonny Chapman in the Broadway production of *Come Back, Little Sheba*. He took over the role on the road. When he returned to New York after the tour, he enrolled at the Actors Studio, where Shelley Winters saw him and recommended him to Universal-International Studios, which offered him a contract in 1952.

● During the dress rehearsal for a *Studio One* production, the young woman hired to do the commercial got stage fright and couldn't say her lines. Betty Furness, who had a role in the show, offered to read the lines from the control booth while the other woman was on-camera, demonstrating refrigerators and washing machines. Soon she was doing the commercials herself.

● When Jan Murray was in high school, his mother became ill and was bedridden for many months. To cheer her up, Murray went to the neighborhood vaudeville house frequently, and re-enacted the entire bill for her when he got home. This created an interest in performing, which led him to the Catskills, where he organized a hotel's recreational program and entertained.

● Storyteller Herb Shriner started as a harmonica player doing seven shows a day in a vaudeville house. He began talking to his audience to stall for time between selections when his mouth was chafed from playing so much. They loved the patter, and soon he just talked.

● Ed Kemmer, who played Commander Buzz Corey in *Space Patrol,* started to act in a German POW camp during World War II. While flying his 48th mission, he was shot down, got captured, escaped, and was recaptured. To pass the time, the prisoners put on stage shows. His interest in acting started there.

● Art Carney was doing an impression of Edward G. Robinson for a Rotarians meeting in Mount Vernon, New York. In the audience was orchestra leader Horace Heidt, who hired Carney immedi-

Betty Furness, in what was to become a familiar—some might say classic—pose. Whose refrigerator looks anything like that?

ately. Carney toured with Heidt for three and a half years.

● Phil Silvers made his "debut" singing with a street gang on the boardwalk at Coney Island at the age of 14. One day a stranger threw him a dime, handed him a business card, and said, "Drop around and see me, kid." On the card was the name of Gus Edwards. Phil didn't know that Edwards' vaudeville act, "The School Days Review," played the famous old Palace Theater. But he dropped around anyway. Ten days later, he was making $40 a week as one of Edwards' singing newsboys at the Palace—then the goal of every old trouper.

● Originally Ann B. Davis wanted to be a doctor and enrolled at the University of Michigan, where her twin sister, Harriet, was studying to become an actress. An older brother, Evans Davis, was dancing in *Oklahoma!* in Chicago, and the sisters visited him during Christmas vacation. By its end, Harriet had decided against show business, and Ann dropped thoughts of doctoring or doing anything but acting.

● Richard Simmons, who would become Sergeant Preston of the Yukon, was a young pilot, spending his vacation at a dude ranch near Palm Springs. The owners had an Arabian stallion that hadn't been broken. Simmons, who had ridden in rodeos, got on and broke him in an hour. One of the guests watching was Louis B. Mayer, who offered Simmons a contract at twice his pilot's salary.

● "We never pushed either of the boys into this. As a matter of fact, the idea of their being on the show started with the boys themselves. Bing Crosby guested on our radio show one week and the script called for an actor to play Bing's son, Lindsay. But Lindsay showed up and played himself. He was around 10 at the time. We had young actors playing Dave and Ricky, but the minute they saw Lindsay up there in front of those mikes, they wanted in. Dave was 12 and Rick was not quite 9. So we started them that very week. That was back in February or March of 1949." —*Ozzie Nelson, speaking of David and Ricky Nelson, October 13, 1956*

● Robert Horton got his first acting role (and his new stage name) in a stage comedy called *I Give You My Husband,* because the part required somebody with red hair.

● Whenever he would hit a home run while playing with the then Los Angeles Angels, Chuck Connors would celebrate by turning a few cartwheels while rounding the bases. A director in the stands liked the clowning and gave Connors a bit part in a movie. Soon he gave up baseball.

● Just out of high school, Mary Tyler Moore was offered a role as Happy

The Nelsons, in the '50s and 1963.

Hotpoint, the dancing elf in commercials on *The Adventures of Ozzie and Harriet.* She filmed the 39 TV spots in five days, ultimately earning about $6,000 from the first job of her career.

● Working as a scenery painter in Hollywood, Darren McGavin had a job painting backdrops at Columbia Studios. He heard there was a part open in a movie called *A Song to Remember.* He thought he'd try out, and got the part—because the picture was about Poles and he looked Polish.

● Leslie Nielsen, an announcer on a Calgary radio station, later went to a radio school in Toronto; the man running it helped him move on to study in New York, which eventually led to acting in

TV. That radio-school operator was Lorne Greene.

● When Shari Lewis was 16, she broke her ankle. To ease the boredom of being laid up at home, her father bought her a puppet and books on ventriloquism.

● Dyan Cannon (then spelling her first name "Diane") was a showroom assistant for a sweater manufacturer when a man came up to her at lunch one day, explained he was an agent, and said, "Honey, are you in pictures? Because if you're not, you should be." Soon she was appearing on *Matinee Theater* and other TV shows.

● After doing magic and ventriloquism, and working on local radio and TV in Omaha, Nebraska, Johnny Carson went to Hollywood and began writing for Red Skelton. One day Skelton injured himself during a rehearsal, and Carson was selected to go on-air as his fill-in. Soon after, he got his own network show.

● Rose Marie came to Cleveland on a promotional tour for *The Dick Van Dyke Show*. While taping some spots at a local TV station, "I suddenly realized that the stuff I heard coming out of the booth was funnier than what we were doing on stage." The director of the spots was a young guy named Tim Conway. When Rose Marie heard that Conway had done some sketches on Cleveland TV, she got the tapes and brought them to the attention of Steve Allen, who brought Conway out to Hollywood. Conway was a hit. Later, the Allen tapes got Conway the *McHale's Navy* job.

● After winning a hot pepper-eating contest, Donna Douglas traveled around the South, extolling the virtues of this re-gional delicacy, and bearing the title "Hot Pepper Eating Champion." This led to a desire to do modeling in New York, which she did. This, in turn, led to several "elbow-grabber jobs" on New York television: a "Letters Girl" on *The Perry Como Show* and a "Billboard Girl" on *The Steve Allen Show*. New York newspaper reporters named her "Miss By-Line," and she appeared as such on *The Ed Sullivan Show*, where she was seen by Hollywood producer Hal Wallis, who signed her to a contract.

● Linda Evans accompanied a Hollywood High classmate who was going on an interview for a part in a Canada Dry commercial. The interviewers liked Evans and hired her, too. After doing only three commercials, she got roles in *Bachelor Father, Ozzie and Harriet, The Untouchables,* and *The Eleventh Hour,* and finally signed a two-year contract with MGM.

● Burt Ward (who went on to play Robin on the *Batman* series) was a real-estate salesman in Los Angeles. One of only two houses he sold in all of 1965 was to Saul David, a producer at Twentieth Century–Fox, who introduced him to an agent.

● When James Brolin was 15, his parents had producer William Castle over to the house. Castle suggested Brolin consider acting and come to the studio to try out for a part. Brolin did—and was told he wasn't right for it. Angry, Brolin became obsessed with getting to be an actor and proving to those who turned him down that he could do it.

● While working as a copy boy at *Time* magazine, Dick Cavett read that Jack Paar was looking for material. So Cavett sat down, wrote a two-page opening monologue, took it to NBC, met Paar in the hall, and got the job.

● Victor Sen Yung, who played cook Hop Sing on *Bonanza,* was, in 1938, working as a salesperson for a chemical company. He took his samples to the Twentieth Century–Fox studios to try to interest them in a new flameproofing compound. Instead, they handed him a test scene for a new movie, and he got the part as Charlie Chan's "Number Two Son," a role he played in 25 Chan movies.

● Dack Rambo and his brother Dirk were discovered by Loretta Young in Saint Victor's Church in West Hollywood during a Sunday mass. She spied them during the service, and afterward asked if they would like to appear in her new TV series.

● Michael Evans was hitchhiking to school in Venice, California. The man who picked him up was an administrator of a theater workshop. Evans impressed him, and one day the man sent him over to an audition. He got the part—as Lionel on *All in the Family.*

● "There was this girl with an absolutely incredible physique. And one day I was finally able to make conversation with her. We sat for a while in the student union [at Stanford] and then she said, 'That's it. I have to go to an audition.' Wanting to hang on, I said, 'I'll go with you.' So I went and auditioned, too. And they liked me, and gave me a small non-speaking part in a Bertolt Brecht play. I was hooked." —*Ted Danson, October 9, 1982*

● Markie Post, divorced and in need of money, was at home watching the game show *Split Second.* She decided that, since she'd always been good at trivia games and crossword puzzles, she could get to be a contestant on the show and win a car. She wasn't chosen to be on the show—she so impressed the staff, she was hired to *work* for the show. Her acting jobs followed.

● Linda Gray became friendly with a woman in a health-food store. The woman turned out to be Mrs. Dennis Weaver, and through that relationship Gray got a part on Weaver's *McCloud,* and that sent her on her way.

● While studying to be an engineer, Judd Hirsch—whose degree is in physics—had a class scheduling conflict one year and had to take Acting I, and that changed the course of his life.

● Janine Turner—later to star in *Northern Exposure* as Maggie O'Connell—was 17 when she was spotted in a Fort Worth supermarket checkout line by Leonard Katzman, executive producer of *Dallas.* He asked her to audition for a small part on the series, and she got the job.

How They Got That Role

Sometimes actors get a role—sometimes *the* role that makes them famous, puts them over the top—in odd and mysterious ways. Most times, they've worked hard and deserve the break, and have gone the extra mile to make that break happen. Other times, the answer is just blowing in the wind. From articles through the years in *TV Guide,* here are how some familiar actors found themselves in possession of those special roles.

• In its fifth year on the air, *Big Town,* one of the top TV film shows in the early 1950s, replaced Pat McVey with Kenneth Tobey. Reason? The show was switching over to color, and Tobey had colorful red hair.

• Jackie Gleason at first rejected Audrey Meadows for the role of Alice Kramden, because he thought Meadows was too pretty for the part. "Alice," Gleason said, "has gotta be a mess."

Upon hearing this, Meadows hired photographers and set up a few shots to show Gleason. "My hair was uncombed, I wore my oldest clothes, a torn apron and no make-up," Meadows remembered later. "Then I stood in the kitchen and fried eggs. I looked awful. The kitchen looked awful. Even the eggs didn't look edible."

When Gleason saw the photos, he roared, "Any girl who would let herself be seen like that for a job deserves it."

• Buddy Ebsen got the role of Davy Crockett's sidekick, George Russell, after he was nearly hired to play Crockett;

Walt Disney, undecided, almost said yes, then saw Fess Parker in a bit role in the movie *Them!,* and that was that.

• Larry Welk, Lawrence Welk's son, was dating one of the Lennon Sisters. One night he had to pick her up at an Elks meeting, where she and her sisters were singing. Extremely impressed, he tried to get his father to audition them, but Welk was too busy. Then, one day, when Welk was in bed with a cold, Larry got the sisters together, brought them into the sick room, and had them sing. Welk signed them to appear on his next show.

• Guy Williams apparently got the part of Zorro in the Disney series not because of any great acting ability but because, of all the other men who tested for the role, he was the only one who could actually fence, something he'd picked up from his father, a skilled fencer back in his native Italy.

• When Allen Ludden was leaving as host of *The G-E College Bowl* to go to *Password,* Robert Earle, who was working as a community-relations specialist with General Electric in Ithaca, New York, wanted the job. He was told by the producers to send them a film of himself hosting a show. He'd never hosted a TV show, and thus didn't have any film. What he did was: He audiotaped a *College Bowl* game, had the whole show transcribed into script form, went to an Ithaca radio station where he once worked and had Ludden's voice carefully edited from the audiotape. Then he went to WICB-TV, the Ithaca College station, set up a lectern in front of a camera, and ran a cord from a tape recorder with the edited tape in it to a foot pedal behind the lectern. With a camera rolling, he pretended to be hosting that *College Bowl* game. He would ask the questions Ludden had asked (but which had been edited out), using the transcript, and then would step on the foot pedal to activate the tape to hear the students' responses. He did this with perfectly rehearsed precision to make it seem as if a *Bowl* session were going on, with him as host. He sent the film to the producers. He got the job.

● Lassie picked Tommy Rettig for the role of the boy in the *Lassie* series. When four finalists were lined up, Lassie went

Look closely. The first person at the right standing in line—watching active actor Jock Mahoney give a 1965 Film Industry Workshop on falling, slapping, punching, and other stunts—is Lloyd Haynes, who would in a few years star in his own series, Room 222. *More interesting is the third person after him: then unknown Sally Field, Mahoney's stepdaughter, described in a* TV Guide *memo as "one of the more interesting 'fallers.' She's rather clumsy, but awfully cute."*

Buddy Ebsen appears to have just read that Fess Parker, left, and not he had just been given the role of Davy Crockett—as was the case—in this scene from the hugely popular Walt Disney miniseries.

to Rettig and nuzzled him. That was the sign that Rettig was the right one.

● While appearing in a traveling production of *Gentlemen Prefer Blondes* in 1966, David Hartman was offered a job in a commercial for Bell Telephone: all he'd have to do was dress up like a cowboy, sit on a horse, and tell the people in the West how to use the area code. He took the job, which paid $125; the trip cost him $300. But when the producers of *The Virginian* were looking for an actor to play a new character, Hartman sent them his 59-second ad—his only "Western"— in which he appeared for exactly eight seconds, saying, "Howdy, folks. The area code in Denver is 303." He got the job and a seven-year contract with Universal.

● Bob Keeshan was working his way through college, hoping to become a lawyer, when he got a job as an NBC page. One day Buffalo Bob Smith of *Howdy Doody* offered him an extra $5 to hand out prizes and carry out props for the show. Soon, instead of wearing civil-ian clothes to do the job, Keeshan was put in a clown costume, to blend in with the atmosphere. Clarabell was born.

● While in high school, Vicki Lawrence wrote a fan letter to Carol Burnett. Along with the letter she included local newspaper articles that mentioned she resembled Burnett, and said she would soon be participating in a talent contest for Miss Fireball.

Burnett, who was looking for someone to play her sister on her new *Carol Burnett Show,* agreed there was a resemblance and gave Lawrence a call.

"When Carol called and I recognized her voice," Lawrence remembers, "I couldn't make a sound. *Nothing* would come out of my mouth, so I gave the phone to my mom. Carol said, 'Put Vicki back on. I'll talk, she can just listen.'"

Burnett came to see Lawrence perform in—and win—the talent contest. A few months later, Lawrence was invited to audition, and became a member of the *Burnett Show* cast.

● When producers of the new *Mickey Spillaine's Mike Hammer* made-for-TV movie were auditioning actresses to play the macho detective's girl Friday, Velda, one of those who showed up was Lindsay Bloom, a chubby blonde who was dubbed wrong for the part. Six weeks later, the producers were still looking; a voluptuous brunette auditioned. The producers immediately knew they had their Velda. They also had Lindsay Bloom again too. In the intervening month and a half, she'd lost 22 pounds and dyed her hair black, on the advice of her agent.

● John Ratzenberger tried out for the part of Norm when they were casting *Cheers.* He knew he hadn't impressed them, and wasn't going to get the part. "I'm walking out the door and I know I've failed at Norm—not failed exactly, but you know whether you've done something that's got the producers excited or not," Ratzenberger recalled later. "So I thought, 'Give it a shot, John, you're exiting anyway.' I turned around and said, 'Listen, do you have a bar know-it-all?' They said no. I said, 'Every bar has one' and went into a 10-minute dissertation on this guy, picking up things in the office for props. They started laughing and kept laughing." Cliff Clavin was born.

• Patricia Wettig and Ken Olin got their roles in *thirtysomething* in part because their baby boy was best friends in preschool with the producer's daughter, and the adults got to know each other.

• After auditioning four times for the role of Sophia in *The Golden Girls,* Estelle Getty was called in for yet another reading. This time she hired a makeup artist to age her; she went shopping at thrift shops to find a worn polyester dress several sizes too big for her and a handbag. Dressed like that, she shuffled into the audition, stayed in character the whole time—and had the job.

• When Tom Poston was auditioning for a spot on the old *Steve Allen Show,* Allen asked him his name and Poston actually forgot. Allen thought it was so funny he hired him.

• When going for the part of McMurphy on *China Beach,* Dana Delany got her dates confused and showed up at the producer's office a day early. She got to talking with him, and he made up his mind about her even before the others showed up the next day.

• Frank Silva got the part of the evil demon, Bob, on *Twin Peaks* when he was propmaster for the show. David Lynch saw him on the set and knew he'd found his Bob. "David told me to go to the foot of the bed and act scared," explained Silva of Bob's origins.

Barking all the way to the bank (actually the check is for $25, which must be merely a little pocket bone money) is Lassie, accompanied by Tommy Rettig, her first TV human boy, and an unidentified studio payroll clerk.

Stars on the Edge

James Mason looks for a way out when he and his wife and children (portrayed by his then real-life wife, Pamela, and children Portland and Alexander) are trapped on the 22nd floor of a new apartment building on "Marooned," a 1957 episode of the NBC Panic! series.

Unwisely looking down while walking a six-inch-wide ledge with high heels on is Barbara Britton; she and Richard Denning were Pam and Jerry, in Mr. and Mrs. North, on CBS in this 1952 photo.

Bette Davis hangs tough, and high—eight floors high—above a Hong Kong street in an attempt to save her husband in "The Cold Touch," the April 13, 1958, installment of General Electric Theater.

Cowboys . . .

Once they were as plentiful on the vast TV wasteland as were the buffalo they slaughtered on the real American prairie. Soon they were, like the Indians before them, pushed off their turf by the White Coats (doctor shows) and Blue Serge (lawyer shows), blown away like so many holstered and vested tumbleweeds.

Here are some to remember.

It may not yet be time to shed a tear for the passing of the Old West on television, but the situation certainly warrants a lump in the throat and perhaps an audible sigh or two.

We must face the facts bravely, even as did the stalwart men under the Stetsons who, knowing the odds against them, strode bravely forward, leathery brows furrowed over eyes squinted against the hot sun, mouths taut, hands poised over revolver butts, minds alert, waiting, waiting for the soul-wrenching crash of a dropped option, but never missing a cue, never avoiding an opportunity to fight, with their lives if necessary for justice, for order, for another closeup.

Long will we remember the heyday of the Western. That Wonderful Year (forgive us, Garry) 1957, when the season opened with 20 Westerns, 11 of them brand, spanking new. There was 1958, when 11 new Westerns starting in the fall brought the number on the air to 26. In 1959 there were 10 new ones, a total of 27. The fall of 1960 saw only four new ones, for a total of 20. And that was the beginning of the end.

Now, from our far-flung correspondents, from secret sources inside and outside the industry, from confidential charts, restricted bulletins and "for eyes

only" memoranda, passed furtively from network chairman to network president to trade paper reporters, we learn the awful truth. Next season there will be NO new Westerns on the air. Admitted, *Gunsmoke* and *Wells Fargo* are being stretched to an hour. Admitted, there'll be a circus show set in the West. Admitted, *Gunsmoke* half-hour reruns will be shown—as *Marshal Dillon*. But NO new pure Westerns, and a total of only 13 on the air!

Feel that lump in the old throat? Hear those sighs?

Courage, friends. Courage.

August 5, 1961

The Ranger Unmasked

On those occasions when the Lone Ranger didn't send Tonto into town to find out what was up, the Masked Rider would do it himself—but only after putting on an amazingly complex disguise. Despite his concern for camouflage detail, somehow he always looked kind of the same—sounded the same, too—and only a town whose citizenry's collective IQ was the equivalent of a smallish child's shoe size could not be able to see through it. Yet, lucky guy—those were just the places he went to. And, by the way: Where did he get and hide all that makeup, anyway? Maybe that's why he kept sending Tonto into town.

...and Indians (Sort of)

Television has never quite known what to do with ethnic minorities. From the start, TV either avoided casting them or, when an ethnic or an "exotic" was required, somehow passed over an actor of that ethnicity or nationality for the role. Instead, an actor of some vague "different-ness" who looked as if he or she could pass for "near-real" was frequently put in the part. Authenticity seemed to work against getting work.

Then, too, there was the tradition of dialect actors, those performers of many accents and made-up faces who could play any sort of person from any place on earth. Casting directors would hire them because they were known commodities, and highly reliable, and, anyway, the American public wouldn't know or care. One of the best and busiest of these was J. Carroll Naish. Though of Irish descent, he was Italian in *Life with Luigi* (he also played the part on radio); as Rabbi Arnold Fischel, the U.S. Army's first Jewish chaplain, in the historic civil-war drama "With Charity for All," on ABC's *Crossroads* series; and as Charlie Chan in the 1956 series. A footnote: there has never been a Chinese Charlie Chan, although his number-one sons have all been Asian; and when a made-for-TV movie, *Charlie Chan,* was cast in 1971—with the possibility of its being a pilot for a series—the actor selected to play Chan was Ross Martin. Naish was also involved in a proposed series in 1953 called *Señor Paco;* in a 1958 *Desilu Playhouse* drama called "My Father, the

Fool," Naish played the Puerto Rican father of another ethnic poseur: Eli Wallach.

Rita Moreno, of Puerto Rican ancestry, is another one who fell through every ethnic crack. She played, among other things, an Indian exchange student in a *Father Knows Best* episode; Cochise's sister, Sonseeahray, to Mexican Ricardo Montalban's Cochise and John Lupton's Tom Jeffords in the 1956 Twentieth Century–Fox Hour presentation of what later became the series *Broken Arrow;* a

Versatile character actor J. Carroll Naish as Luigi (top), Rabbi Arnold Fischel (above left) and Charlie Chan (above right).

South American beauty contestant on *The Millionaire*; and half-breed Tina Starbuck on "The Samaritan," on *Trackdown*. "I wasn't conscious of casting stereotypes in those days—not that it's completely changed now," Moreno said in a 1983 *TV Guide* interview. "If you were a Latina, you played poor, brown-skinned princesses: Mexican, Spanish, Indian; we all looked alike. Or so they seemed to think." In another interview, she added: "I never objected to playing Latin women, but I wanted to play Latin women that exist in real life—not the stereotype who is eternally snarling, 'Yankee pig!' and 'You stole my people's gold.'"

Sometimes playing an ethnic part—and being very good at it—can lock you into that kind of role for life. Take the case of Michael Ansara, who played the part of Cochise (the part Ricardo Montalban played in the pilot) in the *Broken Arrow* series. Ansara, a Shakespearean-trained actor of Lebanese descent, was then tracked into one American Indian role after another. His first role after *Broken Arrow,* for example, was as a Harvard-educated Indian marshal in a 1959 episode of *The Rifleman,* which led to his own short-lived series, *Law of the Plainsman.* He got a brief respite—playing a retired Cuban bullfighter who thwarts the assassination of a Latin American dictator's son living in New York, in a 1959 episode of *Naked City.* By 1961, he was reported to be balking at playing any more Indians, hoping to establish an identity closer to his true self, but as late as 1978 Ansara was being cast as an Indian in the miniseries *Centennial.*

"I don't mind being an Indian," Ansara told *TV Guide* in 1960. "But with Cochise the acting range was rather limited. Cochise could do one of two things—stand with his arms folded, look-

Rita Moreno cast as an Indian exchange student (top left), Cochise's sister (top right), a South American (bottom left) and a half-breed (bottom right).

ing noble; or stand with arms at his sides, looking noble."

This is all not to say that only American Indian actors should play American Indians, or that only Jewish actors should be permitted to play Jews, and so on. It would be nice, though, if that sort of natural casting could occur more frequently, just for honesty—and, in some cases, to give minority actors a role they could use after a long stretch without a job. Consider: With all the Indians on TV and in the movies from the first silents to the days of color TV, in 1960 there were no more than 14 genuine American Indian actors in Hollywood. And it was a decade more before authentic Native Americans were playing the bulk of Native American roles.

The Leave-Takers

"The road to sitcom hell is paved with bodies of people who left their shows prematurely," said Alan Thicke in the January 18, 1992, *TV Guide*. The same can also be said for many of those who left dramatic series too early. Whether for "artistic reasons" (they didn't get along with the producer or the rest of the cast), "to stretch and grow in my craft" (their latest contract demands weren't met), "to strike out on my own" (they believed they were the reason people tuned in every week, and why should they share billing with a bunch of second-raters), or simply because they were fed up and needed to get out for mental-health reasons, many actors who were very big suddenly became very hard to see after they exited their most famous roles in very popular series. What they learned the hard way is that TV audiences don't automatically tune in to see an actor—they tune in to watch that actor do something interesting. Brand loyalty is weak to nonexistent among TV viewers—just ask Dick Van Dyke and Mary Tyler Moore.

In some cases, the mighty (or those who thought they were mightier than they really were) have indeed fallen. In other instances, they just went on to a happier, scaled-down existence. Here are some of the biggest names who jumped ship—a few for decidedly littler canoes, and some for the *Titanic*:

• Pernell Roberts left *Bonanza* at the peak of his fame, after his and its sixth season, tired of arguing over what he saw as the show's diminishing quality. His expressed intent was to do some serious drama—but he soon showed up on a segment of *The Girl from U.N.C.L.E.* He did a lot of forgettable episodic TV, then finally clicked with his own dramatic series, *Trapper John, M.D.* But it never seemed as if he'd attained the potential he left *Bonanza* for.

• Gary Conway left *Burke's Law* to "go on to a wider spectrum of creative challenges." Actually, it was a taller spectrum: he next starred in *Land of the Giants*.

• Don Knotts left *The Andy Griffith Show* to go on to bigger things. He made some fairly popular light and Disney movies, but never hit it so big again.

Gary Conway becomes a pencil-pusher in this scene from a Land of the Giants *episode. Maybe he's trying to write a message to his agent.*

BOB VOSE

Dennis Weaver (center) gets ready to utter his final "Mr. Dillon" in this, his last scene in the Long Branch on Gunsmoke. *Twice before, he'd left the show, only to return. This time it stuck. With him are, from left, James Arness and, with their backs to us, Amanda Blake and Milburn Stone in this 1963 photo.*

● Dennis Weaver left *Gunsmoke,* struggled for a bit, but succeeded and had a long, fairly interesting TV career of series, miniseries, and made-for-TV movies.

● Jean Hagen left *The Danny Thomas Show* because she was tired of playing a housewife. She was not much seen on TV after that.

● Robert Horton left *Wagon Train,* vowing he would never do another TV series. He was soon back in *A Man Called Shenandoah,* which lasted just a year. He wasn't heard from much after that. He did regional and touring theater and some movies. In 1982, he landed a role on the daytime serial *As the World Turns.*

● Steven Hill, who played Daniel Briggs, the first team leader, left after the first (1966–67) season of *Mission: Impossible,* and was not seen much on TV for a long time after. He later appeared semi-prominently as Michael Steadman's father in *thirtysomething* and in a number of father or grandfather roles.

● McLean Stevenson is often seen by many as the classic example of the actor who left a hit series (M*A*S*H) too soon. "I'm tired of being one of six. I want to be one of one," Stevenson (Lieutenant Colonel Henry Blake) told *TV Guide* in 1976, but a few unsuccessful series attempts later, he had not exactly set the entertainment world on fire. Wayne Rogers (Trapper John) also took an early leave of *M*A*S*H,* had a series failure with *City of Angels,* a moderate success with *House Calls,* and not much else. Then Larry Linville (Major Frank Burns) left after five seasons: "It's been good, but I don't know if it would be good for me as an actor to stay on." His subsequent TV appearances (*Grandpa Goes to Washington, Checking In,* and *Herbie, the Love Bug* among them) have been decided anticlimaxes. Gary Burghoff's departure as Radar after seven years has led to nothing of the same scale.

● Farrah Fawcett-Majors left *Charlie's Angels* after only a year. She felt she was just being used as a sex symbol on the show, that she was a serious actress, and that movies were where it was at. She also said she didn't have a contract to continue the show. After threats of litigation by the producers, an agreement was reached wherein, despite having been replaced by Cheryl Ladd, she made six guest appearances. Later, she made a few movies of little note, but scored on stage in *Extremities,* and came back to TV and showed her dramatic muscle in made-for-TV movies like *The Burning Bed. Good Sports,* her series with long-time paramour Ryan O'Neal, lasted less than a season.

● Barbara Bain and Martin Landau left

Mission: Impossible after its third year. Paramount said Landau left because he wanted more money; Landau says Paramount was going to cut the show's budget and hurt quality, so he left. After the British-made series *Space: 1999,* they were seldom seen on TV. Landau made a comeback in the 1988 Francis Ford Coppola movie, *Tucker: The Man and His Dream,* for which he won an Oscar nomination.

● Mike Evans, who had played Lionel on *All in the Family,* left *The Jeffersons* in 1975 after its 13th episode. Four years later—after living in the desert, away from the TV-and-film community—he bumped into Sherman Hemsley (who played George Jefferson), who suggested Evans come back to the show. Which he did in 1979. He stayed for two seasons, then left again.

● Suzanne Somers left *Three's Company* after her demands for more money and other "perks" were rejected by the producers. She was replaced by Jenilee Harrison. But Harrison was not *the* permanent replacement. Though remaining with the show, she was "sent off to veterinary school" while Priscilla Barnes, as Terri Alden, became the permanent third tenant in the *Three's Company* apartment. Somers had a couple of series that didn't last long, made TV-movies, but mostly concentrated on her nightclub act.

● Rob Reiner and Sally Struthers left *All in the Family.* He went on to direct and become highly successful with such hits as *When Harry Met Sally, Misery, This Is Spinal Tap,* and *Stand by Me.* Struthers found work hard to come by for four years, until she came back to TV as the same character, Gloria Bunker Stivic, in her own one-season series. After that her appearances on TV were limited and intermittent.

● Shelley Long left *Cheers* on the May 7, 1987, show after five years in the role of Diane Chambers. She concentrated mainly on movies of moderate success and a TV appearance every now and then.

● David Hartman left *Good Morning America* and was little heard from again.

Don Knotts takes an awkward swing at a ball—and, later, at an Andy Griffith–less career—as Ronny Howard watches.

Fingerprints All Over

It is almost impossible to envision other actors playing roles that have become cemented to certain personalities. For example, who else but Peter Falk could ever play Lieutenant Columbo? He *is* Columbo. And yet the producers who put the show together didn't think so. He wasn't their first choice at all—Bing Crosby was.

The history of TV is sequined with such instances: people who have become near-icons internationally for their portrayal of now famous fictional TV characters, but who were the second or third—or 100th—choice.

Over the years, *TV Guide* has kept track of such instances of actors being handed scripts for series and miniseries with, as the industry saying goes, other actors' fingerprints all over them. What follows is a sampling of times when those who are famous today were not the first, but the last. It's fun to imagine what the shows would have been like if they'd been cast otherwise.

● Dick Van Dyke, in most minds, *is* Rob Petrie. But in the pilot for what was then called *Head of the Family,* the writer-creator of the show, Carl Reiner, played the part of Petrie. Only when CBS showed little interest in the series did Reiner rethink and cast Van Dyke in the lead.

Meanwhile, Mary Tyler Moore wasn't first pick, either, to play Laura Petrie. *TV Guide* reported on November 22, 1958, that "Jennifer Lea has been signed to play Carl Reiner's wife," then on December 12 that Barbara Britton was to costar.

● E. G. Marshall and Robert Reed played father-and-son law partners in *The Defenders,* but they were the second team to play the roles: in 1957, a *Studio One* two-part drama by Reginald Rose called "The Defender" had the same characters played by Ralph Bellamy and William Shatner.

● Dick Powell, in "Who Killed Julie Greer?" a 1961 installment of *The Dick Powell Show* on NBC, played the role of a rich police officer named Amos Burke. In 1963, that same character, the central character in *Burke's Law,* was played by Gene Barry. But Barry wasn't the first choice to replace Powell. Jackie Cooper had first dibs.

● Dick Powell, again, played the continuing character of nightclub operator Willie Dante during the run of *Four Star Playhouse,* but when that character was later spun off for his own series, *Dante's Inferno,* it was Howard Duff who played the part.

● And, once more, it was Dick Powell who first played *Richard Diamond—*

Private Detective on radio, but David Janssen had the role on TV—working for producer Dick Powell. But even Janssen wasn't Powell's first choice: Don Taylor was. In fact, Janssen wasn't the first, second, third, fourth—or even the 24th—actor to audition for the part. In fact, he was the 25th man tested for the role by Powell.

● James Arness wasn't the first choice for *Gunsmoke*'s Matt Dillon. The producers wanted John Wayne. He didn't want to do a series. This may be just a press agent's story—some say Wayne merely convinced Arness to do the part, but wasn't offered it himself because he was too big a star to consider it. William Conrad, the voice of Matt Dillon on

Yes, there was a time when Paul Newman was not the first casting choice, and this is one of those instances: a last-minute replacement for James Dean in the 1955 Producers' Showcase *production of "Our Town," with Frank Sinatra and Eva Marie Saint.*

radio, was tested. So was Raymond Burr, whose voice was right but who was "too big." An actor named John Pickard almost won, but messed up in a love scene with Miss Kitty.

● When TV wanted to do *The Life of Riley,* the star of the radio show, William Bendix, was too busy with movies. So the role went to a new face on TV in his first series role: Jackie Gleason. Then, when Gleason left the show, Bendix took over.

● Brandon de Wilde was the *Lassie* producers' first choice in 1953 for the role of the young boy before Tommy Rettig got the job.

● Oddly, Ronald Colman and Benita Hume, who originated the lead roles in the radio version of *Halls of Ivy,* were not considered for the leads when the show was being produced for TV. Of the many couples considered for the roles, one pairing under serious consideration was Lilli Palmer and Rex Harrison. Finally, the producers made their choice: Colman and Hume.

● *TV Guide* reported in the March 26, 1954, issue that "Robert Cummings is preparing a new film series, *Phoebe,* in which he'll play a newsman running an advice-to-the-lovelorn column." But it was Peter Lawford who got the role.

● Wanda Hendrix could have been famous by now, but she turned down the original *My Little Margie* role, because she didn't like the script. Gale Storm didn't particularly like it, either, but she figured it would get better as it went along. She was right.

● Elsa Lanchester and Jay C. Flippen were tested for the *Tugboat Annie* film-series leads. Then Flippen was out and

Chill Wills was in. Then both were out and, a year later, it was reported that the pilot film for the series was completed at a cost of $128,865, a hands-down record. Of the total, $72,580 was spent on screen tests and story rights before the film was shot. Finally, Minerva Urecal and Walter Sands signed for TPA's *Tugboat Annie,* and went into production on it on July 15, 1957. And after all that, the show only ran one 39-episode season.

● James Dean was the first choice to play George Gibbs, the young male lead in a 1955 *Producers' Showcase* musical production of "Our Town," with Frank Sinatra as the Stage Manager. George was played on-air by Paul Newman.

● It's nearly impossible to imagine anyone but Raymond Burr in the role of Perry Mason. But Burr was not the first choice to play the role—Fred MacMurray was. Nor was Burr the second choice. Robert Sterling was tested and seriously considered, as were Efrem Zimbalist, Jr., and William Hopper—who ended up getting the role of Paul Drake on the series. The story goes that practically every available leading man in Hollywood and a few from the East Coast went to test for the Mason role. Burr was interested, but executive producer Gail Patrick Jackson wasn't interested very much in him. "All right, we'll humor him," Jackson is supposed to have said to her associates. "If he'll test for [prosecuting attorney Hamilton] Burger, we'll test him for Mason, too." Later, in the projection room, Erle Stanley Gardner, creator of the character, jumped up and started waving his arms and shouting the instant he saw Burr in the test. "That's Perry Mason!" he cried.

● Jerry Mathers was lined up for the Beaver from the start; but the role of Wally was originally cast with an actor named Paul Sullivan.

● Robert Alda was up for the role of Bat Masterson, which Gene Barry ultimately won.

● "Jeanne Crain signed to star in CBS's *Guestward Ho* series, the role originally slated for Nanette Fabray." —*January 18, 1958*

"Desilu has taken over the *Guestward Ho* property from CBS (which failed to make headway toward signing either Nanette Fabray or Jeanne Crain) and plans it as a series to star Vivian Vance for season after next." —*May 31, 1958*

"Vivian Vance is making a new test film for her *Guestward Ho!* series." —*January 16, 1960*

"Joanne Dru replaces Vivian Vance in the remake of the *Guestward Ho!* test film." —*March 5, 1960*

● After one season (1957–58), five actresses and four actors (Zoe Hazlett, Jeanne Baird, Frances Helm, Joyce MacKenzie, Kristine Miller, Chris Warfield, Casey Adams, Ray Montgomery, and Harland Ward) were tested to replace Cloris Leachman and Jon Shepodd as Ruth and Paul Martin in *Lassie*. At the last minute, a sixth pair, June Lockhart and Hugh Reilly, were brought in for tests—and wound up with the roles. Jon Provost, and of course Lassie, stayed on.

● Robert Stack was not the first choice to play Eliot Ness on *The Untouchables*. Van Heflin was offered the job first, and took it, but had to back out when a movie conflict arose. Then Van Johnson was offered it, but decided against it. Fred MacMurray was considered, as were Jack Lord and Cliff Robertson. Then Stack.

• Johnny Carson wasn't the first person approached to take over from Jack Paar to host *The Tonight Show.* Many candidates were considered, and Groucho Marx and Jackie Gleason were seriously talked to.

• Although Morey Amsterdam and Pat Carroll were announced as the title-role voices behind ABC's Hanna-Barbera cartoon series *The Jetsons,* the series ultimately had George O'Hanlon and Penny Singleton doing the honors.

• James Franciscus was first choice to play Dr. Kildare—he had the strong backing of the show's creator and director—but the pilot had to roll immediately and he had to ride out the final 17 days of an option that committed him to another series, which never happened. So the producers went with someone else— Richard Chamberlain. William Shatner had also been offered the lead, but turned it down.

• The voice of the car in *My Mother, the Car* was originally to have been supplied by long-absent screen star Jean Arthur. Ann Sothern got the job.

• Tammy Grimes was the first actress approached to play the part of Samantha in *Bewitched.*

• Jack Lord wasn't the first person considered for Steve McGarrett on *Hawaii Five-O*—Gregory Peck was.

• Lou Gossett was the first actor signed to play Gale Sayers in *Brian's Song,* the role that was eventually played by Billy Dee Williams.

• The first Americanized version of

Britain's popular comedy series *Steptoe and Son* starred Lee Tracy and Aldo Ray in the pilot. It didn't sell. Then, when Norman Lear got his hands on the property, he cast Barnard Hughes and Paul Sorvino in the father-and-son roles. It didn't sell. Then Lear and associates thought of making the junk dealer and his son black—and hired Redd Foxx and Demond Wilson for *Sanford and Son.*

• Gavin MacLeod, who was known for playing villains and heavies, was asked to read for a role on *The Mary Tyler Moore Show*—the Lou Grant role. After he'd read it, he left, then returned and asked if he could read for the Murray Slaughter role. And got it.

• The part of Private Duane Doberman on *The Phil Silvers Show* made a national, recognizable figure out of Maurice Gosfield. But the part was originally filled by Buddy Hackett, who bowed out for a Broadway part.

• Darren McGavin turned down the leads in *Run for Your Life, I Dream of Jeannie,* and *Hogan's Heroes.*

• Edd Byrnes was the host of the *Wheel of Fortune* pilot.

• Gary Owens, announcer for *Rowan & Martin's Laugh-In,* was supposed to be the host of *The Gong Show.* John Barbour, who later cohosted *Real People,* was hired and almost immediately fired. Chuck Barris, the show's cocreator, decided he wanted to do it.

• ABC's first choice for the role of Mr. Roarke in *Fantasy Island* was not Ricardo Montalban—it was Orson Welles.

• Ken Howard and Blythe Danner were

offered the leads in *McMillan and Wife* but declined.

● The part Joe Namath played in a series called *The Waverly Wonders* was first offered to Larry Hagman, who turned it down in favor of another script he'd been sent: *Dallas.*

● John Forsythe was not the first choice for Blake Carrington on *Dynasty.* George Peppard was—and in fact he was already hired to do the pilot when he argued with executives over how Carrington should be played, and then left the show.

● "I asked my agents to investigate," Richard Chamberlain told *TV Guide* in 1980. "They discovered that 'Shogun' was indeed going to be filmed, but that I was at the end of a long line of actors being considered for Blackthorne. Well, to shorten a very long tale, I guess I just outwaited everybody else. . . . Finally, there was only one actor left in line ahead of me: Sean Connery. Good fortune intervened and Mr. Connery accepted another film, leaving the part open. Blackthorne was at last mine."

● Sherman Hemsley was not the first actor hired to play George Jefferson on *All in the Family.* Avon (Sportin' Life) Long had the part, but it didn't work out.

● Veronica Hamel rejected the original *Charlie's Angels* role later filled by Jaclyn Smith.

● *Quincy* had been conceived as an *NBC Mystery Movie* for Robert Wagner, a swinging-bachelor type. But Wagner was otherwise engaged, and Jack Klugman was offered the part.

● *Terrible Joe Moran,* about an elderly ex–boxing champ, seemed like a natural

for James Cagney. But the script was written for, and was meant to be starred in by, Katharine Hepburn as a former world-famous tennis player. An injury in a fall kept her from doing it. The producers thought of Cagney.

● Michael J. Fox, who became famous as Alex P. Keaton on *Family Ties,* was not who the producers had their sights on for the part—it was originally to be played by Matthew Broderick, who decided he didn't want to commit himself to a long TV run and instead played in Neil Simon's *Brighton Beach Memoirs* and *Biloxi Blues* on Broadway.

● Jerry Van Dyke turned down the role of Gilligan in *Gilligan's Island.* Instead, he took the role in *My Mother, the Car.* Later, he was the first choice for the role of George, the janitor, in *Newhart,* but he blew the audition and the role went to Tom Poston.

● It came down to two young actresses for the role of Winnie Cooper in *The Wonder Years,* but Danica McKellar got the role. The loser? Her sister, Crystal— who later got the role of the mean Becky.

● Melanie Mayron wasn't the first choice to play Melissa on *thirtysomething.* The producers wanted Polly Draper, who eventually played Ellyn Warren on the show, for the Melissa role.

● The producers of *Coach* didn't only have Craig Nelson in mind for the role of Hayden Fox. Gerald McRaney, Burt Reynolds, James Farentino, David Rasche, Ron Leibman, Tom Skerritt, Gary Lockwood, Jim Stafford and Richard Crenna were all approached to do the role.

Chimps

"There's not enough talent to go around. All you see is talking horses, talking jackasses, monkeys running around. Of course, I'd rather watch monkeys these days than most of the actors," said Sir Cedric Hardwicke in 1962.

It's not easy to determine, on a Freudian level, why TV audiences over the years have found chimpanzee-watching to be a favorite spectator sport. But it has been, since the very beginning of broadcast television. It seems we haven't been able to get enough of these hairy, athletic, big-eared, long- and rubber-limbed equatorial anthropoids—especially when they're dressed in human clothes—and TV producers have accommodated our obsession by casting them wherever possible.

Do we laugh at them because they make us seem superior to an underclass race? Do we identify with them? Do we revel in their anarchy, and live vicariously through their rules-be-damned, swing-from-the-chandeliers behavior. Do we envy the free-spirited, loose-jointed way they swing through life? Are they a mirror, are they a memory?

To those questions, the networks reply: Freudian, shmeudian—who cares? All they know is, when Dave Garroway brought J. Fred Muggs on the *Today* show, ratings went up two points. When that information made its way through the halls of ABC, CBS, NBC, and the DuMont networks, the rush was on.

The human heart and one of its more intimate acquaintances were the subjects of a recent Dick Cavett interview on PBS. The interviewee was Dr. Christiaan Barnard, the South African surgeon of heart-transplant fame.

We caught only the last five minutes of the show, but they were more affecting than any other few minutes we have seen on television lately.

When we tuned in, Dr. Barnard was talking about a subject that some people find repugnant and even grotesque—his experiments using ape hearts in human patients.

Barnard had discovered that there was a considerable difference between chimpanzees and baboons. He no longer used chimps, he said. Why was that, Cavett asked.

Heinie the chimpanzee seems to be checking to see if Marlin Perkins is feverish ("Take two bananas and see me in the morning") in this Zoo Parade *scene from 1952.*

Because, said Dr. Barnard, the chimps are too much like people. At one point he had had two chimps in adjacent cages, and when one was removed for an operation, the other chimpanzee was so distraught that it cried for several days.

As he related this story, Barnard's voice faltered, and it became apparent that his own heart was having its problems—with the memory of one doomed and one disconsolate chimpanzee.

Cavett looked away for a moment, but turned back to confront those emotions. "Do you mind my mentioning that you have slight tears in your eyes now?"

The camera turned to Barnard. His mouth opened, but no words came out. He was hardly the picture of the unfeeling researcher for whom a patient—or an animal—was mere experimental fodder. It was a small but real moment of drama—the kind seen all too rarely in TV's slick packages.

An unfancy, low-budget PBS show. Two people sat and talked about the human heart. They were discussing its physiology—but what they revealed was the more complex anatomy of its vulnerabilities.

June 3, 1978

J. Fred Muggs became the hairy toast of early-rising America as the ratings-winning oddity on the Today *show. Here he seems to be heading to work in a custom-made Corvette. If he was such a big star, you'd think he'd have a driver.*

Tamba has a script change, and it probably couldn't hurt, as Johnny Weissmuller seems to agree in this publicity still for Jungle Jim.

Almost unbearably cute, Kokomo, Jr., was also said to be a lot more docile than the temperamental J. Fred Muggs, and so replaced him on Today. *He also made guest appearances on other NBC shows, including* Howdy Doody.

Zippy the Chimp's human caretaker got drafted into the army and brought Zippy along—into Bilko's platoon for a series of 1959 episodes of The Phil Silvers Show.

The Marquis Chimps—Charlie, Enoch, and Cindy—had an entire show written around their talents: ABC's 1961-season comedy The Hathaways, *in which they played the quasi-children of couple Peggy Cass and Jack Weston.*

Clowns

The greasepaint, frilly collar, bulbous nose, and intermittent hair of the circus clown were all too much of a temptation for many TV celebrities. There were those who applied the clown white because that was their job—for some, it was a first big break in show business. Others portrayed clowns on episodes of TV programs. Still others put on the striped or spotted sack shirt and baggy pants for a special occasion, or just for the fun of it. After all, all the world loves one.

Here, underneath the goo and gum, are some famous faces caught for the pages of *TV Guide*.

This is Howdy Doody's first Clarabell (top left), and underneath that makeup is also the man who became TV's one and only Captain Kangaroo: Bob Keeshan.

Jean Hagen seems amused, Danny Thomas doesn't, in this scene from The Danny Thomas Show (top right).

Which is the real Willy? That's Emmett Kelly on the right, and Henry Fonda on the left playing him in the Kelly biography, "Clown," the March 27, 1955, production of General Electric Theater (left). Kelly served as technical adviser on this, the most expensive half-hour drama ever filmed for TV up to that time.

Carol Burnett (top left), one of TV's greatest comedienne/clowns, put on full makeup for a publicity shoot for TV Guide *in 1977.*

Some backbiters may say his role hasn't changed all that much over the years, but, hey, he's the guy giving away (and earning) million-dollar checks, not us. Pre-Johnny Carson, this was Ed McMahon (top right) in 1956, on the Philadelphia-originated CBS circus series, Big Top.

Don't leave home with this on—that's Karl Malden (left), made up for a 1976 episode of The Streets of San Francisco.

What can you say—TV's two greatest clowns in one scene (above): Red Skelton was the guest on "Lucy Goes to Mexico," a segment of the Westinghouse Lucille Ball–Desi Arnaz Show.

THE PANTHEON

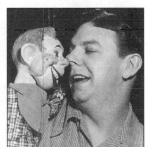

Lucille Ball

If you sat down to watch all the TV shows Lucille Ball starred in, shown one after another without pause, you wouldn't get up again for 10 days and 15½ hours.

Lucille Ball and Desi Arnaz together made $4,000 a week during *I Love Lucy*'s first season—which is $26,000 less than Roseanne Barr Arnold takes in per episode.

"It is so important to have what I like to call the enchanted sense of play. Many, many times you should think and react as a child in doing comedy. All the inhibitions and embarrassments disappear. We did some pretty crazy things in *I Love Lucy,* but we believed every minute of them. It's like getting drunk without taking a drink.**"** — *Lucille Ball, 1959*

"It was romance—out of step. It was romantic, and fun, occasionally. It was emotional. But our senses of values were different.**"** —*Lucille Ball about her marriage to Desi Arnaz, 1962*

Jack Benny

"To me, a special is when coffee is marked down from 89 cents to 54 cents a pound.**"** *—Jack Benny*

"I'm not *too* worried about going on TV. I figure I can't be any worse than anyone else.**"** *—Jack Benny, 1950*

Milton Berle

In 1951, Milton Berle signed a 30-year contract with NBC for $200,000 a year. Though it was later renegotiated downward, he collected $4.8 million—or $200,000 less than Johnny Carson earned from NBC in 1988 for doing *The Tonight Show.*

66Television has made me realize that Mr. and Mrs. American TV audience have a much higher IQ than they are credited with having. I've learned TV is a great way to reach millions of people—who, luckily, can't reach me.**99** —*Milton Berle, 1953*

66He's done everybody's act. He's a parrot with skin on.**99** —*Fred Allen, on* The Milton Berle Show, *1953*

66At first, the pace of doing 39 shows a season was tremendous. The minute you got through with one you started working on the next. There was no chance for me to sit down; I couldn't do it. There was no chance for me to play golf. There was no chance for me to see much of my wife, Ruth. There were times when I was sick and had to go on without an audience knowing it, times when I had pains in my head, my legs aching from rehearsing 96 or 100 hours on one show and doing it for 58 minutes. Later, after the arguments and the shouting and the tension, I'd sit exhausted in my dressing room, wearing a terrycloth robe, and ask myself, 'Is it worth it?'**99** —*Milton Berle, 1956*

Carol Burnett

“I don't think crossing my eyes is worth 50 cents, let alone the money I get.**”** —*Carol Burnett, 1967*

“She has *got* to be a star. She's wholesome—I know the word has the connotation of the kiss of death; she's cute—nothing of the masculine about her as there is in so many female comics. And she's disciplined—she has the greatest respect for that particular show-business tradition. . . . She's got a glimmering, but no *real* idea how important she's become.**”** —*Garry Moore, about Carol Burnett, 1961*

“I'll *never* do a TV series. That's it. Once you've been a series character, you're that character for *life*. They would probably name me *Gertrude* or *Agnes*, and that's all I'd be forever.**”** —*Carol Burnett, 1963*

Sid Caesar

Sid Caesar studied at the Juilliard School of Music, then played the saxophone with the Charlie Spivak, Shep Fields, and Claude Thornhill orchestras.

"Laughter in a can is like freedom in Russia—they can turn it on and off at will." —*Sid Caesar, 1961, on* TV Laughtracks.

Johnny Carson

REVIEW: THE JOHNNY CARSON SHOW

Johnny Carson, the star—naturally!—of CBS's summertime *Johnny Carson Show,* is a young comedian who has been compared to such established TV funnymen as George Gobel and Herb Shriner. It's true that he uses their relaxed tempo, rather than the mile-a-minute style of gagsters like Bob Hope and the pre-conversion Milton Berle, but his brand of humor is strictly his own.

He's a personable, pleasant young man whose forte seems to be whimsy and satire, rather than so-called "sight gags" and slapstick. However, his material isn't always up to par. Not all his opening monologs come off and his sketches are sometimes unamusingly familiar.

So far he has done his best work in parodies of TV shows like *Person to Person* and *You Are There.* At his best, he's first-rate, but it still remains to be seen whether he'll evolve a suitable format before the end of his summertime tenure.

August 20, 1955

"Johnny Carson, a bright young comic, gets his laughs from ideas and situations, rather than rapid-fire jokes. This type of comedian, I feel, will outlive most of the others.**"** *—Jack Benny, 1955*

"Different times on TV demand different things. During the day you have to assume that maybe the audience is busy with other things, watching with one eye, listening with half an ear. You have to keep it brisk. Along about 8 o'clock at night, the audience demands more. You have to keep hitting them with strong things, build a good cast around you the way Perry Como has and the way Bob Newhart had better if he wants to keep going. Late at night your tempo is less urgent. You get away with more. You can use satire, attack sacred cows.**"** *—Johnny Carson, 1962*

Jackie Gleason

When Jackie Gleason, who hardly ever rehearsed his lines for *The Honeymooners,* would forget his lines on-air, he would signal to either Art Carney, Audrey Meadows, or Joyce Randolph by patting his stomach. Then they'd have to jump in and save the scene.

❝I'd hate to do something on our show that was a laugh on someone else's.**❞** —*Jackie Gleason, explaining his opposition to a laugh track for* The Honeymooners, *1955*

❝I'm funnier when I'm fat but I don't enjoy myself.**❞** —*Jackie Gleason, 1956*

❝I'm 53 years old. I love what I do. I have all the money I'll ever need. I'm not looking for challenges. I do what I do very well and I think I get better at it. My weight doesn't bother me because I don't mind it. I like good food so I eat it. I smoke because it's a habit I'm too old to break and I enjoy cigarettes, too. I drink because it's a lot of fun. I admire great boozers. Guys who can go all day and never show it. I play golf every day and am more fascinated with it all the time. Everything I've wanted to do I've had the chance to do. Life ain't bad, pal.**❞** —*Jackie Gleason, 1969*

Howdy Doody

The morning sun shone lemon-yellow over the town of Doodyville, Texas. In a small wooden shack a ranch hand named Doody smiled down at his wife who had just presented him with twin sons. The date was December 27, 1941.

"Howdy," said the father to the squalling babies. At the sound of his voice they began to chortle. "That's what we'll call 'em, honey," Mr. Doody said to his wife. "Howdy will be the first one's name and since his brother is a twin we'll call him Double."

The boys grew up on the ranch where their parents earned a living doing chores. When they were six the boys were enrolled in the Doodyville Public School.

One day, after classes, they found their dad sitting quietly on the porch. In his hand was a telegram.

"Boys," he said, "you never knew your uncle. When he struck oil near Doodyville they named the town after him. He went East before you were born." Here Mr. Doody wiped away a tear. "I have just had word that your uncle is dead. He has willed you a small plot of land smack dab in the middle of New York."

That night Howdy and Double lay in bed talking about what they'd do with the property.

"If I had the land I'd run a circus on it," Howdy sighed. "Take it," said Double. "I like Texas."

One week later a letter arrived from the National Broadcasting Company. They

wanted to buy the land to build a television studio. Calling Howdy and Double to his side, Mr. Doody asked them their opinion. Double told him of Howdy's wish. That night Mr. Doody wrote to NBC, explaining that they could have the use of the land if they'd give Howdy an opportunity to run a circus.

The men in charge at NBC readily agreed to Mr. Doody's terms. They constructed a circus grounds and surrounded it with television cameras and equipment.

Buffalo Bob Smith, who was appointed Howdy's guardian by NBC, met Howdy in the big city and thus began a friendship that has lasted until this day.

Howdy loves New York because it's a million cities in one. Best of all, it's the center of TV and lets him enter 60 cities at once on eight million kids' TV screens.

November 23, 1951

Ernie Kovacs

Ernie Kovacs was happiest when he was creating new effects with television cameras. He started about 10 years ago and was still pioneering at the end—in those half-hour specials he agreed to do because he was promised an absolutely free hand.

Actually he didn't much want to perform. That was for money. He wanted to direct, and once he turned down a multimillion-dollar network offer because the network insisted he perform as well as direct and write.

Ernie did his own writing. Sometimes he had help, but the bulk of it came from his typewriter—in the early hours of the morning. He wrote countless radio and television shows, a couple of books that way.

He worked hard. One year in New York he did three network morning shows and a nighttime network show on television and 15 hours on radio each week. Another year he did 10 hours a week on television.

Doing movies was going to be a cinch for him—and it was. He took it easy, spent time with the children and wife he adored, and became a movie star. But he couldn't stay away from television. He was offered so much money "just to preside" over a silly quiz show that he couldn't turn it down. He wound up writing the show, acting in skits, even writing and acting in the commercials. Finally he got the specials he loved to do. He knew they wouldn't attract great audiences, but he had fun and so did his fans. And television had some excitement. Something new was being tried.

They called him "zany." He wasn't, really. He was gentle and soft-spoken and witty and thoughtful, and tremendously talented.

We'll miss him.

February 10, 1962

"10 5/8 years ahead of my time.**"** —*Ernie Kovacs*

"I'm almost normal. Is that good?**"** —*Ernie Kovacs*

Edward R. Murrow

"When I was quite young and about to make my first trip abroad, a very famous judge told me, 'Ed, you're going to meet kings, queens, millionaires, and movie stars. Don't let 'em throw you. Don't be nervous.' The way I've found it easy to keep a level head is always to imagine that the person you're speaking to is standing there in his underwear.**"** —*Edward R. Murrow, 1956*

Ed Sullivan

Ed Sullivan was a twin, but the other half, Daniel, died before his first birthday.

ED SULLIVAN SHOW FIRSTS

First to stage an ice show on TV.

First to present ballet and opera stars on TV.

First to inject dramatic skits and excerpts from Broadway productions into a TV variety show.

First to take his TV show on the road.

First to present politically and racially unpopular performers, thus defying blacklists.

66Ed Sullivan will be around as long as someone else has talent.**99** —*Fred Allen, 1958*

66A dog could do that, if you rubbed meat on the actors.**99** —*Fred Allen, typifying Ed Sullivan's emceeing as consisting only of pointing at performers, 1963*

66Next week, the Beatles and the Pietà.**99** —*Ed Sullivan, at the end of one of his shows, 1964*

66Let's hear it for the Lord's Prayer!**99** *Ed Sullivan, after Sergio Franchi sang it on the 1965 Christmas show*

66Everything went along fine—until the first show. They told me to look the camera dead in the eye. I looked—and froze. It was some freeze. It took me six years to thaw out.**99** —*Ed Sullivan, 1955*

Danny Thomas

The title of Danny Thomas's show, *Make Room for Daddy,* came from Thomas's wife. Whenever he was on the road doing club dates, one of his young daughters would sleep with her mother. When Thomas came home, his wife would move the daughter out again, saying, "We must make room for Daddy."

"If you gotta have a nose, *have* one." —*Danny Thomas*

AUDIO

"Say goodnight, Gracie."

Catch Phrases

Sometimes a phrase, a sentence, even just one word spoken in just such a way by a TV character or personality can simply capture America's imagination (or, some critics might say, lack of it). And, before you know it, it's become part of the language—at least for this season—and you can't go anywhere, do anything, or speak with anyone without its popping up in conversation. Sometimes you just want to scream from the overuse. How many times in the 1960s could you have handed people something and had each one of them respond, in imperfect Maxwell Smart imitation, "Thanks—I needed that," before thoughts of mayhem would have risen to your surface?

Some of these catch phrases wilt and die on the popular-culture/faddism vine; others, decades old, still slip into discussions from time to time, to one's utter amazement and odd pleasure, showing the power and influence of TV, and how fully we want to be like it and be accepted as part of the whole it makes of us.

Following are some of the most popular, oft-repeated catch phrases in TV history. Some were designed by writers specifically to trigger response and take American tongues by storm; others simply happened, and were happily cultivated by the lucky shows and stars who happened to fall into them. These are powerful slogans, packed solid with nostalgia, and we defy you to read them and not hear the TV voices of the past who became famous for saying them. And we predict you will be helpless to avoid imitating those voices. It's sort of like channeling.

"Well, I'll be a dirty bird."
"You don't hardly get those no more."
　　—George Gobel on
　　　The George Gobel Show

"Would you believe . . . ?"
"Sorry about that, Chief."
"Thanks—I needed that."
"And I'll be *loving* it."
　　—Maxwell Smart (Don Adams) on
　　　Get Smart

"Dy-no-mite!"
　　—J.J. (Jimmie Walker) on *Good Times*

"Mister Dillon!"
　　—Chester (Dennis Weaver) on
　　　Gunsmoke

"Aaayhh!"
　　—Fonzie (Henry Winkler) on
　　　Happy Days

"To the moon, Alice!"
"One of these days, one of these days—POW!—right in the kisser!"
"Baby, you're the greatest."
　　—Ralph Kramden (Jackie Gleason)
　　　on *The Honeymooners*

"Peace."
　　—Dave Garroway on *Today*

"Well!"
　　—Jack Benny on *The Jack Benny Show*

"Who loves ya, baby?"
　　—Kojak (Telly Savalas) on *Kojak*

"What a revoltin' development this is!"
—Chester A. Riley (William Bendix)
    on *The Life of Riley*

"Mmmmwwahh."
—Dinah Shore

"Say goodnight, Gracie."
—George Burns to Gracie Allen on
    *The George Burns and Gracie Allen
    Show*

"Work!?!!"
—Maynard G. Krebs (Bob Denver)
    on *The Many Loves of Dobie Gillis*

"Na nu, na nu."
—Mork (Robin Williams) on
    Mork and Mindy

"You bet your bippy."
"Look that up in your Funk and
Wagnalls."
"Sock it to me."

Flip Wilson as Geraldine: "The Devil made me do

"Verrry interrresting."
—*Rowan & Martin's Laugh-In*

"Cowabunga!"
—Chief Thunderthud on
    Howdy Doody

"And that's the way it is. . . . "
—Walter Cronkite on *CBS News*

"How sweet it is!"
"And away we go!"
—Jackie Gleason on
    The Jackie Gleason Show

"The Devil made me do it."
"What you see is what you get."
—Flip Wilson on *The Flip Wilson Show*

"Just the facts, ma'am."
—Joe Friday (Jack Webb) on *Dragnet*

"Va-va-va-voom!"
—Newton-the-Waiter and Charlie
    (both Art Carney) on *The Morey
    Amsterdam Show;* later, Ed Norton
    on *The Honeymooners*

"I don't fool around, boy."
—Ricky Nelson on *Ozzie and Harriet*

"My name—José Jimenez."
—Bill Dana on *The Steve Allen Show*

"Yabba-dabba-doo!"
—Fred Flintstone on *The Flintstones*

"Smarter than the average bear."
—Yogi Bear

"Nussing. I know nussing!"
—Sergeant Schultz (John Banner) on
    Hogan's Heroes

"I kid you not."
—Jack Paar

"I'll kwill you a mwillion times!"
—Milton Berle

"Hello dere."
—Marty Allen of Allen and Rossi

"Son of a gun."
—Joey Bishop

"Meathead."
"Stifle yourself."
—Archie Bunker (Carroll O'Connor)
on *All in the Family*

"On ahr stage tonight . . ."
"A really big shew . . ."
—Ed Sullivan

"God is going to get you for this."
—Maude (Bea Arthur) on *Maude*

"Well, kiss mah grits!"
—Flo (Polly Holliday) on *Alice*

"Come on down!"
—Johnny Olsen on *The Price Is Right*

"Yuucchh!"
—Richard Deacon as Mel Cooley to
Morey Amsterdam's Buddy Sorrell
on *The Dick Van Dyke Show*

"Holy [fill in the blank]!"
—Robin on *Batman*

"Walkies!"
—Barbara Woodhouse on
Training Dogs the Woodhouse Way

"Cheeseburgie, cheeseburgie . . . No
Coke—Pepsi."
"Generalissimo Francisco Franco is
still dead."
"Candy-gram."
"I'm Chevy Chase and you're not."
"Jane, you ignorant slut."
"Never mind."
"Yah, yah, that's the ticket!"
"Now, isn't that special?"
"Could it be . . . SATAN?!"
"You look mah-velous."
"I hate when that happens."

"We are two wild and crazy guys."
"But, no-o-o-o-o-o . . ."
—Various cast members on
Saturday Night Live

"I pity the fool. . . ."
—Mr. T on *The A Team*

"Heeeerrrre's Johnny!"
—Ed McMahon on *The Tonight Show*

"Where's the beef?"
—Clara Peller in a Wendy's
commercial

"Doan be reedeeculus!"
—Balki Bartokomous (Bronson
Pinchot) in *Perfect Strangers*

"Oh, just one more thing . . ."
—Lieutenant Columbo (Peter Falk)
on *Columbo*

"Homey don't play that."
—Homey the Clown (Damon Wayans)
on *In Living Color*

"I've fallen and I can't get up."
—Mrs. Fletcher

"Good night, David."
"Good night, Chet."
—Chet Huntley and David Brinkley,
NBC News

Chevy Chase on Saturday Night Live's *"Weekend Update": "Franco is still dead."*

Unseen Voices

Though TV is a visual medium, often it has been a disembodied or at least an incognito voice that has captured viewers' imaginations. Actors lend their voices to cartoon characters all the time, and do voice-overs for commercials. But it's the actors whose voices emanate from odd or mysterious sources that intrigue us and make us remember them—and even help make the shows they "appear" in successful or at least remembered beyond normal expectations. When it comes to TV, forget that old piece of etiquette: sometimes it is better to be heard and not seen.

Back in the 1950s and early '60s, the gimmick of the unseen voice was all the rage. Turn on your set and you could hear Cleo, the wryly commenting basset hound, on *The People's Choice;* the person behind the voice was actress Mary Jane Croft. Horace Fenton, the never-seen owner of the hotel where Buddy Hackett's *Stanley* ran his newsstand, was given vocal life by the off-screen voice of Paul Lynde. In *The Plainclothesman,* the TV audience lived inside the skull and looked out through the eyes of the lead character, the Lieutenant—what he saw, we saw, but we never saw him, and only heard the voice of actor Ken Lynch saying his lines.

Mary Tyler Moore became famous for being "Sam," the alluring female who gave *Richard Diamond—Private Detective* his assignments. Only Sam's legs were seen, and only Moore's voice was heard. The purpose was not to make Sam a character that would take away from Diamond, but in the end viewers and TV writers were intrigued about who Sam was. Moore became somewhat of a celebrity, and her face appeared in many publications—thus defeating the whole Sam scheme. Moore capitalized on the publicity and left the show after 13 episodes to go on to other things; Roxanne Brooks took over.

Paul Frees, one of Hollywood's busiest and highest-paid voice characterizers, was the voice of Cap'n Crunch, the Pillsbury Doughboy, Ludwig von Drake, and Boris Badenov, but was also the voice of John Beresford Tipton of *The Millionaire.* When actor Peter Duel died during the filming of his series, *Alias Smith and Jones,* Frees imitated Duel's voice and saved an entire episode.

Allan "Rocky" Lane, an old movie cowboy, was the uncredited voice of Mr. Ed, and actor John Irwin was the original voice of Morris the Cat of cat food commercial fame.

In the talking-object category, Ann Sothern was *My Mother the Car,* speaking to son Jerry Van Dyke; William Daniels spoke for KITT, the supercar in *Knight Rider;* and Majel Barrett was the voice of the Starship *Enterprise*'s computer in both the original *Star Trek* and *Star Trek: The Next Generation.*

Many people wish their bosses would disappear, but two shows granted their employees that request: the never-seen Charlie on *Charlie's Angels* and the present-by-telephone-only Hollywood film-studio head John Bracken of *Bracken's World* were played, respectively, by John Forsythe and Warren Stevens. Bracken was only invisible

They even look like them—the unseen voices of Fred and Wilma Flintstone were provided by Alan Reed and Jean Vander Pyl.

for the show's first season, though; in its second, and last, Leslie Nielsen gave flesh to the character.

Shaaron Claridge's voice was one heard frequently on the *Adam-12* police-story series: hers was the police radio-operator's voice heard in the patrol car. It was apt casting—Claridge reported to Universal Studios once a week to tape her part, then headed off to her four-to-midnight shift as a police radio-operator at the Los Angeles police station in Van Nuys.

Lorenzo Music, the writer/producer of *Rhoda,* became the voice of unseen Carlton the Doorman when, with time running out till the first episode was to be shot, he couldn't find the right person. He read the part during rehearsals, it got laughs, and he stayed in the role and became an actor—which is what he'd come to Hollywood to be in the first place.

Daniel Stern was the adult voice of teenage Kevin Arnold in the voice-over narrations on *The Wonder Years*.

And even though Michael Saint Gerard was the one seen on the 1990 ABC series *Elvis,* he wasn't the one who did the singing of Presley's songs. And it wasn't Elvis, either. It was an Elvis impersonator, country-and-Western singer Ronnie McDowell. In fact, McDowell had been the voice of Elvis singing on every TV-movie or miniseries about Presley that had been broadcast since Elvis's death in 1977.

CHEERS: And farewell to Jim Backus, Vic Perrin and Mel Blanc, a talented trio of TV-voice artists. Besides appearing in the sitcoms *I Married Joan* and *Gilligan's Island,* Backus provided the voice of curmudgeonly cartoon character Mr. Magoo. Perrin is best remembered for his chilling introduction to *The Outer Limits:* "We can control the horizontal. . . . We can control the vertical." Blanc, of course, was the "Man of a Thousand Voices" who gave vivid life to innumerable cartoon characters, among them Bugs Bunny, Yosemite Sam and Porky Pig. The passing of these men, all within a week of one another this summer, silenced three great voices.
—*August 26, 1989*

We are asked to believe that there's no such thing as a loud commercial.

When you're sitting there watching a program and the sound comes on, blasting you out of your seat, waking the baby, and cracking a few glasses on the kitchen shelf—forget it. It's just an aural illusion.

They tell us nobody deliberately records sound at a level higher than program sound level. It just *seems* that way. The announcer is talking fast, or into an echo chamber, and you may have the *feeling* that the sound is up, but it isn't. It's your imagination.

There are quality standards for recording sound set by the Society of Motion Picture and Television Engineers. And they tell us most engineers adhere to these standards. But there are pitfalls. For one thing, one has to consider the *average* sound level, not the peaks. Another thing, there are two different recording systems, variable density and variable area, and when a commercial made with one system follows a commercial made with the other system, there may be the impression that the sound has suddenly been turned up.

We don't know a thing about the technical problems in sound recording. We do know that we are annoyed when we are forced to turn the volume knob down for commercials, up for programs.

Engineers have spanned bays with bridges, tunneled through mountains, sent man into space and made it possible to send television pictures across oceans. Certainly the men who record the sound and those who transmit it have the ability, if someone would give them a shove, to keep the sound on a commercial down to the level of the rest of the program.

Please—no more double-talk or explanations or excuses. Just *do* it.
December 15, 1962

TV Music

One of the oddest subsidiary money-making perks of TV stardom has been the signing of hot television celebrities to recording contracts—even when those actors couldn't carry a tune if the fate of the earth depended on it . . . which, thankfully, it does not.

It's good for the record company, signing a big name that can sell records no matter what's on them to enough people to swing a profit. And it's a way to earn extra bucks and pump up egos for the stars, who, like the clown who wanted to play Hamlet, deep down inside (and in the privacy of their own showers) believe they can croon. Some—a very rare some—actually can, and have.

Some of the records that have come out of these arrangements have been straight stuff, singing with musical accompaniment; others have been half-singing/half-recitation with orchestral backing; and some have been novelty items, often tied to the char-

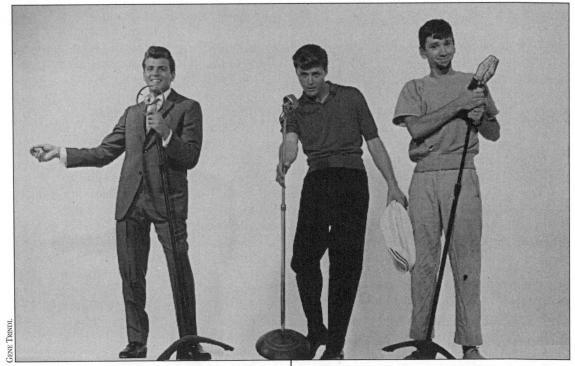

GENE TRINDL

Fabian (left), the only true recording artist in this group, swings it while Bob Denver (right) looks for the beat and Edd "Kookie" Byrnes has a brush with musical fame.

acters the actors play in their hit series. A flurry of them came out in the 1950s, linking the current heart throbs with the rock-and-roll rage, thus producing some wimpy, echo-chambered voices on anemic records. And, like many of the series, the records end up, all too quickly, as forgotten oddities in the remainder bin.

In 1954, Art Carney released, through Columbia Records, a *Honeymooners*-related record: "Va Va Va Voom" backed with "Song of the Sewer." This followed the earlier Jackie Gleason record: "And Awa-a-ay We Go."

Garry Moore put out a record album in 1955 titled *Music I Like,* in which he sang and played the drums.

Hugh O'Brian, TV's *Wyatt Earp,* recorded an album for ABC-Paramount in 1957.

Jackie Cooper—then of *The People's Choice*—conducted an orchestra for a 1957 album of 12 of the nation's favorite standards, to be selected by a poll. Album's title: *The People's Choice.*

Kathy Nolan of *The Real McCoys* cut her first rock-and-roll record in December 1958.

Jack Webb cut a 1958 album for the Warner Brothers label called *You're My Girl: Romantic Reflections by Jack Webb,* with lush orchestrations of classic ballads while he recited, but did not sing, the lyrics.

Several recording companies in 1959 wanted to release Efrem Zimbalist, Jr.'s classical compositions to take advantage of *77 Sunset Strip*'s success.

Vince Edwards, better known as Ben Casey, recorded with Decca Records, beginning in 1962. That same year, his competition, Richard Chamberlain, sold nearly a million copies of a ver-. sion of the *Dr. Kildare* theme that had words set to it. Then, during Christmas 1962, he had an album, *Richard Chamberlain Sings.*

The cast of *Bonanza* recorded an album of country music in 1962, and Lorne Greene and Pernell Roberts got individual contracts after the success of that album.

William Frawley, a one-time singing vaudevillian, recorded an album at the height of his *I Love Lucy* popularity.

Paul Petersen of *The Donna Reed Show* recorded the rock-and-roller "She Can't Find Her Keys."

Lori Martin, of *National Velvet,* made one called "God Bless America, the Home of the Boy I Love."

Tim Considine, of *My Three Sons,* recorded "Take It from a Guy Who Knows."

Shelley Fabares of *The Donna Reed Show* sold a million copies of "Johnny Angel."

Rosemary Prinz, Penny Hughes Wade in *As the World Turns,* in 1964 recorded her first album, *TV's Penny: Rosemary Prinz Sings.*

Fess Parker, then star of the new *Daniel Boone* series, signed an exclusive recording contract in 1964 with RCA Victor. His first album: *Fess Parker Sings About Daniel Boone, Davy Crockett, Abe Lincoln, and Other American Heroes.*

Jim Nabors, who could really sing, cut an album in 1965 for Columbia called *Shazam!* in which he sang songs like "Gomer Says Hey!" in his Gomer voice.

Sebastian Cabot, who was then playing Mr. French, the butler in *Family Affair,* in 1966 put out *Sebastian Cabot, Actor . . . Bob Dylan, Poet,* an album of readings of "It Ain't Me, Babe," "Blowin' In the Wind," and others to a chamber-music accompaniment.

The *Star Trek* crew took advantage of

their popularity: Leonard Nimoy released *Mr. Spock's Music from Outer Space,* which included the song "Music to Watch Space Girls By"; Nichelle Nichols put out an album of harp music; and William Shatner overdramatically recited such songs as "Lucy in the Sky with Diamonds" and Bob Dylan's "Mr. Tambourine Man" in his album, *The Transformed Man,* on Decca Records in 1968.

Soap queen Eileen Fulton (of CBS's *As the World Turns*) had her first record, *The Same Old World,* released in September 1970, to coincide with publication of her first book, *How My World Turns.* Later, she had a single out called "Some Dreams Never Come True."

Bill Bixby and Brandon Cruz of ABC's *The Courtship of Eddie's Father* did a duet on a record, "Daddy, What If," in 1970.

Telly Savalas, based on his Kojak popularity, put out an album in 1975 on Audio Fidelity Records appropriately entitled *Telly Savalas.*

Ted Knight, bumbling newscaster Ted Baxter on CBS's *The Mary Tyler Moore Show,* became a singer, too. He recorded two songs—"Hi Guys" and "I'm in Love with Barbara Walters."

Lorenzo Music, who provided the voice for Carlton the Doorman on the *Rhoda* series, put out a record in 1976 called "Who Is It?" full of Carltonisms.

Mary Kay Place did an album called *Tonight! At the Capri Lounge . . . Loretta Haggers,* which was based on her *Mary Hartman, Mary Hartman,* character. The album was nominated for a Grammy.

Cheryl Ladd made an album, riding on the crest of her *Charlie's Angels* popularity, as did Philip Michael Thomas and Don Johnson, using their *Miami Vice* popularity as springboards.

In March 1983, 10 of ABC's daytime series stars put out an album, *Love in the Afternoon.*

It had a good beat and you could dance to it— American Bandstand, *with Dick Clark at the podium, began in this Philadelphia studio (top), complete with painted music-store backdrop. Meanwhile (above), caught for a 1959 TV Guide article on local teen dance shows, is a future National League baseball all-star catcher and network sports announcer, Tim McCarver, on Top 10 Dance Party, WHBQ-TV, Memphis.*

You, Too, Can Speak Dragnet

You've heard of a French-English dictionary? A Spanish-English dictionary? Here, as a TV GUIDE public service, is a Dragnet-English dictionary.

Every viewer of the popular NBC detective show will be interested in knowing what Jack Webb means when he mutters: "We thought he was an ordinary 4127A LAMC without a package, but the make showed the caper was a 211, a carry away. When R and I checked, the FBI kickback had him a muscle-happy big time."

But the serious student of Dragnetese, a language spoken by some TV actors and the Los Angeles Police Department, will use this dictionary to help him become a well-rounded Dragneter. The secret is all in the sound of the words and your facial expression. For practice, dip your face in paste (flour and water will do) and stand in front of a mirror while you utter the Dragnet words in perfect monotone.

Students—get to work.

AID—Accident Investigation Division.

APB—All Points Bulletin.

BIA—Bureau of Internal Affairs.

Big Time—Has served time in any state pen.

Booster—Shoplifter.

Bunco—A crime where money or other valuables are taken from victim under misrepresentation.

Caper—A crime.

Carry Away—Carry safe away before working on it.

Code 3—Emergency call using siren and red light.

Dip—Pickpocket.

DR Number—Division record number.

FBI Kickback—In all arrests, fingerprints are sent to Washington where they're checked to see if they are on record from some other state. Information is then sent back.

Fish—New man in prison.

Grifter—Con man.

Hang-on Citation—Parking citation issued without signature of driver.

Heavy Squad—Robbery Squad.

Heel and Toe Job—Hitting a cash register.

High Power Tank—Where prisoners under heavy bond are kept.

I Sheet—Identification sheet which gives suspect's physical description.

ID Card—Identification of police officers.

Jail Prowler—Officer who makes jail rounds checking.

KMA 367—Radio identification.

Make—Identification of suspect or car.

Muscle Happy—Guy who belongs to the gym team in prison.

MWA—Male, White, American.

Oddity File—Special file maintained of physical oddities.

Package—Criminal record.

Paper Hanger—Check forger.

P&F Ward—Police and Fire Ward.

Punch Job—Punch dial out of safe.

R and I—Record and identification.

Rip Job—Rip safe or peel.

SD—Scientific investigation.

Small Fry Pushers—Narcotic peddlers.

Soup Job—Use nitroglycerine on safe.

Statts Office—Statisticians' office compiles crime reports on solved and unsolved crimes.

Steer—Steer victim to confidence man.

Vag Charge—Vagrancy.

To Qualify—Police officers must qualify in shooting each month.

F car—Felony car.

K car—Night detective car.

T car—Traffic car.

R car—Radio car.

TT—Teletype.

WIC—Welfare & Institution Code.

32 S&W—32-caliber Smith and Wesson revolver.

211—Robbery—penal code section 211.

311—Lewd conduct.

390—Drunk.

390 W—Drunk woman.

415—Disturbing the Peace.

459—Burglary

484—Theft.

484 PS—Purse Theft.

510 (also called mama sheet)—Authorization form filled in by investigating officers.

4172 LAMC—A drunk.

July 3, 1953

ADDITIONAL POLICE CODES
AND SIGNALS
(AS HEARD ON *ADAM-12*)

Code 2—Urgent. No red light or siren.

Code 4—No further assistance needed.

Code 5—Stake out. Other cars avoid.

187—Homicide.

237—Narcotics.

261—Rape.

417G—Suspect with a pistol.

417K—Suspect with a knife.

502—Drunk driving.

927—Investigate, unknown trouble.

10-4—OK.

10-22—Take no further action.

10-23—Stand by.

10-28—Check full registration.

10-97—Arrived at scene of crime.

10-98—Finished with last assignment.

February 5, 1972

CENSORS AND SPONSORS

"Let us assume (as seems likely) that the reformers will eventually win their crusade against jiggly sex on TV. What then will the programmers have left to keep the populace in thrall . . .? Take away violence, take away sex, and you have taken away the two main motivating impulses of the long history of human drama. Granted *Charlie's Angels* comes a lot closer to King Leer than King Lear. Still, they were holding our attention in a manner that video-taped highlights of the summer macramé class at Apple Farm, say, would not.**"**

—*Ron Powers, August 5, 1978*

A visitor from Mars, looking at our television, would have to come to the conclusion that in America, violence is good. Sex is bad.

He would see that the human body must be a shameful thing and cannot be shown on television. It's perfectly all right, though, to bruise, cut, maim or even destroy the human body on a television show.

It's permissible for a man to stab or shoot a woman—but he must be very careful about caressing her.

Gangsters in a crime drama may plan felonies, and no one minds. But let a man and a woman discuss abortion pro and con and the roar of disapproval from special groups forces many stations to drop the program.

Our Martian would find that it's allowable to leer at a shapely woman on the air, it's acceptable to tell mildly dirty jokes, but

when a program deals with a serious though nonexplicit dramatic situation that concerns sex, the American audience is shocked. Or at least the habitual letter-writers are.

And, of course, nothing scares easier than a television advertiser. If a few viewers write him that his 30-second spot announcement is going to appear in a program that might conceivably offend some left-handed boilermaker in Plymouth, Wis., he'll cancel the ad. You can't blame him—he's not spending his ad money to offend people. But you'd think more advertisers would realize that a few screams don't necessarily reflect public opinion.

Each of us certainly has a right to his or her personal opinion, his or her personal standards. Do we have the right, though, to decide what our neighbor may see on the air? If there's something we don't like on our screen we can switch it off. What might baffle the Martian is why more of us don't control our own screen and let our neighbor worry about his.

October 6, 1973

Without going into the pros and cons of rock 'n' roll music, which still has some hold in teen-age circles, we'd like to mutter a word or two about one of its by-products, Elvis Presley.

Presley, for those over 18 who may not have been subjected to his whine 'n' writhe interpretations of the music, is a skinny young man in a fancy jacket, tight pants, blue suede shoes, a haircut not quite as attractive as the going-away portion of a duck, and sideburns that extend below his ears. He first was introduced to national TV audiences on CBS's *Stage Show* late last January.

The teen-agers, bless their hearts, face a great number of problems these days; and, for some reason, the problems have brought them an overwhelming urge to be part of the crowd. It is the crowd that desires recognition, not the individual.

So the crowd goes for rock 'n' roll, and Elvis Presley. Fine. So long as no one is harmed, the youngsters can have fun listening to records, dancing, clapping hands and making noise. But what of Presley and his ilk on TV?

What the continuity acceptance departments of the networks must consider, we believe, is whether Presley-type singing and contortions are in keeping with the general standards of the medium. Is the fact that he is popular with an important age group enough to justify exhibiting him to the general public? Are we to accept as television entertainment anything at all that is popular? Should we deny teen-agers their favorite because it might offend some older viewers?

Judging the matter is not easy, and we're glad it's not our job to do it. If the decision is to let Presley continue appearing, however, let the grownups be given fair warning.

July 7, 1956

A Few Words from Our Sponsor

In the early days of commercial TV, the advertiser was king (today it's more like the royal consort). Advertisers wielded far greater power then than they do now. Essentially, the networks were little more than technology-filled outlets dealing in the renting out of time—they had the cameras, the control panels, the technicians, and the airwaves—and they sold large chunks of that time to advertisers or advertising agencies. The advertisers controlled that time—be it a half-hour, hour, 90 minutes, or longer—and then could, for all intents and purposes, put whatever show they wanted in that time slot. Advertisers determined program content, made creative decisions, ordered script changes, could hire and fire, and pretty much ran the show.

But this sort of absolute power tends to corrupt, and often, in the name of protecting the product against the insidious inroads of its competition, the advertiser, or executives at the ad agency, would push through changes in the shows to make the programs conform to what was considered the best interests of the company. Often they were innocuous. Sometimes they were ludicrous. Occasionally they were flat-out censorship.

TV Guide loved to bring to light bizarre, humorous, or bothersome advertiser heavyhandedness that threatened to have a chilling effect on the nascent art form of the exciting new television medium.

Some of the better examples:

While filming an episode of *Make Room for Daddy,* Danny Thomas had to refer to Sir Winston Churchill as a member of the British House of Commons, instead of the usual "member of Parliament." One of his sponsors was a cigarette company that didn't want to mention, even almost subliminally, a competing brand on the program.

Tad Mosel, who wrote a TV-play called "The Haven" for *TV Playhouse* in 1953, was worried that its theme of marital infidelity might not be cleared by NBC.

Garry Moore brought his sponsor's famous slogan to life on I've Got a Secret by presenting persons whose names combined to form "Winston Tastes Good Like a Cigarette Should"—or almost did.

In one of TV's most famous commercial images, this man floated downward as Hertz put him in the driver's seat. Actually, this 1963 commercial was made by putting him in the car and pulling him out diagonally using wires attached to a crane. Then the film was run backward.

But there was only one objection— where a character in the play referred to "an old Chevy," he was asked to change it to read "an old car."

On *Kraft Television Theater,* a character's name was changed at the last minute because it had been Borden.

A variety show was forced by its sponsor, Studebaker, to fire its band singer, Joey Nash, because he had the last name of a competing car company.

Studio One, sponsored by Westinghouse, had to change the name of Rudyard Kipling's *The Light That Failed* to "The Gathering Night." Another *Studio One* script was turned down when an adman found that the plot revolved around a leaky refrigerator.

The announcer for the General Motors–sponsored college football telecasts found himself in a dilemma when the quarterback of the Pittsburgh team was named Henry Ford.

Ronson, the cigarette-lighter sponsor,

In this memorable ad, when the guy gives the young woman the old line about having run out of gas, she goes out and checks the oil filter, which was the sponsoring product.

was reported to have written all the matches out of a *Playhouse 90* script and put cigarette lighters in.

Frank Sinatra changed the name of his Kent Productions to Hobart Productions. Reason: his TV sponsor was Chesterfield.

A telegrapher in the background of a *Casey Jones* episode kept pounding out

The way Maxwell House offered a "cup and a half of flavor" was to superimpose two coffee cups: one was a bottomless cup, and coffee was poured into it; the other was a cup through which a glass cylinder filled with coffee was pushed up. Together, they gave the desired effect.

the same message over and over in Morse code: "Buy the sponsor's product."

Merv Griffin, early in his TV career, was hired as a featured vocalist on Kate Smith's show. Unfortunately for him, the show was sponsored by Esquire Shoe Polish—Griffin was the name of a competing brand. He was let go.

The *Hallmark Hall of Fame* was doing a production of George Bernard Shaw's *Man and Superman*. At one point in the play there is a terrific tirade against mothers, describing them as dreadful

Early studies showed that viewers liked and remembered animated commercials, and soon they were all over the TV schedule, like these two popular ads promoting the spicy nature of one product and bee's wax in another.

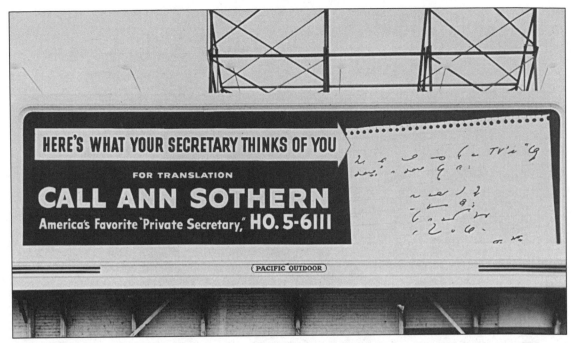

This billboard at Hollywood and Vine, in Gregg shorthand, reads: "If you are anything like my boss on TV's Private Secretary, *your secretary probably thinks: You are smart and efficient/In so many ways;/But you sometimes forget/The value of praise. Ann Sothern."*

harpies who sell their daughters in marriage to the highest bidders. A man from the advertising agency insisted the speech had to be taken out. He argued that Mother's Day was a very important holiday in the greeting-card business, and the show would antagonize every mom in America. Luckily, the company overrode the adman's objections and the speech stayed in.

Woody Woodpecker cartoons, set to be shown on ABC in the late afternoon in 1957, ran into advertiser-caused censorship problems. The ad people deleted 25 sequences from the 52 cartoons showing in rotation on the show. The sequences included tipsy horses, tobacco-spitting grasshoppers, and neurotic birds. Even though the cartoons had passed the motion-picture industry's Breen and Johnston offices, had received the Purity Seal, and had been shown all over the world without a critical comment, the advertisers felt the cartoons were not beneficial for their products.

What TV Won't Let You See

In Crime Shows: Criminals and crime presented in a sympathetic light. Law enforcement not being upheld; criminals going unpunished. Detailed descriptions that could lead to imitation of lawbreaking, gambling, narcotics usage and murder.

In Variety Shows: Off-color comedy, whether contained in gags, songs, expressions or gestures. Overly nude costumes, disrobing scenes, sexy dancing or glorified drunkenness. Even pre-broadcast studio shows ("warm-ups") must be kept clean.

In Dramatic Shows: Marriage and family life being presented in a disrespectful manner, offensively or suggestively. Derogatory situations concerning any race, religion, profession, industry or physical affliction.

In Children's Shows: Anything detracting from a youngster's respect for adult authority, good behavior and clean living. Incidentally, networks insist that juvenile material be cleared anywhere from 13 days (NBC) to six weeks (ABC) ahead.

In Movies on TV: Suggestive costuming, risqué themes and certain social problems—even though they may have gotten by Hollywood's own tough Production Code. Many old movies and musical short subjects were made in pre-censorship days.

In Commercials: Advertising for fortune tellers, hard liquor, firearms, intimate personal products, medical men. DuMont, by the way, won't accept brassiere ads that use live models. Other networks will, if they're in good taste.

One network editor sums it up with: "We won't let you see anything on TV you wouldn't want your mother to."

August 11, 1951

The Federal Trade Commission, oozing righteous indignation, has ruled that advertisers may not use camera tricks or gimmicks in television commercials to exaggerate what a product is, looks like or can do.

It was sandpaper that went against the FTC's grain. The commercial in question allowed as how Palmolive shaving cream was so potent it could be used to shave sandpaper—and sure enough, there was a shot of a piece of sandpaper being shaved.

Most of us thought the idea of shaving sandpaper was a fairly logical way of leading up to the fact that the shaving cream would do wonders for men with sandpaper beards. To the FTC, apparently, this might deceive the millions of Americans who are known to buy shaving cream for the sole purpose of shaving sandpaper.

It was learned that—brace yourself—shaving cream does NOT work for sandpaper shaving! FTC technicians tried and tried, but Palmolive didn't do the job. For beards, yes. For sandpaper, no. Furthermore, it was learned that in making the commercials, real sandpaper wasn't used—it was Plexiglas covered with sand.

Result: the ruling against camera tricks. A ruling, incidentally, which was needed, but which perhaps is too broad because it could lead to some very dull commercials if it were taken too literally. After all, who'd want a cigarette that doesn't dance or pop out of a pack by itself or come with a beautiful blonde to blow smoke in your face?

January 27, 1962

NAMING
NAMES

The original TV name-namer: Richard Carlson as FBI counterspy Herbert Philbrick, in a den of conspiring Commies in I Led Three Lives.

The Name's Familiar, But I Can't Place the Face

Even before Rod Serling, there was something very *Twilight Zone*–ish about TV. It was not uncommon for shows to sign off the air on one day, or week or season, and then, the next regularly scheduled time that show came on, to have one of the characters on it being played by a different person. Same name, different face. And we were supposed to accept it, and go on as if this new person were the old person, as if nothing had happened and such changes occurred in life all the time.

The thing is, we *did* accept it, and still do, especially the wholesale resurfacing of soap-opera roles. If such a thing were ever to happen in real life—if, say, you woke up one morning to find that your spouse, your parents, and your best friend were now being played by totally different people claiming to be the ones you knew as the real McCoys—you'd be running down the road like Kevin McCarthy in *Invasion of the Body Snatchers,* looking for pods and afraid to go to sleep.

But TV has that power to comfort us and make everything all right and believable—and believed.

Here are some examples of our willingness to suspend our disbelief, prime-time style.

● Herb Ellis was hired in the fall of 1952 to play the role of Officer Frank Smith opposite Jack Webb's Joe Friday on *Dragnet*. Soon after, Ben Alexander replaced him in the role, and stayed for the remainder of the show's original run.

● When Dorothy Malone left *Peyton Place* because of illness during the 1965 season, Lola Albright stepped in and played the same role, Constance Mackenzie, for shows aired between December 9, 1965, and January 10, 1966, until Malone returned.

● Donna Reed took over for Barbara Bel Geddes as Miss Ellie on *Dallas* during the 1984–85 season. Next season, Bel Geddes decided to come back, and Reed was unceremoniously dumped.

● When Philip Loeb was blacklisted for left-leaning affiliations, near-look-alike Harold Stone stepped into the role of Jake without explanation on *The Goldbergs*. Stone was later replaced by Robert H. Harris.

● Larry Keating replaced Fred Clark as Harry Morton in *The Burns and Allen Show.* Clark himself replaced John Brown, who had stepped in for Hal March in 1951.

● Mary K. Wells, Julie Stevens, Jane Nigh, Beverly Tyler, and Trudy Wroe all played Lorelie Kilbourne in the six-year run of *Big Town*.

● Minerva (*Tugboat Annie*) Urecal replaced Hope Emerson as *Peter Gunn*'s "Mother."

● *Petticoat Junction* had perhaps the most same-name, different-face turnovers of any nighttime series. Sharon Tate was first announced in the role of daughter Billie Jo Bradley; but by airtime, that role was played by Jeannine Riley. In 1965, Billie Jo was played by Gunilla Hutton, and the next year by Meredith MacRae. In the meantime, the original Bobbie Jo (Pat Woodell) left in 1965, to be replaced by Lori Saunders. Fortunately, Betty Jo—Linda Kaye—stayed the same throughout; maybe it had something to do with the fact that Linda Kaye was actually Linda Kay Henning, daughter of the show's producer.

● After Roger Carmel and the producers of *The Mothers-in-Law* couldn't come to terms on a new contract, Carmel was replaced with Richard Deacon in the same role, Roger Buell, husband of Kaye Ballard in the series.

● After playing the part of Lionel on *All in the Family* and *The Jeffersons,* Mike Evans left the latter early on in its run. He was replaced as Lionel by Damon Evans.

● After three episodes, Meg Foster, playing the role originated in the 1981 pilot TV-movie by Loretta Swit, was replaced by Sharon Gless in *Cagney & Lacey.* Gless had also just finished doing *House Calls,* having replaced Lynn Redgrave in that.

● When Al Corley, who played Steven Carrington on *Dynasty,* left the show, Carrington suddenly had a new face—Jack Coleman's. Al Corley then returned to the role in *Dynasty: The Reunion.*

● Right after J.R. was shot on the classic *Dallas* cliffhanger, Larry Hagman decided to renegotiate his contract. When the filming for the next season's shows were to begin, he and the producers hadn't come to terms. In case Hagman didn't re-sign, the producers had a plan; according to producer Philip Capice: "J.R.'s ambulance, traveling at breakneck speed, would have been hit by another vehicle en route to the hospital. As a result of the accident, J.R. would have needed plastic surgery. We could have kept his face in bandages for several more shows, then unveiled a new actor in the role when the time was right. Would it have worked? Fortunately, we never had to find out."

● When *Diff'rent Strokes* moved from NBC to ABC in 1985, Mary Ann Mobley replaced Dixie Carter as Conrad Bain's wife.

● When Pamela Sue Martin left the cast of *Dynasty,* her character, Fallon Carrington Colby, was disposed of in a plane crash. However, when *Dynasty II: The Colbys* became a spin-off series, Fallon was resurrected, in the person of Emma Samms. Since the two *Dynasty* shows were related, they changed the portrait of Fallon seen in *Dynasty* from Martin to Samms, and totally refilmed certain old scenes from when Martin was on the show, now using Samms in her place—exactly duplicating the shots to use for flashback sequences.

● Nearly six years passed between ABC's multipart miniseries *The Winds of War* and its equally massive follow-up, *War and Remembrance.* The sequel picked up the story at about the time the original ended, but some of the actors who played in the original were unavailable or had grown too old to fit their parts. Jane Seymour replaced Ali MacGraw as Natalie; Hart Bochner substituted for Jan-Michael Vincent as Natalie's husband, Byron; and Sir John Gielgud replaced John Houseman as Aaron Jastrow.

P.S. In a switch—same face, different name—Ray Milland was Professor Ray McNutley in *Meet Mr. McNutley* in 1953. Next season, when the show's name was changed to *The Ray Milland Show*, he was Professor Ray McNulty.

"Didn't You Used to Be...?"

Actors and celebrities change their names for a lot of reasons—most of them good. Here's a list of some of our most popular TV personalities, and the names they left behind.

Don Adams — *Donald James Yarmy*

Edie Adams — *Edith Elizabeth Enke*

Nick Adams — *Nicholas Aloysius Adamshock*

Eddie Albert — *Edward Albert Heimberger*

Alan Alda — *Alphonso D'Abruzzo*

Fred Allen — *John Sullivan*

Mel Allen — *Melvin Israel*

Ed Ames — *Edmund Urick*

Eve Arden — *Eunice Quedens* (she got "Eve" from "a book I don't remember" and "Arden" from a jar of cosmetics)

Beatrice Arthur — *Bernice Frankel*

Kaye Ballard — *Gloria Katherine Balotta*

Anne Bancroft — *Anna Maria Italiano*

Sandy Baron — *Sanford Beresofky*

Gene Barry — *Eugene Klass* ("Barry" came from "Barrymore")

Jack Benny — *Benjamin Kubelsky*

Milton Berle — *Milton Berlinger*

Joey Bishop — *Joseph Gottlieb*

Taurean Blacque — *Herbert Middleton, Jr.*

Janet Blair — *Martha Janet Lafferty*

Amanda Blake — *Beverly Louise Neill*

Robert Blake — *Michael James Vijencio Gubitosi*

Whitney Blake — *Nancy Whitney*

Pat Boone — *Charles Eugene Boone*

Sullivan and Kubelsky

Morgan Brittany — *Suzanne Cupito* ("Morgan Brittany" came from the name of a character in a romance novel, *Floodtide*)

James Brolin — *James Brunderlin*

Mel Brooks — *Melvin Kaminsky*

George Burns — *Nathan Birnbaum*

Red Buttons — *Aaron Chwatt*

Edd Byrnes — *Edward Breitenberger*

Rory Calhoun — *Francis Timothy Durgin*

Dyan Cannon — *Camille Diane Friesen*

Judy Carne — *Joyce Botterill*

Vikki Carr — *Florencia Bisenta de Casillas Martinez Cardona*

Diahann Carroll — *Carol Diahann Johnson*

Richard Chamberlain — *George Chamberlain*

Charo — *Maria Rosario Pilar Martinez*

Cher — *Cherilyn LaPiere Sarkisian*

Robert Clary — *Robert Max Widerman*

Lee J. Cobb — *Leo Jacob*

Dorothy Collins — *Marjorie Chandler*

Mike Connors — *Krekor Ohanian*

Ben Casey's *Vincento Eduardo Zoino* and Hawaii Five-O's *John Joseph Ryan*.

Robert Conrad — *Conrad Robert Falk*

Michael Constantine — *Constantine Joanides*

Tim Conway — *Tom Conway*

Alistair Cooke — *Alfred Alistair*

Glenn Corbett — *Glenn Rothenburg*

Howard Cosell — *Howard Cohen*

Linda Cristal — *Marta Victoria Moya Peggo Bouges*

Ken Curtis — *Curtis Gates* (changed by Tommy Dorsey, whose orchestra he sang with)

Dagmar — *Virginia Ruth Egnor* (previous stage name: Jennie Lewis)

Vic Damone — *Vito Farinola*

Bill Dana — *William Szathmary* ("Dana" came from a reworking of his mother's first name, "Dena")

James Darren — *James Ercolani*

Dennis Day — *Owen Patrick Eugene Dennis McNulty*

Doris Day — *Doris von Kappelhoff*

Yvonne De Carlo — *Peggy Middleton* ("De Carlo" was her mother's maiden name)

Angie Dickinson — *Angeline Brown*

Troy Donahue — *Merle Johnson, Jr.*

Donna Douglas — *Doris Smith Bourgeois*

Mike Douglas — *Michael Delany Dowd*

Michael Dunn — *Gary Neil Michael Joseph Alvious A'Dunn Miller*

Barbara Eden — *Barbara Huffman*

Vince Edwards — *Vincento Eduardo Zoino*

Dale Evans — *Frances Butts*

Linda Evans — *Linda Evanstad*

Chad Everett — *Raymond Cranton*

Tom Ewell — *Yewell Tompkins*

Jamie Farr — Jameel Joseph Farah

Totie Fields — *Sophie Feldman*

June Foray — *June Forer*

Demi James Sposa (left), with Paul Winchell, Jerry Mahoney and wrestler.

Redd Foxx — *John Elroy Sanford*

Anthony Franciosa — *Anthony Papaleo*

Arlene Francis — *Arlene Kazanjian*

James Garner — *James Scott Bumgarner*

Ben Gazzara — *Biagio Anthony Gazzara*

Gentle Ben — *Bruno*

Gale Gordon — *Charles T. Aldrich*

Lee Grant — *Lyova Haskell Rosenthal*

Robert Guillaume — *Robert Williams* ("Guillaume" is the French form of "William")

Buddy Hackett — *Leonard Hacker*

Ty Hardin — *Orison Whipple Hungerford, Jr.* ("Ty" is short for "Typhoon," a childhood nickname)

Mary Hart — *Mary Johanna Harum*

Helen Hayes — *Helen Brown*

Peter Lind Hayes — *Joseph Conrad Lind*

Joey Heatherton — *Davenie Johanna Heatherton*

David Hedison — *Ara Heditsian*

Skitch Henderson — *Lyle Russell Cedric Henderson*

Pee-wee Herman — *Paul Reubens*

Barbara Hershey — *Barbara Herzstein*

Robert Horton — *Meade Howard Horton*

John Houseman — *Jacques Haussmann*

Susan Howard — *Jeri Lynn Mooney*

Rock Hudson — *Roy Scherer, Jr.* (later took "Roy Fitzgerald" as his legal name)

Jeffrey Hunter — *Henry H. McKinnies, Jr.*

Tab Hunter — *Arthur Kelm* (although later his divorced mother reassumed her

maiden name, Gelien, and so did he)

Will Hutchins — *Marshall Lowell Hutchason*

Dennis James — *Demi James Sposa*

John James — *John James Anderson*

David Janssen — *David Meyer*

Spike Jones — *Lindley Armstrong Jones*

Tom Jones — *Thomas Jones Woodward*

Alan King — *Irwin Alan Kniberg* (his first stage name was "Earl Knight")

Zalman King — *Zalman King Lefkowitz*

Ted Knight — *Tadewurz Wladyzui Konopka*

Cheryl Ladd — *Cheryl Jean Stoppelmoor* (she also used the stage name "Cherie Moore")

Michael Landon — *Eugene Maurice Orowitz*

Robert Lansing — *Robert Howell Brown, Jr.* ("Lansing" came from the Michigan city)

Piper Laurie — *Rosetta Jacobs*

Steve Lawrence — *Sidney Leibowitz*

Pinky Lee — *Pincus Leff*

Sheldon Leonard — *Sheldon Leonard Bershad*

Jerry Lewis — *Joseph Levitch*

Gary Lockwood — *Gary John Yurosek*

Liberace — *Wladziu Valentino Liberace*

Hal Linden — *Harold Lipshitz* (changed his name after seeing "Linden"—a New Jersey town—on a gas-storage tank)

Person to Person *with Wladziu Valentino Liberace.*

Denise Lor — *Denise Jeanne Marie Briault*

Jack Lord — *John Joseph Ryan*

Tina Louise — *Tina Blacker*

Joan Lunden — *Joan Blunden*

Ted Mack — *William Edward Maguinness*

Guy Madison — *Robert Moseley*

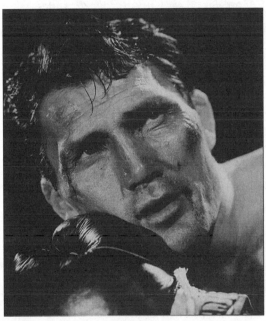

Walter Palanuik in Requiem for a Heavyweight.

Karl Malden — *Malden Sekulovich*

Dean Martin — *Dino Crocetti*

Ross Martin — *Martin Rosenblatt*

Walter Matthau — *Walter Matuschanskayasky*

Jim McKay — *James Kenneth McManus*

Donna Mills — *Donna Miller*

Eli Mintz — *Edward Satz*

Mr. T — *Lawrence Tureaud*

Cameron Mitchell — *Cameron Mitzell*

Garry Moore — *Thomas Garrison Morfit*

Rita Moreno — *Rosita Dolores Alverio*

Harry Morgan — *Harry Bratsburg*

Greg Morris — *Gregory Allan Williams*

Morris the Cat — *Lucky*

Ken Murray — *Kenneth Abner Doncourt*

Edward R. Murrow — *Egbert Roscoe Murrow*

Harriet Nelson — *Peggy Lou Snyder*

Bob Newhart — *George Newhart*

Julie Newmar — *Julie Newmeyer*

Kathleen Nolan — *Joycelyn Joan Schrum*

Hugh O'Brian — *Hugh Krampke*

Ryan O'Neal — *Patrick Ryan O'Neal*

Charles Osgood — *Charles Osgood Wood III*

Gary Owens — *Gary Altman*

Jack Palance — *Walter Palanuik*

Betsy Palmer — *Patricia Betsy Hrunek*

Bert Parks — *Bert Jacobson*

Minnie Pearl — *Sarah Ophelia Cannon*

Stefanie Powers — *Stefania Zofja Federkievicz*

Dirk and Dack Rambo — *Orman and Norman Rambo*

Tony Randall — *Leonard Rosenberg*

Martha Raye — *Margaret Theresa Yvonne Reed*

Donna Reed — *Donna Mullenger*

Robert Reed — *John Rietz*

Roy Rogers — *Leonard Slye*

Susan Saint James — *Susan Miller*

Soupy Sales — *Milton Hines*

Emma Samms — *Emma Samuelson*

John Saxon — *Carmine Orrico*

Connie Sellecca — *Concetta Sellecchia*

Jane Seymour — *Joyce Penelope Wilhelmina Frankenberg*

Martin Sheen — *Ramon Estevez* (named after Bishop Sheen)

Dinah Shore — *Fannie Rose Shore*

Phil Silvers — *Philip Silversmith*

Suzanne Somers — *Suzanne Mahoney*

Jack Soo — *Carl Suzuki*

Ann Sothern — *Harriette Lake*

David Soul — *David Solberg*

Barbara Stanwyck — *Ruby Stevens*

Jean Stapleton — *Jeanne Murray*

Connie Stevens — *Concetta Ann Ingolia*

Ray Stevens — *Ray Ragsdale*

Gale Storm — *Josephine Owaisca Cottle*

Robert Taylor — *Spangler Arlington Brugh*

Lauren Tewes — *Cindy Tewes*

Danny Thomas — *Muzyad Yakhoob*

Vera Vague — *Barbara Jo Allen*

Vivian Vance — *Vivian Roberta Jones*

Clint Walker — *Norman Walker*

Nancy Walker — *Anna Myrtle Swoyer*

Burt Ward — *Bert John Gervis, Jr.*

Jack Warden — *Jack Warden Lebzelter*

Tuesday Weld — *Susan Ker Weld*

Jack Weston — *Jack Weinstein*

Andy Williams — *Howard Andrew Williams*

Cara Williams — *Bernice Kamiat*

Guy Williams — *Armando Catalano*

Jane Wyman — *Sarah Jane Fulks*

Ed Wynn — *Isaiah Edwin Leopold*

Gig Young — *Byron Barr*

The Name of the Game

Obviously, people are paid to write TV scripts. But, for some reason, there seems to be an entire cadre of fiddlers, fussers, fumblers, and fixers who make the big bucks by changing shows' titles—over and over, back and forth, looking for that magical combination of consonants and vowels (and maybe numerology—who knows?) that will ensure a hit. They appear to spend more time repairing titles than they do repairing the shows. And they go about it with the utter seriousness of people who don't want to be reminded that they are doing something silly.

What follows is a partial list of title-fiddling over the years. Some make sense; with the others, you wonder why they bothered.

● *You're the Top* was the first but never-used name for Ed Sullivan's *The Toast of the Town.*

● The first title for *The Flintstones* was *The Flagstones.*

● The 1964 show *Kentucky Jones* with Dennis Weaver was originally entitled *Kentucky's Kid,* and designed to star Jack Carson.

● The original name for the *Today* show was to be *The Rise and Shine Revue.*

● CBS's *Morning Show* in 1954 had a pre-airing title of *Eye-Opener.*

● The Mickey Mouse Club serial, "Spin and Marty," was originally called "Marty Markham."

● NBC's 1957 dramatic series replacing *Noah's Ark* went through three nerve-racking titles. Originally called *Impact,* it was changed to *Crisis.* Then to *Panic!*

● NBC's John Payne series, first titled *The Six Shooter* and then *Restless Gun,* was changed to *The Westerner*—then back to *Restless Gun.*

● *Wally and the Beaver* was the original title of *Leave It to Beaver.*

● *Gunn For Hire* was the original title for *Peter Gunn.*

● A show called *Sunset 77* was announced for the fall of 1958 by ABC. It of course became *77 Sunset Strip.*

● *Diamond Head* became *Hawaiian Eye.*

● The first title for *Make Room for Daddy* was *The Children's Hour.*

● *McHale's Navy* was first called *McHale's Men.*

● The first name for *Petticoat Junction* was *Ozark Widow.* Then followed *Dern Tootin'* and *Whistle Stop.*

● For the 1963–64 season, ABC bought a

series called *Please Stand By.* This was changed to *Beyond Control,* and, finally, to *The Outer Limits.*

● *Mr. Solo* and just plain *Solo* were the first stabs at a name for *The Man from U.N.C.L.E.*

● The first title for what eventually became *I Spy* was, of all things, *Danny Doyle.*

● *The Wild West* gained another *Wild* between pilot and series.

● *Lost in Space* was first known as *Space Family Robinson.*

● *Green Acres* was first called *Country Cousins* then *The Eddie Albert Show.*

● *It Takes a Thief* started out life as *Once a Crook.*

● *What's My Line?* was sold to CBS under the title *Occupation Unknown.*

● *Julia,* which starred Diahann Carroll, was first called *Mama's Man.*

● The pilot for what was to become *The Brady Bunch* was called *The Brady Brood.*

● *Nanny and the Professor* first was called *Nanny Will Do.*

● *Family Business* was retitled *The Partridge Family.*

● *All in the Family* was originally titled *Those Were the Days* (the British show it was based on was called *Till Death Do Us Part*).

● *The Waltons,* which was adapted from the special *The Homecoming: A Christmas Story,* was originally to be called *Spencer's Mountain,* which is the name of the Henry Fonda–starring movie the characters were first shown in.

● Originally, the CBS series was to be called *The Chimp and I.* But human star Ted Bessell's agent advised Paramount that his client wasn't about to take second billing to an ape. The project became *Me and the Chimp.*

● *Cyborg* was the first name for *The Six Million Dollar Man.*

● Before settling on the name *Monty Python's Flying Circus,* the comedy group toyed with giving their show one of the following names: *Owl Stretching Time, Toad Elevating Moment, Sex and Violence, A Horse, a Spoon and a Basin, Unlike a Bloody Stumbling Boot,* and *Gwen Dibley's Flying Circus.*

● *Charlie's Angels* was originally known as *The Alley Cats.*

● *Diff'rent Strokes* was first called *45 Minutes From Harlem.*

● *Dynasty*'s first title was *Oil.*

● *Here's Boomer* was originally called *Here's Johnny* (the dog's name was really Johnny) but it was too close to the Carson signature introduction. The name "Boomer" was invented.

● The original title for *Happy Days* in the pilot was *New Family in Town.*

● *Simon & Simon* was originally called *Pirate's Key.*

NUMBERS

There are seven basic scheduling rules that the television brass tried to—but couldn't always—observe in setting their schedules.

1. In any given time period the success of a show will depend solely on its competition. In other words, you can have a hit at 8 P.M. Wednesday simply because your show is the best among three bad shows. So don't waste your best show if you don't need to.

2. More than three-fourths of the new programming will fail. So don't cancel an old show unless you must.

3. Never reschedule a whole night.

4. Never schedule one comedy by itself. Have a minimum of two—and, if possible, three or four—in a row.

5. Never start feature movies at the beginning of the evening, because so many of them do not appeal to the younger people.

6. Try to protect a new program by scheduling it between established shows.

7. Remember, the position a program is assigned is far more important than the content of the program itself.

Michael Dann, former head
of programming at CBS, September 17, 1977

"Suppose you could continue to have only one of the following—radio, television, newspapers, or magazines—which one of the four would you most want to keep?"

That was one of a series of questions asked by Elmo Roper and Associates of 2000 adults, a group the research firm selected carefully to be a statistically accurate cross section of our population.

The answers: 42 percent would keep television, 28 percent newspapers, 22 percent radio, 4 percent magazines and 4 percent didn't know.

Another question had to do with news. "If you got conflicting reports of the same news story from radio, television, the magazines, and the newspapers, which of the four versions would you be most inclined to believe—the one on radio or television or magazines or newspapers?"

The answers: 39 percent would believe

television, 24 percent newspapers, 12 percent radio, 10 percent magazines and 17 percent didn't know.

A related question was, "Which of the four would you be *least* inclined to believe—the one on radio, television, magazines or newspapers?"

The answers: 28 percent would be least inclined to believe the newspapers, 25 percent the magazines, 9 percent radio, 7 percent television and 32 percent didn't know.

We report the survey results to you because we believe they indicate that television is accepted by the American public as more than an entertainment medium. It is accepted as our most reliable and fastest source of news.

Another reason we're reporting on the survey is that you may have missed reading about it in the newspapers or in other magazines.

March 17, 1962

Let's consider a study, one that somehow has escaped public attention. It wasn't a very formal study—just an angry Chicago advertising man busy with his television and a week of newspapers in the fall of 1961.

The ad man, Dr. Jaye S. Niefeld, read this quote from FCC chairman Minow: "They [the TV broadcasters] want to be treated like journalists . . .

They ought to act like journalists . . . I've been told that if you survey the *Chicago Sun-Times* to see what's the most popular feature in it, it's the comics, followed by advice to the lovelorn. That doesn't mean the *Sun-Times* turns the whole paper over to 'em. But television does."

Niefeld didn't study the *Sun-Times*. He studied the *Chicago Tribune* for a week. Then he studied the CBS station in Chicago, WBBM-TV. All in all he surveyed 100,000 column inches of newspaper space and 500,000 seconds of television time.

The *Tribune* devoted 6 percent of its total weekly space to general news of international, national and local events— that's just straight news, not financial or sports. The television station devoted 9 percent of its time to the same subject. The *Trib* devoted 72 percent of its space to advertising. The station devoted 14 percent of its time to commercials. The station spent 2 percent of its total time on programs depicting crime and violence. More than 1 percent of the newspaper's space went to stories of thefts, murders, muggings, etc.

All this was not to criticize the *Chicago Tribune,* one of our great newspapers, but to indicate that broadcasters *should* be treated as journalists.

July 21, 1962

The High and the Mite-y

Everyone on television looks to be somewhere between three and six inches tall—maybe a foot, foot and a half if you have one of those large-screen or projection TVs. Of course, no one on TV is shown actual size, except for certain puppets and cartoon characters, perhaps, and, probably, Dr. Ruth.

It's difficult to tell who's tall, who's small on the home screen, and that's probably why *TV Guide* over the years has been scrupulous about including stars' heights in interviews and profile stories. Stars' weights were often mentioned, too, although over time those might fluctuate—as in the case of Jackie Gleason, or Andy Devine, who topped the scale at 330 pounds—by 100 pounds or more. And, in the early years, female performers' measurements were prominently displayed (Dagmar's 42-inch bust and 23-inch waist made it into print innumerable times) but vanished from *TV Guide*'s pages in the 1970s, when such things (though still of interest among certain circles) became politically incorrect.

It's a tall man's business, that's for sure. Heights above six feet are practically the norm, with six feet four inches seemingly not out of the ordinary.

As a readers' service, we've pulled together the reported heights of many of the stars spotlighted in *TV Guide* in its 40 years and display them here, (a) to get a little perspective on comparative heights, and (b) so you'll know, when you see the reruns, who were as they appeared to be, who benefited from judicious editing and flattering camera angles, and who had to stand on a stepstool or knee-deep in a ditch to make eye contact with costars.

- Emmanuel Lewis—3'4" (during his *Webster* years)
- Michael Dunn—3'10", 78 lbs.
- Herve Villechaize—3'11"
- Gary Coleman—4'8"
- Nancy Walker—4'11"
- Danny DeVito—5'
- Estelle Getty—5'
- Shari Lewis—5'

- Sally Struthers—5'1 1/2"
- Dorothy Collins—5'2"
- Carol Kane—5'2"
- Dudley Moore—5'2"
- Connie Stevens—5'2"
- Michael J. Fox—5'4"
- Arte Johnson—5'4"
- Cheryl Ladd—5'4"

- Donna Mills—5'4"
- Shelley Winters—5'4"
- Victoria Jackson—5'4 1/2"
- Rod Serling—5'5 1/2"
- Courteney Cox—5'5"
- Linda Purl—5'5"
- Marlo Thomas—5'5"
- Melanie Mayron—5'5 1/2"
- Morey Amsterdam—5'6"
- Donna Douglas—5'6"
- Joe E. Ross—5'6"
- Junior Samples—5'6"
- Joan Van Ark—5'6"
- Vanna White—5'6"
- Henry Winkler—5'6 1/2"
- Jim McKay—5'6 3/4"
- Chuck Barris—5'7"
- Meredith Baxter—5'7"
- Carol Burnett—5'7"
- Dick Cavett—5'7"
- Bob Costas—5'7"
- John Hillerman—5'7"
- Garry Moore—5'7"
- Howard Morris—5'7"
- Betsy Palmer—5'7"
- Richard Simmons—5'7"
- Martin Balsam—5'7 1/2"
- Linda Gray—5'7 1/2"
- Nick Adams—5'8"

- Eve Arden—5'8"
- Tim Conway—5'8"
- Veronica Hamel—5'8"
- Elizabeth Montgomery—5'8"
- Burt Ward—5'8"
- Mary Alice Williams—5'8"
- Robin Williams—5'8"
- Dagmar—5'8 1/2" (5'11" in heels)
- Tina Louise—5'8 1/2"
- Lee Meriwether—5'8 1/2"
- Harry Morgan—5'8 1/2"
- Diana Rigg—5'8 1/2"
- Don Adams—5'9"
- Beatrice Arthur—5'9"
- Edward Asner—5'9"
- Fred Astaire—5'9"
- Richard Basehart—5'9"
- Ken Berry—5'9"
- Charles Bronson—5'9"
- Sebastian Cabot—5'9", 240 lbs.
- William Conrad—5'9"
- Sarah Purcell (*Real People*)—5'9"
- Diane Sawyer—5'9"
- Connie Sellecca—5'9"
- Tom and Dick Smothers—5'9" each
- Linda Thorson—5'9"
- David Birney—5'10"
- Pat Harrington, Jr.—5'10"
- Julie Newmar—5'10"

- John Saxon—5'10"
- Jean Smart (*Designing Women*)—5'10"
- Inga Swenson (*Benson*)—5'10"
- George Wendt—5'10"
- Roy Clark—5'11"
- Lisa Todd—5'11"
- Lindsay Wagner—5'11"
- Marsha Warfield—5'11"
- Kurt Russell—5'11 1/2"
- Larry Linville—6'
- Gary Sandy—6'
- Peter Bonerz—6'1"
- David Carradine—6'1"
- Dan Haggerty—6'1"
- Jim Henson—6'1"
- Patrick MacNee—6'1"
- Irish McCalla (*Sheena, Queen of the Jungle*)—6'1"
- Ed O'Neill—6'1"
- Telly Savalas—6'1"
- Betty Thomas—6'1"
- Jonathan Winters—6'1"
- Mike Connors—6'1 1/2"
- Claude Akins—6'2"
- Alan Alda—6'2"
- Bruce Boxleitner—6'2"
- Joseph Campanella—6'2"
- Gary Collins—6'2"
- Frank Converse—6'2"
- Peter Cook—6'2"

- Ted Danson—6'2"
- Patrick Duffy—6'2"
- Dennis Farina—6'2"
- Tony Franciosa—6'2"
- Charlton Heston—6'2"
- Patrick McGoohan—6'2"
- Greg Morris—6'2"
- Roger Mosley—6'2"
- Ron Perlman—6'2"
- Rob Reiner—6'2"
- Charles Robinson (*Night Court*)—6'2"
- Robert Urich—6'2"
- Raymond Burr—6'2 1/2"
- Dennis Weaver—6'2 1/2"
- Steve Allen—6'3"

Six-foot-one Irish "Sheena" McCalla and her Mexican stunt double.

- Ed Begley, Jr.—6'3"
- Richard Boone—6'3"
- Buddy Ebsen—6'3"
- Mike Farrell—6'3"
- Elliott Gould—6'3"
- Peter Graves—6'3"
- Alan Hale, Jr.—6'3"
- Ernie Kovacs—6'3"
- Peter Marshall—6'3"
- Wayne Rogers—6'3"
- Guy Williams—6'3"
- James Garner—6'3 1/2"
- Harry Anderson—6'4"
- Dan Blocker—6'4", 300 lbs.
- Barry Bostwick—6'4"
- James Brolin—6'4"
- Ron Ely—6'4"
- John Gavin—6'4"
- Clint Eastwood—6'4"
- Art Fleming—6'4"
- David Hasselhoff—6'4"
- Rock Hudson—6'4"
- George Kennedy—6'4"
- Durward Kirby—6'4"
- John Larroquette—6'4"
- Peter Lupus—6'4", 50" chest, 33" waist
- Jock Mahoney—6'4"
- Ed McMahon—6'4"
- Jack Palance—6'4"

- Bob Saget—6'4"
- Tom Selleck—6'4"
- Tom Snyder—6'4"
- Arthur Treacher—6'4"
- Lyle Waggoner—6'4"
- Max Baer, Jr.—6'4 1/2"
- Frank Campanella—6'5"
- Andrew Duggan—6'5"
- Lou Ferrigno—6'5"
- Fred Gwynne—6'5"
- David Hartman—6'5"
- Gardner McKay—6'5"
- Merlin Olson—6'5"
- Fess Parker—6'5"
- Sinbad—6'5"
- Forrest Tucker—6'5"
- Clint Walker—6'5"
- Chuck Connors—6'5 1/2"
- Fred Dryer—6'6"
- Jim Fowler—6'6"
- Ken Howard—6'6"
- John Tesh—6'6"
- Garrick Utley—6'6"
- James Arness—6'7"
- Pat McCormick—6'7"
- Hulk Hogan—6'8"
- Richard Moll—6'8"
- Ted Cassidy—6'9"

What Things Cost on TV

● In 1958, Rosalind Russell's costumes for her *Wonderful Town* special cost $25,000; Kathy Nolan's wardrobe on *The Real McCoys* cost $11.46, bought at thrift shops. Her shoes cost 21 cents—with tax.

● Every time a covered wagon was burned on *Wagon Train,* it cost $3,000. More than 100 were burned in the show's eight years.

● On the first Super Bowl, televised on January 15, 1967, commercial time ranged from $37,500 to $42,500 for a 30-second spot; by 1991, a 30-second commercial cost $800,000.

● The first property rehabbed as the initial project on *This Old House* in 1979, in the Boston working-class neighborhood of Dorchester, was purchased for $17,500 and later sold at auction for $55,000. Ten years later, a project in which a barn was taken down and an entirely new one built in its place cost $400,000.

● Cost to outfit Steve Thomas's tool belt on PBS's *This Old House:* web belt, hammer, holster, tool punches, $48.17; graphite hammer, $25.80; combination square, $8.89; three nail sets, $6.24; utility knife, $6.70; bits for cordless drill (two), $7.68; four chisels, $50.64; block plane, $25.36; electrical pliers, $14.22; 25-foot tape, $23.18. Total: $216.88.

● TV news-anchorperson salaries: CNN's

Bob Vila and Norm Abram in happier times, when they worked together rehabbing dilapidated properties on the popular PBS series This Old House.

Bernard Shaw, $500,000; CBS's Dan Rather, $3–4 million; NBC's Tom Brokaw, $2 million; ABC's Peter Jennings, $1.8 million, and more for specials.

● NBC's *Matlock* spends $2,000 for each seersucker suit worn by Andy Griffith, who uses as many as 12 per season. Each suit is then hand-washed and "aged"—to give the impression that Matlock never buys new clothes!

● Cost per five-month season for the Grecian Formula used on The Family Channel's *The New Zorro* to make Zorro's horse very black (so that no reddish hue shows on film): $4,000.

● The average cost of a single episode of a half-hour sitcom ranges from $500,000 to $700,000. The average cost of a one-hour drama: about $900,000 to $1 million.

● Cost of the sneakers worn by Fred Rogers on *Mister Rogers' Neighborhood:* $29.95.

● Ted Danson's reported salary on NBC's *Cheers:* $450,000 per episode. Number of episodes in a season: 26. Grand total: $11.7 million per season.

● Cost of the doughnuts on *Twin Peaks:* $150 a week.

● The theme song for a long-running half-hour show generates $1300 per airing, divided between the songwriters and music publishers.

● Cost of the Aristo stopwatch on CBS's *60 Minutes:* $130.

● NBC's *Empty Nest* spent $2,000 for the stethoscopes, scales, jars of cotton balls, uniforms, etc., used regularly on the show. Other costs range from $20 for a retractable syringe to $2,500 for an intensive-care hospital-bed setup.

● Weekly wardrobe budget for the four women stars on CBS's *Designing Women:* $12,000–13,000 (including rentals).

● Cost of a necktie worn by Elliott (Timothy Busfield) on ABC's *thirtysomething:* $52.

● Fox's *The Simpsons* costs "less than $20,000 per minute" to animate, or "$30,000 to $50,000 a minute," depending on whom you ask. The costs of animating a half-hour animated show (22 minutes, minus commercials) run from $350,000 on the low end (CBS's *Teenage Mutant Ninja Turtles*) to $500,000 on the high (the syndicated *Tiny Toon Adventures*). Those really bad Saturday-morning cartoons run about $200,000–$250,000 for a half-hour.

● Cost of the Plexiglas desk used by *Entertainment Tonight*'s Mary Hart, John Tesh, and Leeza Gibbons: $2,000.

● Screening, logging, editing, and paying a producer to review and select 45 clips (out of thousands submitted) for *America's Funniest Home Videos* on ABC costs about $7,500 per clip aired.

● Dean Stockwell's gold-and-silver shoes on NBC's *Quantum Leap* cost $125 a pair; he wears 12 per season. Season total: $1,500. His Zino cigars are handmade in Honduras and cost $185 a box. He smokes one box per episode.

● Cost to ABC's *The Wonder Years* for Federal Expressing schoolwork and tests for Josh Saviano (to New Jersey) and Fred Savage (to Brentwood, California): $50 per week.

- Cost of Jeff Smith's pepper mill on PBS's *The Frugal Gourmet:* $40.

- ABC's sportscasters pay about $200 for a blazer.

- Keeping staffers awake on ABC's *Nightline* costs $120 a month for coffee.

- Cost of Sally Jessy Raphael's identical red eyeglasses: about $5,000–$7,000 per year. Why so much? Extra pairs are kept in the studio, at home, and for travel— and still more are left with her husband, assistant, and publicist. A special glare coating runs up the price.

- Annual cost of Kleenex on *Sally Jessy Raphael* (handed out to crying guests and gum-chewing audience members): $200.

- Cost of costuming Katey Sagal and Christina Applegate for one episode of Fox's *Married . . . with Children:* approximately $2,500.

- Cost of the suspenders worn by Bill Cosby on NBC's *The Cosby Show:* $30–$70.

- Cost of making a music video: ranges from $18,000 (for nobody you ever heard of) to $300,000 (for somebody like Janet Jackson or Madonna). A typical video runs $90,000–$120,000.

THIS IS ONLY A TEST

TV Guide's Tough and Tricky TV Trivia Test

Here's a chance to pit your memory and couch-potato skills against 166 challenging—and occasionally sly—questions, all based on information gleaned from articles, interviews, and items that appeared in *TV Guide* issues over the past 40 years.

For those keeping score at home, and awarding one point per correct response (with one point for each extra-point and bonus-point question answered accurately), rate yourself as follows:

0–50: You enjoy watching TV, but have other interests that occupy your time. You read *TV Guide* mostly for the listings.

51–100: You love TV, have great powers of recall, and voraciously read *TV Guide* cover to cover.

101–140: Maybe you love TV a tad too much. You are practically a genius when it comes to TV information. TV is clearly your basic source of entertainment, and *TV Guide* is always by your side.

Above 140: You are among the most knowledgeable humans when it comes to TV, and even though we admire your vast pool of learning, may we suggest that you consider getting a life? And thanks for making *TV Guide* your soulmate for the past four decades.

1. Jim Anderson (Robert Young in *Father Knows Best*) held what job?

2. What daughter had a part in the TV version of a hit movie her father had starred in? For extra points, name his and her character names.

3. Flub-A-Dub was a character on *The Howdy Doody Show,* of a very odd anatomical structure—he/she/it seemed to be made up of parts of other animals. Name those parts and those animals.

4. On *Howdy Doody,* what was Clarabell's last name?

5. Name three other puppet regulars on *Kukla, Fran and Ollie.* And what was the collective name used for the entire cast of that show?

6. In *Time for Beany,* who provided the voice for Cecil the Seasick Sea Serpent for more than five years? And what was the name of Beany and Cecil's ship?

7. Popular puppet character from TV's early days, Rootie Kazootie, had a different name when he first made the scene. What was it?

8. Ted Mack showcased talent on *The Original Amateur Hour.* But what was his talent that brought him fame before he joined this show?

9. What was the musical theme to *The Late Show*?

10. Who sponsored *Amos 'n' Andy* on TV?

11. On *What's My Line?*, what did it mean when John Daly tugged on his ear?

12. Who was the first actress to play Alice Kramden in *The Honeymooners*? And who was the first to play Ed Norton's wife?

13. On what television show did Lucille Ball make her video debut?

14. In what TV series of the 1950s did a star's real-life daughter play her sister?

15. Who were the only two celebrities honored on *This Is Your Life* who were purposely tipped off ahead of time, and why?

16. Join the cowboy pardners:

Wild Bill Hickok	El Toro
Roy Rogers	Pancho
The Lone Ranger	Pat Buttram
Hopalong Cassidy	Jingles
Gene Autry	Pat Brady
The Cisco Kid	Red Connors
Kit Carson	Tonto

17. Jack Paar always talked lovingly of his daughter. What was her name?

18. Who played Sergeant Joe Friday's first girlfriend on *Dragnet*? And what was the character's name?

19. Who were Sergeant Joe Friday's partners during the run of *Dragnet,* and who played them?

20. What TV production device commonly found in every studio today was unveiled for the first time during the 1952 political conventions?

21. What TV-show actor/host was also President Eisenhower's television coach?

22. What later well-known comedienne was the first "live-test-pattern girl"—on whom cameramen trained their lenses to make certain their colors were true—in a 1942 CBS color-TV demonstration for the Federal Communications Commission?

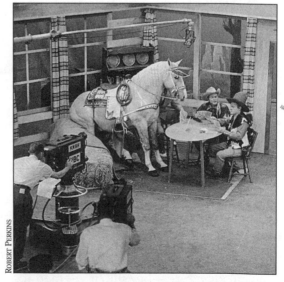

Hiding an ace up his fetlock, Trigger calls and raises Bob Hope as Roy Rogers kibitzes during a December 30, 1951, comedy/variety special that kicked off the Roy Rogers Show *on NBC.*

23. Who was the first comedian to imitate Ed Sullivan on Sullivan's show?

24. What two men played Davy Crockett for the Disney company? And who sang the hit record of the Davy Crockett theme?

25. What was the name of Captain Midnight's sidekick, and who played him?

26. How was host Hal March presented with the questions on *The $64,000 Question*? And for extra points, who broke March's nose?

27. In the 1955–56 season of *Our Miss Brooks,* Miss Brooks left one school to take a job at another. What were the names of both schools? Who were the principal and vice-principal at the new school?

28. When a musical version of *Our Town* aired in 1955, one song in it became a huge hit, and a long-lasting signature song, for Frank Sinatra, who played the Stage Manager in the production. What was that song?

29. Humphrey Bogart played Captain Queeg in the movie made of Herman Wouk's *The Caine Mutiny Court Martial.* Who played the role in the 1955–56 TV-season production? And who played it in a 1980s TV version?

30. Name, in chronological order, the five men who have played the Lone Ranger on radio and TV.

31. How did Wyatt Earp's appearance change in the first few episodes of the 1956–57 season?

32. What baseball teams did *General Hospital*'s John Beradino play for before

he became an actor? And, for extra points, whom did Chuck Connors play for?

Long before The Rifleman, *still a good shot: Chuck Connors in 1941.*

33. Who is credited with being the first performer on TV to use cue cards?

34. Everybody knows Dick Clark was the host of *Bandstand*—but there was another show by that name on NBC in the 1950s. How did the music differ, and who was its host?

35. Name all the boys who played Little Ricky on *I Love Lucy.*

36. Spin and Marty spent the summer at what Western camp?

37. Name the two TV series that took place on a cruise ship.

38. What are the first names of the Lennon Sisters? For extra points, what was the name of the singing group their father sang with professionally? And, for a bonus point, what did the sisters save up their pay for?

39. Why is the award of the Academy of Television Arts and Sciences called an "Emmy"?

40. Johnny Carson's big break was hosting *Who Do You Trust?* But who was the first emcee of that show under its original title, *Do You Trust Your Wife?*

41. On *Gunsmoke,* what was Chester's last name? And why did he limp?

42. Who of the performers associated with *Gunsmoke* was on the show the longest?

43. "Sugarfoot" was merely the nickname of the character in the Western series *Sugarfoot*—what was the character's real name? And what was he studying via correspondence course?

44. Before she became well known as "Lassie's mother" in the *Lassie* series, what was Jan Clayton most famous for?

45. Both *Wyatt Earp* and *The Adventures of Jim Bowie* had the same group provide music for them. Who were they, and what made them unique?

46. What was the full name of Yancy Derringer's Indian sidekick, who played him, and what did that Indian name mean?

47. Two Western series on the air during the same season took place in Dodge City, presumably around the same time in history, yet in each show Dodge City had a different law-enforcement officer keeping the peace. Which series were these, who were the lawmen, and how was the law-enforcement bottleneck freed up?

48. Name five professional athletes who went on to become stars of non–sports-related TV series.

49. In 1959, Darren McGavin was actively working as the star of two different film series. What were they?

50. Edd Byrnes became famous as Kookie on *77 Sunset Strip.* But he played another part in that series. What was it? And, for extra points, what was Kookie's full name?

51. Johnny Carson appeared on the August 19, 1959, *I've Got a Secret* with a secret to stump the panel. What was his secret?

52. In *Tightrope!,* where did the hero, played by Mike Connors, hide his gun?

53. What was Tony Randall's first TV series?

54. Before *The Andy Griffith Show* began its run, it previewed on another popular series. What was that series?

55. Rod Serling planned to stop being the on-camera host of *The Twilight Zone* beginning in the 1960–61 season. Whom had he planned to have replace him?

56. Name the six women who, over the years, played Sid Caesar's wives.

57. What was the name of Paladin's servant in *Have Gun Will Travel?* And, for extra points, who played him?

58. *Look Who's Talking,* with the gimmick of having the audience hear the thoughts of a baby, was a big movie hit that spawned the TV show *Baby Talk.* But this was not the first time this gimmick had been tried on TV. What show used it first?

59. The summer-1960 replacement for Perry Como was a Western called *Tate.* What was the show's big gimmick?

60. What popular talk-show host was also, early in his career, the emcee of a CBS-network religious TV show?

61. Who were the stars who founded Four Star Productions, producer of such shows as *Richard Diamond—Private Detective, The Rifleman,* and *Wanted— Dead or Alive?*

62. What was the name of the first host of *Death Valley Days,* and who was the actor who played him?

63. On which show did Clint Eastwood make his TV debut?

Clint Eastwood, costume-hunting, pre-Rawhide.

64. Back in 1961, a rare event occurred: the costars of one TV show switched in midseason to another show in the same time period on the same network and for the same sponsor. Can you name the two series, and the two stars?

65. Mitch Miller became famous for his TV sing-alongs. Before that, he was a symphonic musician. What instrument did he play?

66. Beginning with the 1961–62 season, *The Flintstones* began having "guest stars"—celebrities whose voices were heard and whose likenesses were seen in cartoon fashion. Can you name them?

67. What popular TV actor earlier in his career played Matt Dillon on radio?

68. Gertrude Berg returned to TV in 1961 with a series called *Mrs. G. Goes to College* (later, *The Gertrude Berg Show*). What did the "G" stand for?

69. Who succeeded Dave Garroway as host of the *Today* show? And what was the line of male-host succession after him?

70. Which actor replaced Edd "Kookie" Byrnes as the valet parker on *77 Sunset Strip,* and what was the name of the character he played? Also, what happened to Kookie?

71. What was Ben Casey's medical specialty?

72. Who was the spunky Hispanic singer who appeared regularly on ABC's *Surfside 6,* what was her real name, and what was the name of the nightclub she performed in?

73. *The Eleventh Hour,* a series starring Wendell Corey as a psychiatrist, was a spin-off from what hit series?

Edd Byrnes as Kookie, valet of the dolls.

74. Which network televised the first Super Bowl on January 15, 1967?

75. Name two shows that had rodeo riders as leads, and tell who starred in them.

76. Who took over when Johnny Carson left *Who Do You Trust?* to become host of *The Tonight Show*?

77. What was the name of the perfume that Bob Barker, host of the daytime *Truth or Consequences,* gave to each loser?

78. What was the name of the nearly comatose, immobile shaggy dog who was, with his trainer, a comedy staple on *The Ed Sullivan Show* for years? And what was his trainer's name?

79. During the 1962–63 season, Raymond

Burr had to have surgery and was out of *Perry Mason* for a while. Who were the guest stars who took over for him as defense attorneys?

80. Car 54, the actual police car used by actors Fred Gwynne and Joe E. Ross in *Car 54, Where Are You?,* was an exact duplicate of an actual New York Police Department vehicle, except for one thing. What was that?

81. On *The Beverly Hillbillies,* who played the part of Jethro's little baby sister, Jethrene?

82. Who hosted *Shindig*?

83. Who played the blacksmith in *Gunsmoke,* and what was the character's full name?

84. After J. Fred Muggs left the scene, the *Today* show featured a troupe of puppets on occasion. What was the name of that troupe?

85. ABC was the last of the three networks to go from 15 minutes to a half-hour of evening news, on January 9, 1967. Who was the anchorman on-air when that change occurred?

86. What two performing brothers, who both later starred in popular sitcoms, both hosted TV quiz shows earlier in their careers—and what were those shows?

87. By *77 Sunset Strip*'s last season, who from the original cast was still on the show?

88. In which medical facility did Dr. Kildare work?

89. What was it that made Jack Benny angry enough to take his TV show and leave CBS for NBC in 1964?

90. Bill Hanna and Joe Barbera were responsible for the creation of Huckleberry Hound, Yogi Bear, the Flintstones, the Jetsons, etc. When they were story men at MGM in the 1940s, what famous cartoon-character team did they create?

91. What was Rob Petrie's brother's name?

92. In *The Munsters,* how old were Lily and Herman supposed to be?

93. Who was the singing group—sort of the equivalent of Lawrence Welk's Lennon Sisters—on *The Danny Kaye Show*?

94. When Pernell Roberts left *Bonanza,* how was the sudden absence of Adam Cartwright explained on the show?

95. In its last season, ABC's *Burke's Law* had a title change, and the lead character, Amos Burke, switched jobs. What were they?

96. Who played *The Fugitive*'s one-armed man, and how did he lose that arm? Which arm was missing? And what other regular job in show business did the actor have?

97. What was the name of the submarine on *Voyage to the Bottom of the Sea*?

98. In 1965, CBS took one of its daytime serials, *As the World Turns,* and ran a nighttime version of it twice-weekly, in imitation of ABC's *Peyton Place* success. What was the name of that show?

99. Who was the "*Hullabaloo* girl" who danced the Frug in a raised cage every week on the show?

100. Which nighttime drama underwent a title change during its run, then, when canceled, switched networks and was turned into a daytime serial?

101. Which TV detective kept an ocelot as a pet?

102. What was the semi-popular song recorded by Soupy Sales? And, for extra points, can you name any other Sales songs?

103. Which tights-wearing arch-villain wreaked havoc in the pilot episode for *Batman*? And who played that villain?

104. How did Peter Falk lose his eye? And which one is it?

105. What was the name of Reginald Van Gleason III's father, and who played him?

106. In an attempt to find someone to replace Pernell Roberts in *Bonanza,* the producers introduced a Cartwright cousin to the Ponderosa, but it didn't work out and he didn't last long. Who played that cousin?

107. What actor played a cat in two series?

108. Who, for one episode, portrayed Larry Hagman's mother in *I Dream of Jeannie*?

109. Who was the first female regular to move into the previously all-male Douglas household on *My Three Sons,* who played her, and what was she doing there?

110. Though he handled and explained many different kinds of animals during the runs of both *Zoo Parade* and *Wild Kingdom,* what was zoologist Marlin Perkins' true area of specialization? And what was that of his assistant, Jim Fowler?

111. Chuck Barris, of *The Gong Show* fame, wrote a very big rock-and-roll hit. What was it?

112. Who was the first woman to win $64,000 on *The $64,000 Question* and what was her category of knowledge? And what other well-known female TV personality of the 1960s also won the top $64,000 prize, and what was her specialty?

113. In *The Avengers,* what were they avenging?

114. What was the first TV show—in fact, the first TV or movie production in history—to have real American Indians playing all the roles of Indians, not only as extras but in speaking parts as well?

115. During the 1960s, one TV star became the highest-earning entertainer in the history of show business. Who was that performer?

116. On what show of the 1970s did Fred Astaire, himself in his 70s, become a semi-regular? And what role did he play?

117. They played the same roles together in the play version on Broadway, in the filmed version in the movies, and in the series version on TV. Who are these two actresses, and what is the name of the show/movie/series they re-created their roles in?

118. How much money did Jed Clampett make from the discovery of oil on his property on *The Beverly Hillbillies*?

119. In 1971, when Milburn Stone underwent heart surgery and had to be out of *Gunsmoke* for a while, who filled in for him as the town's medic, and what was the reason given for Doc's absence?

120. After Barbara Bain left *Mission:*

Impossible, who replaced her? And, after one season, who replaced the replacement?

121. Who were the only husband and wife ever to host a Miss America telecast?

122. Who was the first person seen doing the first joke on the very first *Laugh-In*?

123. And who were the only original *Laugh-In* cast members to stay on the show through its entire run?

124. Who was the only individual *Laugh-In* performer to win an Emmy?

125. Who were the original cast of PBS's *The Electric Company* when it premiered in October 1971?

126. What instrument did Joey Bishop occasionally play on his shows?

127. Who were the last actors to portray Drs. Kildare and Gillespie on TV?

128. Who played Wonder Woman on TV?

129. Which relatively unknown young writer—who would later become a top television producer—and which other young director, who would later become a fabulously successful movie director—were involved in the creation of the first series episode of *Columbo* in 1971?

130. Who were the first hosts of ABC's first morning-program competition against the *Today* show? And what was the show called?

131. When *What's My Line?* became a syndicated series in the 1970s, who was the only one of the original series' panelists to be on the new panel?

132. Which three members of the same acting family each starred in dramatic series that aired on Monday nights at 10:00 P.M. on CBS in different seasons?

133. Which actor played the same character on two different but related shows that were on during the same season?

134. Kate Jackson, Farrah Fawcett-Majors, and Jaclyn Smith were the stars of *Charlie's Angels*—but what were the names of the characters they played?

135. Who was the last person to leave the house on the final episode of *Upstairs, Downstairs*?

136. Who is the only on-screen *Star Trek* actor to play a Vulcan, a Klingon, *and* a Romulan? And what original-series guest star became a regular on *Star Trek: The Next Generation*?

137. What was the highest-rated news telecast of all time?

138. Who was the first actor to be cast as David, the oldest son in *Eight Is Enough,* and why did he leave the show?

139. What was the real name of the Love Boat?

140. In *Star Trek,* the Klingons and Romulans were, at various times, the chief enemies of Good. Who were the unspeakably evil futuristic villains of *Battlestar Galactica*?

141. How many versions of and/or sequels to Irwin Shaw's *Rich Man, Poor Man* were made for TV?

142. Name two of the actors who have starred as Elvis Presley on TV in movies or series.

143. What were the names of the two robots in *Buck Rogers in the 25th Century*?

144. On *Mork & Mindy,* who played Mork's son, and what was the son's name?

145. What kind of automobile—year, model—was the "General Lee," the car used and abused by the stars of *The Dukes of Hazzard*? What kind of car was KITT, on *Knight Rider*? And what kind of car did Lieutenant Columbo drive?

146. On how many networks did *The Paper Chase* TV series appear?

147. Which soap opera was Carol Burnett so wrapped up in that she decided to play a part in it? And what character did she play?

148. What was highly unusual about the first episode of the soap opera *Loving*?

149. Who replaced Herve Villechaize as Mr. Roarke's sidekick on *Fantasy Island*?

150. What is the unusual connection between Morgan Brittany's appearances in the movies *Gable and Lombard* and *Day of the Locust,* and the TV miniseries *Moviola*?

151. Who are the three women who played Jenna Wade, Bobby Ewing's childhood sweetheart, during the run of *Dallas*?

152. When the Beatles appeared for the first time on *The Ed Sullivan Show,* on February 9, 1964, they sang five songs. What were they?

153. In the Robert Guillaume series, what was Benson's last name?

154. Who played Dr. J. T. McIntyre, son of Pernell Roberts, in the series *Trapper John, M.D.,* and what series did he star in later?

155. When American Express started its famous "Do you know me?" ad campaign in 1974, which famous unknown did the first commercial?

156. Before *Miami Vice*'s soundtrack album hit number one on the *Billboard* charts in 1985, what was the last series to produce a top-selling soundtrack album?

157. Who was the first black female regular on *Saturday Night Live*?

158. Just before its 1980 season, *The Facts of Life* eliminated four of the original seven girls who had costarred in the series. One of those four went on to very big things in the movies. Who is she?

159. Who was daytime drama's first homosexual continuing character, and on what show did he appear?

160. Before they were together again in *Designing Women,* what TV series had Dixie Carter, Delta Burke, and writer/producer Linda Bloodworth all been involved in? And of the four original female stars of *Designing Women,* who was the only one who was not from the South?

161. Both Raymond Burr and Charles Durning, in different teleplays and portraying the character at different times in his life, played the same man of the cloth. Who was he?

162. Before Marsha Warfield's bailiff, Roz, on *Night Court,* which two actresses played the bailiff's role and why did they leave the show?

163. Geraldo Rivera has a tattoo. What is it of, and where is it located?

164. What does the family in *The Simpsons* have in common with the family on *Father Knows Best*—other than both being families, of course?

165. On *Hill Street Blues,* Sergeant Esterhaus used to end his roll call by saying, "Let's be careful out there." What did his replacement, Sergeant Jablonski, say?

166. What program, in 1991, became the longest continually running show on national TV still presided over by its original host?

Craig Stevens and Lola Albright on Peter Gunn.

ANSWERS

1. He was an agent for the General Insurance Company.

2. Jamie Lee Curtis was in *Operation Petticoat* on TV, playing Lieutenant Barbara Duran; Tony Curtis was in the movie version, playing Lieutenant Nick Holden.

3. Head of a duck with a pot of flowers on it; neck of a giraffe with rings around it; body of a dachshund; flippers of a seal; tail of a pig; four webbed feet; ears of a dog; elephant's memory; cat's whiskers; raccoon's tail on his head of hair.

4. Hornblow.

5. Madame Ophelia Ooglepuss, Clara Coo Coo, Mercedes, Colonel Cracky, Fletcher Rabbit, Buelah Witch, and Cecil Bill—along with the stars of the show—made up the Kuklapolitan Players.

6. Stan Freberg was the voice; the *Leakin' Lena* was the ship.

Hal March asks the big one on The $64,000 Question.

7. Rootie Tootie.

8. He played saxophone and clarinet with the Ben Pollack Band, then toured with his own orchestra before acting as MGM's musical director.

9. LeRoy Anderson's "Syncopated Clock."

10. Blatz Beer.

11. That one of the panelists was getting risqué, and that he or she should change the subject.

12. Pert Kelton; Elaine Stritch.

13. *Pantomime Quiz,* in the summer of 1949.

14. *I Married Joan,* in which Beverly Wills played the younger sister of her off-screen mother, Joan Davis.

15. Lillian Roth, to get permission from her to tell about her struggle with alcoholism; and Eddie Cantor, for fear that, if the surprise were sprung on him, his bad heart could give out. By the way, the Roth *This Is Your Life* appearance was re-created in the 1955 movie *I'll Cry Tomorrow,* with Susan Hayward playing Roth.

16. Wild Bill Hickock—Jingles; Roy Rogers—Pat Brady; Lone Ranger—Tonto; Hopalong Cassidy—Red Connors; Gene Autry—Pat Buttram; Cisco Kid—Pancho; Kit Carson—El Toro.

17. Randy.

18. Dorothy Abbott played Ann Baker.

19. Barton Yarborough was Detective Sergeant Ben Romero, as he was on radio, until his death

Amateur Hour's Ted Mack and one-man band, 1956.

on December 22, 1951; he was replaced by Barney Phillips as Sergeant Ed Jacobs; he was replaced by Herb Ellis and then Ben Alexander, both as Officer Frank Smith; finally, Harry Morgan played Officer Bill Gannon.

20. The TelePrompTer.

21. Robert Montgomery.

22. Nanette Fabray. In 1949, she performed the same task for RCA's experiments in compatible color broadcasts.

23. Frank Fontaine—Crazy Guggenheim of *The Jackie Gleason Show*—in 1948.

24. Fess Parker played Crockett in the 1950s, Tim Dunigan when Disney tried to revive the excitement in the 1980s. Bill Hayes had the hit record.

25. Ikky, played by Sid Melton.

26. The first four questions were "dealt" by an IBM computer; the remainder were presented by a bank executive flanked by two bank guards. Jackie Gleason did the breaking. March guested once on Gleason's old *Cavalcade of Stars,* where Jackie was to hit him on the schnozz with a breakaway bottle. Seems the bottle didn't break away.

27. She left Madison High for Mrs. Nestor's Private Elementary School, where her former boss, Osgood Conklin (Gale Gordon), had become principal, and Oliver Munsey (Bob Sweeney) was the vice-principal.

28. "Love and Marriage," by Jimmy Van Heusen and Sammy Cahn.

29. Lloyd Nolan; Brad Davis.

30. George Stenius (later known as George Seaton, film director), Earle W. Graser, Brace Beemer, Clayton Moore, John Hart, and Clayton Moore (he gave it up, then resumed it). Several sources claim that a Jack Deeds and Jim Jenell (program director of radio station WXYZ, Detroit) also played the part, however briefly.

31. He wore an eyepatch, a result of an auto accident Hugh O'Brian was in.

32. Beradino played for the Saint Louis Browns from 1939 to 1948 (with time out for the Navy), then was sold to the Cleveland Indians, where he

stayed until 1952; after that he played a while with the Pittsburgh Pirates. Connors was on the Brooklyn Dodgers then was sold to the Chicago Cubs, where he hit .233 in 70 games in the majors; eventually he was shipped to Los Angeles, where the Cubs had a minor-league team.

33. Ed Wynn, who also used them in his Broadway shows.

34. Big-band orchestras played; Bert Parks emceed.

35. James John Gouzer, 18 days old, was Little Ricky on January 19, 1953, the day of Little Ricky's birth; Richard Lee and Ronald Lee Simmons, twins, played Little Ricky from March 1953 until the summer of that year, when Mike and Joe Mayer, also twins, were hired; they played the role for three seasons. In 1956, Richard Keith, five years old, got the role.

36. The Triple R Ranch.

37. *The Love Boat,* and *The Gale Storm Show (Oh, Susanna).*

38. Peggy, Janet, Kathy, Dianne. Their father's group was—naturally—The Lennon Brothers. And the girls wanted to use their money to add a room to their family's old two-bedroom house.

39. It's a corruption of the word "immy," television jargon for the image-orthicon camera tube.

40. Edgar Bergen.

41. His last name was Goode. The limp was a

Rod Serling, Ralph Nelson, Ed and Keenan Wynn in the 1960s' "The Man in the Funny Suit."

device said to have been created by producer/director Charles Marquis Warren to explain how Chester could seem so physically robust yet constantly hang around in the marshal's office.

42. George Walsh, the show's announcer, who also was the announcer on the radio-show version.

43. Tom Brewster; law.

44. As a singer, she was the lead on Broadway in Rodgers and Hammerstein's classic *Carousel.*

45. The Ken Darby Singers, who had no instrumental accompaniment: they just sang and mostly hummed.

46. X. Brands played Pahoo-Ka-Ta-Wah, which in Pawnee language means Wolf Who Stands in Water.

47. Both Wyatt Earp and Matt Dillon roamed Dodge City in their respective series; at the beginning of the 1959–60 season, Wyatt Earp moved to Tombstone.

48. Chuck Connors (*The Rifleman*), John Beradino (*General Hospital*), Ed Marinaro (*Hill Street Blues, Sisters*), Merlin Olsen (*Aaron's Way, Father Murphy*), Muhammad Ali (did the voice of himself for the animated *The Adventures of Muhammad Ali*), Joe Namath (*The Waverly Wonders*), Alex Karras (*Webster*), Bob Uecker (*Mr. Belvedere*), Fred Dryer (*Hunter*), Joe Garagiola (*Today*), Roosevelt Grier (*Daniel Boone*), Tony Danza (*Who's the Boss?*) and Fred Williamson (*Julia*) are among the most well-known.

49. *Riverboat* for NBC, and the syndicated *Mike Hammer.*

50. In *Girl on the Run,* which was originally produced as a feature picture but which became the series' first episode, airing on October 10, 1958, he played a killer. But preview audiences were so taken with him, the producers found a way to work him into the show. Kookie's full name was Gerald Lloyd Kookson III.

51. His secret was that he was an expert archer, and to prove the point, he did a William Tell and shot an apple off the head of Garry Moore, who—just to be on the safe side—sat behind an inch-thick transparent shield.

52. Tucked into the back of his belt, where the bad guys always somehow failed to look or frisk.

53. *One Man's Family,* from 1950–52.

54. *The Danny Thomas Show.*

55. He invited Orson Welles to be the host.

56. Imogene Coca, Nanette Fabray, Janet Blair, Audrey Meadows, Giselle Mackenzie, and, in a few instances, Patricia Barry.

57. Hey Boy was played by Kam Tong.

58. *Happy,* starring Ronnie Burns and the Born twins—Steven and David—as the "talking" Happy.

59. Tate was a one-armed gunslinger; his left arm had been wounded into uselessness in the Civil War, and he had it covered in black leather, suspended in a sling.

60. Merv Griffin hosted *Look Up and Live.*

61. There were only three stars—Dick Powell, Charles Boyer, and David Niven. They wanted to find another star to invest in the company and rotate in a weekly half-hour series. But, in 1951, few movie idols would risk both money and reputation on TV.

62. The Old Ranger was played by Stanley Andrews.

63. Eastwood, who became popular on *Rawhide,* had his first bit part on *Highway Patrol.*

64. *Acapulco* began February 27, 1961, in the Monday-night time slot previously occupied by *Klondike,* both of which starred James Coburn and Ralph Taeger.

65. The oboe.

66. Hoagy Carmichael—the first, on September 15, 1961—then Ann-Margret (as Ann Margrock) and Tony Curtis (as Stoney Curtis).

67. William Conrad.

68. Mrs. Green.

69. John Chancellor followed Garroway, and was followed in turn by Hugh Downs, Frank McGee, Jim Hartz, Tom Brokaw, and Bryant Gumbel.

70. When Kookie was "promoted" to full-fledged private eye and became a member of the Bailey and Spencer detective agency on October 13,

1961, J. R. Hale—played by Robert Logan—got his old job.

71. He was a neurosurgeon.

72. Margarita Sierra played Cha Cha O'Brien, who sang and danced in the Boom Boom Room.

73. *Dr. Kildare.*

74. Two networks did: CBS and NBC, each having shown games of the competing leagues—CBS the NFL, NBC the AFL—during the regular season.

75. Earl Holliman starred in *The Wide Country;* Jack Lord was *Stoney Burke.*

76. Woody Woodbury.

77. Jungle Gardenia.

78. Bob Williams was the human; Louie was the dog.

79. Bette Davis, Walter Pidgeon, Michael Rennie, and Hugh O'Brian.

80. It was painted dark red and white—instead of the real cars' green and white—so, while the show was filming on location, New York citizens would not be confused and think it was an actual police car; since the program was filmed in black and white, home viewers couldn't tell the difference.

81. Max Baer, Jr., who also played Jethro.

82. Los Angeles deejay Jimmy O'Neill.

83. Burt Reynolds played Quint Asper.

84. The Muppets.

85. Peter Jennings, during the first of his two tours of duty as ABC anchor.

86. Dick Van Dyke once hosted *Mother's Day;* Jerry Van Dyke hosted *Picture This.*

87. Only Efrem Zimbalist, Jr.; the others—Roger Smith, Edd Byrnes, Louis Quinn, Jacqueline Beer, even the offices next to Dino's restaurant—had been let go by Warner Brothers.

88. Blair General Hospital.

89. He was incensed that CBS would schedule *Petticoat Junction* to air between his and Red Skelton's shows, and when he asked CBS to move it, the network wouldn't. So he did.

90. Tom and Jerry.

91. Stacy.

92. She was 156 years old; he was built in 1818.

93. The Clinger Sisters.

94. He was supposed to be away at a university in Europe.

95. When Burke left the police force, he went to work for a U.S. intelligence agency, and the show's name was changed to *Amos Burke—Secret Agent.*

96. Bill Raisch—who also was Burt Lancaster's regular stand-in—had his right arm amputated after he was severely burned fighting a shipboard fire during World War II.

97. The *Seaview.*

98. *Our Private World.*

99. Lada Edmund, Jr.

100. CBS's *The Nurses* became *The Doctors and the Nurses,* then became an ABC soap opera with an all-new cast.

101. Honey West.

102. "The Mouse" was Sales' biggest hit (and a minor dance craze); he also sang "Hey, Pearl," and "My Brains Fell Out."

103. Frank Gorshin was the Riddler.

104. When he was three years old, Falk underwent surgery to remove a tumor in his right eye. The eye was removed.

105. Art Carney was Sedgwick Van Gleason.

106. Guy Williams, former Zorro.

107. Robert Loggia; he starred in *The Nine Lives of Elfego Baca,* known as "El Gato," which is "cat" in Spanish; and in *T.H.E. Cat* during the 1966–67 season.

108. Spring Byington.

109. Tina Cole played Katie, who married son Robbie Douglas (Don Grady) and moved into the Douglas house with him.

110. Perkins—curator of Chicago's Lincoln Park

Zoo, and then of the Saint Louis Zoo—was a herpetologist: snakes were his specialty. Fowler, aptly named, was an ornithologist: birds were his specialty.

111. "Palisades Park."

112. Dr. Joyce Brothers won for knowing a lot about boxing. *Get Smart*'s Barbara Feldon won in the Shakespeare category.

113. In the very first episode, a woman engaged to marry a doctor was murdered, and the doctor retained Steed to track down the killer, thus avenging her death. As a side note, the actress who played the murder victim was Kate Woodville, *Avengers* star Patrick MacNee's real-life wife.

114. A fall-1968 episode of *The Virginian* used 37 American Indian actors, including folksinger Buffy Sainte-Marie.

115. Dean Martin signed a three-year, $34-million contract with NBC, plus earnings for records, Las Vegas appearances, etc.

116. He was Alister Mundy, the father of Robert Wagner's Alexander Mundy, in the last season of *It Takes a Thief.*

117. Monica Evans and Carole Shelley played the Pigeon sisters in all three versions of *The Odd Couple.*

118. $25 million.

119. Pat Hingle, as a visiting physician, took over for Doc, who had gone back east to study advanced medical techniques.

120. Lesley Ann Warren replaced Bain; Lynda Day George replaced Warren.

121. Gary Collins and Mary Ann Mobley, who was Miss America 1959, hosted the 1971 Miss America broadcast.

122. Announcer Gary Owens. He appeared in an announcer booth, hand cupped to ear, reading the words, "What you are about to see is true," as the word "FALSE" crawled across the screen.

123. Ruth Buzzi, Gary Owens, and Rowan and Martin were the last.

124. Arte Johnson.

125. Bill Cosby, Rita Moreno, Jim Boyd, Lee Chamberlain, Morgan Freeman, Judy Graubart, and Skip Hinnant.

126. The mandolin.

127. Mark Jenkins was Kildare, Gary Merrill was Gillespie, in a syndicated prime-time-access series shot on videotape in 1972–73.

128. Two women did: Cathy Lee Crosby, then Lynda Carter.

129. Steven Bochco, who would later provide TV with *Hill Street Blues* and *L.A. Law,* wrote the episode, and Steven Spielberg directed.

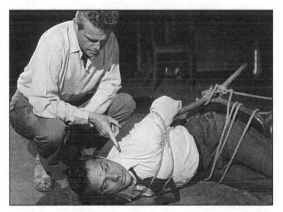

James Daly gets direction in Foreign Intrigue, *1955.*

130. Bill Beutel and Stephanie Edwards hosted *AM America.*

131. Arlene Francis; Dorothy Kilgallen and Bennett Cerf had died.

132. James Daly starred in *Medical Center,* Tyne Daly starred in *Cagney & Lacey,* and Timothy Daly starred in *Almost Grown.*

133. Richard Anderson played Oscar Goldman on both *The Six Million Dollar Man* and *The Bionic Woman.*

134. Sabrina Duncan (Jackson), Jill Munroe (Fawcett-Majors), and Kelly Garrett (Smith).

135. Rose, played by Jean Marsh, who also created the series.

136. Besides his recurring role as Sarek, Spock's

father, Mark Lenard also played a Romulan commander in the episode "Balance of Terror" and the Klingon captain in *Star Trek: The Motion Picture.* And Diana Muldaur, who played the parts of Dr. Ann Mulhall and Dr. Miranda Jones in two original-series episodes, returned 20 years later for a season as Dr. Katherine Pulaski.

137. The one-minute *NBC News Update* that was shown in the middle of *Gone With the Wind, Part I,* on November 7, 1976.

138. Mark Hamill got out of his five-year contract for the show because he'd just made a movie he thought would be successful and there might be a sequel he would be prevented from being in because of the series. The movie: *Star Wars.*

139. The *Pacific Princess,* then, later, the *Royal Princess.*

140. The Cylons.

141. Three. The original miniseries version of *Rich Man, Poor Man,* starring Nick Nolte and Peter Strauss in 1976; a sequel of sorts, *Rich Man, Poor Man—Book II,* which was not based on Shaw's book at all but was created by other writers; and *Beggarman, Thief,* a TV-movie that was based on Shaw's sequel to *Rich Man, Poor Man.*

142. Kurt Russell in the 1979 ABC TV-movie, *Elvis;* Don Johnson in the 1981 NBC TV-movie, *Elvis and the Beauty Queen;* Dale Midkiff in the 1988 *Elvis and Me;* and Michael Saint Gerard in the ABC series *Elvis.*

143. Twiki, the little one, which actually had a chimpanzee inside; and Crichton, which was fully automated.

144. Jonathan Winters played Mearth.

145. The "General Lee" was a bright-orange 1969 Dodge Charger with a Confederate flag on the roof and racing numbers on the doors. Dozens of them were used, and wrecked, during the show's run. KITT was a black Pontiac Trans-Am. Columbo drove a 1960 Peugeot 403.

146. Three—it ran originally on CBS, it was rerun on PBS, and then new episodes were filmed for a run on Showtime in 1983.

147. Burnett played Miss Johnson, a hospital patient, in 1976, and then in 1983 played Verla Grubbs, the daughter of an ex–carnival performer, in several appearances on *All My Children.*

148. The first episode was a two-hour ABC prime-time movie that aired on June 26, 1983, and starred Lloyd Bridges and Geraldine Page. The very next day, it began its life as a half-hour daytime drama on ABC, without Bridges and Page.

149. Christopher Hewett, six feet two, played the gentleman's gentleman Lawrence, replacing the three-foot-eleven Villechaize's Tattoo.

150. In all three, she played actress Vivien Leigh.

151. Morgan Fairchild during the 1978 season, Francine Tacker during the 1979 season, and Priscilla Presley starting in 1983.

152. "All My Loving," "Till There Was You," "She Loves You," "I Saw Her Standing There," and "I Want To Hold Your Hand."

153. DuBois.

154. Timothy Busfield played the role, and later starred as Elliott Weston in *thirtysomething.*

155. William Miller, Barry Goldwater's vice-presidential running mate.

156. *Peter Gunn,* in 1959.

157. Danitra Vance.

158. Molly Ringwald.

159. Hank Eliot was the first such character, on *As the World Turns,* in November 1988.

160. *Filthy Rich;* Jean Smart.

161. Pope John XXIII—Durning played him in the 1987 PBS presentation *I Would Be Called John: Pope John XXIII,* and Burr played him in *A Man Whose Name Was John,* a 1973 ABC TV-movie.

162. Selma Diamond and Florence Halop had the role, and both died of cancer.

163. Half-Jewish Rivera has the Star of David tattooed at the base of his thumb on his left hand.

164. Both live in the mythical town of Springfield, U.S.A.

165. "Let's do it to them before they do it to us."

166. *Firing Line,* with William F. Buckley, Jr.

TIMELINE

1816 Swedish chemist Baron Jöns Jakob Berzelius discovers a new element he calls "selenium," which will become an important component of television.

1847 In England, F. C. Bakewell invents the concept of "scanning," the earliest known direct antecedent to TV.

FEBRUARY 11, 1847 Thomas Alva Edison is born in Milan, Ohio.

1862 Abbé Caselli transmits the first picture (between Amiens and Paris) through a wire using electricity.

1875 The first primitive television system, using selenium cells and lamps to mimic the human eye, is proposed by G. R. Carey.

1876 The telephone is patented by Alexander Graham Bell.

1877 M. Senlecq invents the "Telectroscope," a crude, selenium-using television system.

1878 The beginning of cathode-ray tube development begins, based on rays generated by Sir William Crookes.

1878 David Hughes invents the first microphone.

1884 Paul Nipkow patents the first scanning disc, opening the door to the television age.

MARCH 18, 1886 Edward Everett Horton born in Brooklyn, New York.

1889 Edison films the first motion picture—a man sneezing—in his West Orange, New Jersey, laboratory.

OCTOBER 2, 1890 Groucho Marx born in New York City.

MARCH 10, 1891 Sam Jaffe born in New York City.

JANUARY 31, 1892 Eddie Cantor born in New York City.

FEBRUARY 9, 1892 Peggy Wood born in Brooklyn, New York.

FEBRUARY 27, 1892 William Demarest born in Saint Paul, Minnesota.

FEBRUARY 14, 1894 Jack Benny born in Chicago, Illinois.

APRIL 4, 1895 Arthur Murray born in New York City.

MAY 8, 1895 Bishop Fulton J. Sheen born in El Paso, Illinois.

JANUARY 20, 1896 George Burns born in New York City.

1898 Sir Oliver Lodge comes up with a workable method for tuning.

MAY 25, 1898 Bennett Cerf born in New York City.

JUNE 11, 1900 Lawrence Spivak born in Brooklyn, New York.

AUGUST 18, 1900 A Frenchman named Perskyi stitches together Latin and Greek words and comes up with a new term: "television."

OCTOBER 10, 1900 Helen Hayes born in Washington, D.C.

AUGUST 9, 1901 *My Little Margie*'s Charles Farrell born in Onset Bay, Massachusetts.

JANUARY 14, 1902 Frances "Aunt Bee" Bavier born in New York City.

AUGUST 11, 1902 Lloyd Nolan born in San Francisco, California.

SEPTEMBER 28, 1902 Ed Sullivan born in New York City.

MARCH 11, 1903 Lawrence Welk born near Strasburg, North Dakota.

MARCH 20, 1903 Edgar Buchanan born in Humansville, Missouri.

MAY 29, 1903 Bob Hope born in London.

1904 Ribbe invents a one-channel, two-way television system.

MAY 21, 1904 Robert Montgomery born in Beacon, New York.

AUGUST 15, 1904 Bil Baird born in Grand Island, Nebraska.

1905 Albert Einstein publishes his theory of the photoelectric effect, which will be vital for the development of the television camera.

JANUARY 3, 1905 Ray Milland born in Neath, Wales.

1906 Lee de Forest invents the

"audion," a vacuum tube that will become central to radio and TV systems.

JANUARY 12, 1906 Henny Youngman born in Liverpool, England.

JANUARY 22, 1906 Ann Sothern born in Valley City, North Dakota.

FEBRUARY 2, 1906 Gale Gordon born in New York City.

APRIL 4, 1906 John Cameron Swayze born in Wichita, Kansas.

SEPTEMBER 15, 1906 Kathryn Murray born in Jersey City, New Jersey.

NOVEMBER 13, 1906 Hermione Baddeley born in Broseley, Shropshire, England.

1907 Russian physicist Boris Rosing patents a television system that is not too different from modern equipment.

FEBRUARY 22, 1907 Robert Young born in Chicago, Illinois; Sheldon Leonard born in New York City.

MAY 1, 1907 Kate Smith born in Greenville, Virginia.

JULY 16, 1907 Barbara Stanwyck born in Brooklyn, New York.

AUGUST 30, 1907 Shirley Booth born in New York City; Fred MacMurray born in Kankakee, Illinois.

SEPTEMBER 29, 1907 Gene Autry born in Tioga, Texas.

1908 American engineer Eugene Lauste invents the first talking motion pictures.

APRIL 2, 1908 Buddy Ebsen born in Belleville, Illinois.

APRIL 22, 1908 Eddie Albert born in Rock Island, Illinois.

APRIL 25, 1908 Edward R. Murrow born in Greensboro, North Carolina.

JULY 12, 1908 Milton Berle born in New York City.

SEPTEMBER 14, 1908 Clayton Moore born in Chicago, Illinois.

OCTOBER 20, 1908 Arlene Francis born in Boston, Massachusetts.

NOVEMBER 18, 1908 Imogene Coca born in Philadelphia, Pennsylvania.

NOVEMBER 20, 1908 Alistair Cooke born in Manchester, England.

APRIL 29, 1909 Tom Ewell born in Owensboro, Kentucky.

JUNE 9, 1910 Bob Cummings born in Joplin, Missouri.

JUNE 11, 1910 Jacques-Yves Cousteau born in Saint-André-de-Cubzac, France.

JUNE 18, 1910 E. G. Marshall born in Owatonna, Minnesota.

JULY 4, 1911 Mitch Miller born in Rochester, New York.

AUGUST 6, 1911 Lucille Ball born in Jamestown, New York.

DECEMBER 9, 1911 Broderick Crawford born in Philadelphia, Pennsylvania; Lee J. Cobb born in New York City.

APRIL 30, 1912 Eve Arden born in Mill Valley, California.

MAY 11, 1912 Phil Silvers born in Brooklyn, New York.

MAY 18, 1912 Perry Como born in Canonsburg, Pennsylvania.

JULY 17, 1912 Art Linkletter born in Moose Jaw, Saskatchewan, Canada.

AUGUST 1, 1912 Henry Jones born in Philadelphia, Pennsylvania.

AUGUST 12, 1912 Jane Wyatt born in Campgaw, New Jersey.

AUGUST 15, 1912 Julia Child born in Pasadena, California.

Cooking show host Julia Child.

AUGUST 24, 1912 Durward Kirby born in Covington, Kentucky.

OCTOBER 25, 1912 Minnie Pearl born in Centerville, Tennessee.

OCTOBER 31, 1912 Dale Evans born in Uvalde, Texas.

NOVEMBER 5, 1912 Roy Rogers born in Cincinnati, Ohio.

DECEMBER 14, 1912 Morey Amsterdam born in Chicago, Illinois.

JANUARY 6, 1913 Loretta Young born in Salt Lake City, Utah.

JANUARY 15, 1913 Lloyd Bridges born in San Leandro, California.

JANUARY 18, 1913 Danny Kaye born in Brooklyn, New York.

MARCH 15, 1913 Macdonald Carey born in Sioux City, Iowa.

MARCH 22, 1913 Karl Malden born in Chicago, Illinois.

JUNE 13, 1913 Ralph Edwards born in Merino, Colorado.

JULY 3, 1913 Dorothy Kilgallen born in Chicago, Illinois.

JULY 4, 1913 Virginia Graham born in Chicago, Illinois.

JULY 13, 1913 Dave Garroway born in Schenectady, New York.

JULY 18, 1913 Red Skelton born in Vincennes, Indiana.

AUGUST 10, 1913 Noah Beery, Jr., born in New York City.

JANUARY 4, 1914 Jane Wyman born in Saint Joseph, Missouri.

JANUARY 6, 1914 Danny Thomas born in Deerfield, Michigan.

FEBRUARY 4, 1914 Ida Lupino born in London, England.

FEBRUARY 20, 1914 John Daly born in Johannesburg, South Africa.

MAY 12, 1914 Howard K. Smith born in Ferriday, Louisiana.

JULY 18, 1914 Harriet (Hilliard) Nelson born in Des Moines, Iowa.

AUGUST 31, 1914 Richard Basehart born in Zanesville, Ohio.

SEPTEMBER 16, 1914 Allen Funt born in New York City.

DECEMBER 30, 1914 Bert Parks born in Atlanta, Georgia.

JANUARY 31, 1915 Garry Moore born in Baltimore, Maryland.

FEBRUARY 12, 1915 Lorne Greene born in Ottawa, Ontario.

MARCH 31, 1915 Henry Morgan born in New York City.

APRIL 10, 1915 Harry Morgan born in Detroit, Michigan.

SEPTEMBER 3, 1915 Kitty Carlisle born in New Orleans, Louisiana.

DECEMBER 12, 1915 Frank Sinatra born in Hoboken, New Jersey.

JANUARY 3, 1916 Betty Furness born in New York City.

FEBRUARY 26, 1916 Jackie Gleason born in Brooklyn, New York.

JULY 27, 1916 Keenan Wynn born in New York City.

NOVEMBER 4, 1916 Walter Cronkite born in St. Joseph, Missouri.

MARCH 1, 1917 Dinah Shore born in Winchester, Tennessee.

MARCH 12, 1917 Desi Arnaz born in Santiago, Cuba.

APRIL 13, 1917 Howard Keel born in Gillespie, Illinois.

MAY 21, 1917 Raymond Burr born in New Westminster, British Columbia, Canada; Dennis Day born in New York City.

JUNE 17, 1917 Dean Martin born in Steubenville, Ohio.

JUNE 18, 1917 Richard Boone born in Los Angeles, California.

AUGUST 25, 1917 Don Defore born in Cedar Rapids, Iowa.

OCTOBER 13, 1917 Burr Tillstrom born in Chicago, Illinois.

NOVEMBER 24, 1917 Howard Duff born in Bremerton, Washington.

DECEMBER 22, 1917 Gene Rayburn born in Christopher, Illinois.

JANUARY 29, 1918 John Forsythe born in Penn's Grove, New Jersey.

FEBRUARY 3, 1918 Joey Bishop born in the Bronx, New York.

MARCH 20, 1918 Jack Barry born in Lindenhurst, New York.

APRIL 14, 1918 Mary Healy born in New Orleans, Louisiana.

MAY 1, 1918 Jack Paar born in Canton, Ohio.

MAY 9, 1918 Mike Wallace born in Brookline, Massachusetts.

MAY 29, 1918 Herb Shriner born in Toledo, Ohio.

JULY 27, 1918 Skitch Henderson born in Birmingham, England.

NOVEMBER 4, 1918 Art Carney born in Mount Vernon, New York.

NOVEMBER 7, 1918 Billy Graham born in Charlotte, North Carolina.

DECEMBER 31, 1918 Marie Wilson born in Anaheim, California.

JANUARY 13, 1919 Robert Stack born in Los Angeles, California.

JANUARY 14, 1919 Andy Rooney born in Albany, New York.

JANUARY 25, 1919 Edwin Newman born in New York City.

FEBRUARY 5, 1919 Red Buttons born in New York City.

FEBRUARY 12, 1919 Forrest

Tucker born in Plainfield, Indiana.

FEBRUARY 13, 1919 Tennessee Ernie Ford born in Bristol, Tennessee.

MARCH 17, 1919 Nat "King" Cole born in Montgomery, Alabama.

MAY 16, 1919 Liberace born in West Allis, Wisconsin.

MAY 20, 1919 George Gobel born in Chicago, Illinois.

JUNE 14, 1919 Dorothy McGuire born in Omaha, Nebraska.

OCTOBER 17, 1919 Radio Corporation of America (RCA) founded.

NOVEMBER 19, 1919 Alan Young born in North Shields, England.

JANUARY 20, 1920 DeForest Kelley born in Atlanta, Georgia.

FEBRUARY 18, 1920 Jack Palance born in Lattimer, Pennsylvania; Bill Cullen born in Pittsburgh, Pennsylvania.

FEBRUARY 26, 1920 Tony Randall born in Tulsa, Oklahoma.

MARCH 22, 1920 Werner Klemperer born in Cologne, Germany.

MARCH 25, 1920 Howard Cosell born in New York City.

JULY 10, 1920 David Brinkley born in Wilmington, North Carolina.

SEPTEMBER 27, 1920 William Conrad born in Louisville, Kentucky.

OCTOBER 27, 1920 Nanette Fabray born in San Diego, California.

NOVEMBER 25, 1920 Ricardo Montalban born in Mexico City, Mexico.

DECEMBER 19, 1920 David Susskind born in New York City.

JANUARY 27, 1921 Donna Reed born in Denison, Iowa.

FEBRUARY 14, 1921 Hugh Downs born in Akron, Ohio.

FEBRUARY 24, 1921 Abe Vigoda born in New York City.

APRIL 10, 1921 Chuck Connors born in Brooklyn, New York.

APRIL 18, 1921 Barbara Hale born in Dekalb, Illinois.

JUNE 14, 1921 Gene Barry born in New York City.

AUGUST 28, 1921 Nancy Kulp born in Harrisburg, Pennsylvania.

SEPTEMBER 15, 1921 Jackie Cooper born in Los Angeles, California.

OCTOBER 1, 1921 James Whitmore born in White Plains, New York.

NOVEMBER 14, 1921 Brian Keith born in Bayonne, New Jersey; Johnny Desmond born in Detroit, Michigan.

DECEMBER 26, 1921 Steve Allen born in New York City.

JANUARY 19, 1922 Guy Madison born in Bakersfield, California.

FEBRUARY 11, 1922 Leslie Nielsen born in Regina, Saskatchewan, Canada.

MARCH 20, 1922 Carl Reiner born in the Bronx, New York; Ray Goulding born in Lowell, Massachusetts.

MARCH 31, 1922 Richard Kiley born in Chicago, Illinois.

APRIL 5, 1922 Gale Storm born in Bloomington, Texas.

APRIL 27, 1922 Jack Klugman born in Philadelphia, Pennsylvania.

MAY 7, 1922 Darren McGavin born in San Joaquin, California.

MAY 10, 1922 Nancy Walker born in Philadelphia, Pennsylvania.

JULY 2, 1922 Dan Rowan born in Beggs, Oklahoma.

JULY 26, 1922 Jason Robards, Jr., born in Chicago; Blake Edwards born in Tulsa, Oklahoma.

JULY 27, 1922 Norman Lear born in New Haven, Connecticut.

AUGUST 1, 1922 Arthur Hill born in Melfort, Saskatchewan, Canada.

AUGUST 18, 1922 Shelley Winters born in Saint Louis, Missouri.

SEPTEMBER 1, 1922 Yvonne De Carlo born in Vancouver, British Columbia, Canada.

SEPTEMBER 8, 1922 Sid Caesar born in Yonkers, New York.

OCTOBER 31, 1922 Barbara Bel Geddes born in New York City.

DECEMBER 9, 1922 Redd Foxx born in Saint Louis, Missouri.

DECEMBER 21, 1922 Paul Winchell born in New York City.

JANUARY 8, 1923 Larry Storch born in New York City.

JANUARY 19, 1923 Jean Stapleton born in New York City.

JANUARY 30, 1923 Dick Martin born in Detroit, Michigan.

MARCH 6, 1923 Ed McMahon born in Detroit, Michigan.

MAY 13, 1923 Beatrice Arthur born in New York City.

MAY 26, 1923 James Arness born in Minneapolis, Minnesota.

JUNE 24, 1923 Jack Carter born in New York City.

NOVEMBER 30, 1923 Efrem Zimbalist, Jr., born in New York City.

DECEMBER 7, 1923 Ted Knight born in Terryville, Connecticut.

DECEMBER 12, 1923 Bob Barker born in Darrington, Washington.

DECEMBER 29, 1923 Dr. Vladimir K. Zworykin applies for a patent for the "Iconoscope," the all-electronic "eye" that is the granddaddy of modern image-orthicon TV-camera tubes, replacing earlier, mechanical methods of producing television images.

JANUARY 21, 1924 Telly Savalas born in Garden City, New York.

FEBRUARY 19, 1924 Lee Marvin born in New York City.

MARCH 24, 1924 Norman Fell born in Philadelphia, Pennsylvania.

APRIL 3, 1924 Doris Day born in Cincinnati, Ohio.

APRIL 16, 1924 Henry Mancini born in Cleveland, Ohio.

MAY 21, 1924 Peggy Cass born in Boston, Massachusetts.

JUNE 4, 1924 Dennis Weaver born in Toplin, Missouri.

JUNE 25, 1924 Sidney Lumet born in Philadelphia, Pennsylvania.

JULY 19, 1924 Pat Hingle born in Denver, Colorado.

JULY 21, 1924 Don Knotts born in Morgantown, West Virginia.

AUGUST 2, 1924 Carroll O'Connor born in New York City.

AUGUST 31, 1924 Buddy Hackett born in Brooklyn, New York.

OCTOBER 4, 1924 Charlton Heston born in Evanston, Illinois.

JANUARY 21, 1925 Benny Hill born in Southampton, England.

JANUARY 30, 1925 Dorothy Malone born in Chicago, Illinois.

FEBRUARY 8, 1925 Jack Lemmon born in Boston, Massachusetts.

FEBRUARY 17, 1925 Hal Holbrook born in Cleveland, Ohio.

FEBRUARY 18, 1925 George Kennedy born in New York City.

APRIL 14, 1925 Rod Steiger born in Westhampton, New York.

APRIL 19, 1925 Hugh O'Brian born in Rochester, New York.

JUNE 13, 1925 Charles Francis Jenkins oversees the first transmission of moving pictures using motion-picture film; the image of a miniature windmill in motion is sent from Anacostia, D.C., to Washington, D.C., a distance of five miles.

JUNE 25, 1925 June Lockhart born in New York City.

JULY 6, 1925 Merv Griffin born in San Mateo, California.

AUGUST 11, 1925 Mike Douglas born in Chicago, Illinois.

AUGUST 15, 1925 Rose Marie born in New York City; Mike Connors born in Fresno, California.

SEPTEMBER 4, 1925 Howard Morris born in New York City.

SEPTEMBER 28, 1925 Arnold Stang born in Chelsea, Massachusetts.

OCTOBER 16, 1925 Angela Lansbury born in London, England.

OCTOBER 23, 1925 Johnny Carson born in Corning, Iowa.

NOVEMBER 11, 1925 Jonathan Winters born in Dayton, Ohio.

NOVEMBER 17, 1925 Rock Hudson born in Winnetka, Illinois.

NOVEMBER 24, 1925 William F. Buckley, Jr., born in New York City.

DECEMBER 8, 1925 Sammy Davis, Jr., born in New York City.

DECEMBER 13, 1925 Dick Van Dyke born in West Plains, Missouri.

DECEMBER 23, 1925 Harry Guardino born in New York City.

1926 Congress legislates the Federal Radio Commission—later the Federal Communications Commission—into existence.

JANUARY 8, 1926 Soupy Sales born in Franklinton, North Carolina.

FEBRUARY 12, 1926 Joe Garagiola born in Saint Louis, Missouri.

MARCH 16, 1926 Jerry Lewis born in Newark, New Jersey.

MARCH 18, 1926 Peter Graves born in Minneapolis, Minnesota.

APRIL 4, 1926 Cloris Leachman born in Des Moines, Iowa.

APRIL 19, 1926 Don Adams born in New York City.

MAY 5, 1926 Ann B. Davis born in Schenectady, New York.

MAY 8, 1926 Don Rickles born in New York City.

JUNE 1, 1926 Andy Griffith born in Mount Airy, North Carolina.

JULY 10, 1926 Fred Gwynne born in New York City.

AUGUST 7, 1926 Stan Freberg born in Pasadena, California.

AUGUST 10, 1926 Junior Samples born in Cumming, Georgia.

AUGUST 14, 1926 Alice Ghostley born in Eve, Missouri.

AUGUST 18, 1926 A weather map is televised for the first time, sent from Arlington, Virginia, radio station NAA to the Weather Bureau Office in Washington, D.C.

SEPTEMBER 27, 1926 Jayne Meadows born in Wuchang, China.

OCTOBER 17, 1926 Beverly Garland born in Santa Cruz, California.

NOVEMBER 8, 1926 Joe Flynn born in Youngstown, Ohio.

NOVEMBER 15, 1926 The National Broadcasting Company is created.

NOVEMBER 28, 1926 Dorothy Collins born in Windsor, Ontario.

1927 Columbia Broadcasting System (CBS) goes on the air with a 16-station network.

JANUARY 10, 1927 Giselle MacKenzie born in Winnipeg, Manitoba.

JANUARY 27, 1927 The United Independent Broadcasters, Inc., was formed. It was soon to change its name to the Columbia Broadcasting System.

FEBRUARY 15, 1927 Harvey Korman born in Chicago, Illinois.

MARCH 31, 1927 William Daniels born in Brooklyn.

APRIL 7, 1927 TV images for the first time are sent over regular long-distance telephone lines between Washington, D.C., and New York City—the first intercity telecast. Secretary of Commerce Herbert Hoover spoke the first words into the telephone; the *New York Times* reported, "It was as if a photograph had suddenly come to life. . . ."

MAY 5, 1927 Pat Carroll born in Shreveport, Louisiana.

MAY 30, 1927 Clint Walker born in Hartford, Illinois.

JUNE 27, 1927 Bob Keeshan born in Lynbrook, New York.

JULY 4, 1927 Neil Simon born in the Bronx, New York.

JULY 7, 1927 Doc Severinsen born in Arlington, Oregon.

JULY 14, 1927 John Chancellor born in Chicago, Illinois.

SEPTEMBER 16, 1927 Peter Falk born in New York City.

OCTOBER 1, 1927 Tom Bosley born in Chicago, Illinois.

OCTOBER 17, 1927 Tom Poston born in Columbus, Ohio.

NOVEMBER 30, 1927 Richard Crenna born in Los Angeles, California.

DECEMBER 26, 1927 Alan King born in Brooklyn, New York.

DECEMBER 28, 1927 Martin Milner born in Detroit, Michigan.

1928 Baird dabbles with color and 3-D TV, and sends signals across the Atlantic.

JANUARY 13, 1928 The first American home gets a TV set, in Schenectady, New York. On May 11, its one-and-a-half-square-inch screen begins to receive transmissions three afternoons a week from the first U.S. television station with a regular schedule—General Electric's WGY.

FEBRUARY 8, 1928 John Logie Baird sends the first television image from London to Hartsdale, New York.

FEBRUARY 9, 1928 Roger Mudd born in Washington, D.C.

MARCH 19, 1928 Patrick McGoohan born in New York City.

APRIL 7, 1928 James Garner born in Norman, Oklahoma.

APRIL 23, 1928 Shirley Temple born in Santa Monica, California.

JUNE 1928 The first outdoor "location" television shots are taken by John Logie Baird.

JULY 2, 1928 Charles F. Jenkins begins broadcasting the

first regular telecasts designed to be received by the public, using a technique called "Radiovision," a neon-lamp-based system that used a radio station's signals to activate mechanical video equipment that had to be built by the listener/viewer using plans that could be obtained from Jenkins' laboratory.

JULY 7, 1928 Vince Edwards born in Brooklyn, New York.

JULY 22, 1928 Orson Bean born in Burlington, Vermont.

AUGUST 10, 1928 Jimmy Dean born in Plainview, Texas.

AUGUST 13, 1928 WRNY, Coytesville, New Jersey, becomes the first standard broadcast station to televise an image—the face of Mrs. John Geloso, one and a half inches square, blown up by a magnifying glass to three inches so it could be viewed by the 500 people assembled in New York University's Philosophy Hall.

AUGUST 21, 1928 The first newspaper listing of a TV program was in this day's *New York Times.*

AUGUST 22, 1928 The first "remote" television pickup: General Electric Company engineers televised Governor Alfred E. Smith accepting the Democratic nomination for President in the capital building, Albany, New York.

SEPTEMBER 11, 1928 *The Queen's Messenger,* a now forgotten stage melodrama, becomes the first play ever televised, over station WGY, Schenectady, New York.

OCTOBER 1, 1928 George Peppard born in Detroit, Michigan.

OCTOBER 25, 1928 Anthony Franciosa born in New York City.

DECEMBER 9, 1928 Dick Van Patten born in New York City.

APRIL 16, 1929 Edie Adams born in Kingston, Pennsylvania.

JUNE 2, 1929 Chuck Barris born in Philadelphia, Pennsylvania.

JUNE 22, 1929 Ralph Waite born in White Plains, New York.

JUNE 27, 1929 A bouquet of roses and an American flag are the first color pictures shown when Bell Telephone Laboratories in New York City gives the first public demonstration of a crude but working color-TV system.

AUGUST 13, 1929 Pat Harrington, Jr., born in New York City.

SEPTEMBER 5, 1929 Bob Newhart born in Oak Park, Illinois.

SEPTEMBER 27, 1929 Sada Thompson born in Des Moines, Iowa.

OCTOBER 17, 1929 Beverly Garland born in Santa Cruz, California.

NOVEMBER 1, 1929 Betsy Palmer born in East Chicago, Indiana.

NOVEMBER 14, 1929 McLean Stevenson born in Normal, Illinois.

NOVEMBER 15, 1929 Ed Asner born in Kansas City, Kansas.

NOVEMBER 18, 1929 Zworykin demonstrates the "Kinescope," an early picture tube whose face is the "screen"

of home television receivers. Images are produced by a stationary electron gun scanning a fluorescent surface.

NOVEMBER 30, 1929 Ageless Dick Clark is born in Mount Vernon, New York.

DECEMBER 9, 1929 John Cassavetes born in New York City.

JANUARY 3, 1930 Robert Loggia born in New York City.

FEBRUARY 10, 1930 Robert Wagner born in Detroit, Michigan.

MARCH 27, 1930 David Janssen born in Naponee, Nebraska.

MAY 22, 1930 An audience at Proctor's Theatre, Schenectady, New York, becomes the first to see closed-circuit TV projected onto a big screen.

MAY 31, 1930 Clint Eastwood born in San Francisco, California.

JULY 30, 1930 W2XBS, NBC's first TV station, goes into operation.

AUGUST 16, 1930 Robert Culp born in Berkeley, California.

AUGUST 28, 1930 Ben Gazzara born in New York City.

SEPTEMBER 16, 1930 Anne Francis born in Ossining, New York.

DECEMBER 3, 1930 Andy Williams born in Wall Lake, Iowa.

DECEMBER 30, 1930 Jack Lord born in New York City.

FEBRUARY 20, 1931 Amanda Blake born in Buffalo, New York.

MARCH 20, 1931 Hal Linden

born in New York City.

MARCH 22, 1931 William Shatner born in Montreal, Quebec.

MARCH 26, 1931 Leonard Nimoy born in Boston, Massachusetts.

JUNE 3, 1931 John Logie Baird uses television for live transmission from the English Derby.

JULY 8, 1931 Roone Arledge born in Forest Hills, New York.

JULY 21, 1931 W2XAB, CBS's first TV station, starts transmitting in New York, and CBS announces the first regular seven-day-a-week TV broadcasting schedule in America.

JULY 27, 1931 Jerry Van Dyke born in Danville, Illinois.

SEPTEMBER 21, 1931 Larry Hagman born in Fort Worth, Texas.

SEPTEMBER 25, 1931 Barbara Walters born in Boston, Massachusetts.

SEPTEMBER 30, 1931 Angie Dickinson born in Kulm, North Dakota.

OCTOBER 30, 1931 RCA and NBC put a TV transmitter atop the Empire State Building.

OCTOBER 31, 1931 Dan Rather born in Wharton, Texas.

NOVEMBER 8, 1931 Morley Safer born in Toronto, Ontario.

DECEMBER 11, 1931 Rita Moreno born in Humacao, Puerto Rico.

JANUARY 2, 1932 Dabney Coleman born in Austin, Texas.

JANUARY 22, 1932 Piper Laurie born in Detroit, Michigan.

MAY 5, 1932 Will Hutchins born in Los Angeles, California.

AUGUST 23, 1932 Mark Russell born in Buffalo, New York.

OCTOBER 19, 1932 Robert Reed born in Highland Park, Illinois.

NOVEMBER 13, 1932 Richard Mulligan born in New York City.

NOVEMBER 20, 1932 Richard Dawson born in Gosport, Hampshire, England.

NOVEMBER 22, 1932 Robert Vaughn born in New York City.

APRIL 15, 1933 Elizabeth Montgomery born in Hollywood; Roy Clark born in Meherrin, Virginia.

APRIL 26, 1933 Carol Burnett born in San Antonio, Texas.

APRIL 28, 1933 Carolyn Jones born in Amarillo, Texas.

MAY 23, 1933 Joan Collins born in London, England.

JUNE 8, 1933 Joan Rivers born in Brooklyn, New York.

JUNE 12, 1933 Jim Nabors born in Sylacauga, Alabama.

AUGUST 1, 1933 Dom DeLuise born in Brooklyn, New York.

SEPTEMBER 18, 1933 Robert Blake born in Nutley, New Jersey.

SEPTEMBER 19, 1933 David McCallum born in Glasgow, Scotland.

NOVEMBER 5, 1933 Herb Edelman born in Brooklyn, New York.

DECEMBER 8, 1933 Flip Wilson born in Jersey City, New Jersey.

DECEMBER 15, 1933 Tim Conway born in Chagrin Falls, Ohio.

JANUARY 17, 1934 Shari Lewis born in New York City.

JANUARY 20, 1934 Arte Johnson born in Benton Harbor, Michigan.

JANUARY 22, 1934 Bill Bixby born in San Francisco, California.

JANUARY 31, 1934 James Franciscus born in Clayton, Missouri.

FEBRUARY 14, 1934 Florence Henderson born in Dale, Indiana.

FEBRUARY 21, 1934 Rue McClanahan born in Healdton, Oklahoma.

MARCH 26, 1934 Alan Arkin born in New York City.

MARCH 31, 1934 Shirley Jones born in Smithton, Pennsylvania.

APRIL 5, 1934 Frank Gorshin born in Pittsburgh, Pennsylvania.

JUNE 5, 1934 Bill Moyers born in Hugo, Oklahoma.

JULY 1, 1934 Jean Marsh born in Stoke Newington, England; Jamie Farr born in Toledo, Ohio.

AUGUST 23, 1934 Barbara Eden born in Tucson, Arizona.

SEPTEMBER 10, 1934 Charles Kuralt born in Wilmington, North Carolina.

JANUARY 9, 1935 Bob Denver born in New Rochelle, New York.

JANUARY 25, 1935 Dean Jones born in Morgan City, Alabama.

FEBRUARY 16, 1935 Sonny Bono born in Detroit, Michigan.

MARCH 1, 1935 Robert Conrad born in Chicago, Illinois.

MARCH 15, 1935 Judd Hirsch born in the Bronx, New York.

MARCH 31, 1935 Richard Chamberlain born in Beverly Hills, California.

MAY 11, 1935 Doug McClure born in Glendale, California.

MAY 19, 1935 David Hartman born in Pawtucket, Rhode Island.

JULY 15, 1935 Ken Kercheval born in Wolcottville, Indiana.

JULY 17, 1935 Diahann Carroll born in the Bronx, New York.

AUGUST 16, 1935 Julie Newmar born in Los Angeles, California.

DECEMBER 21, 1935 Phil Donahue born in Cleveland, Ohio.

JANUARY 27, 1936 Troy Donahue born in New York City.

JANUARY 28, 1936 Alan Alda born in New York City.

FEBRUARY 11, 1936 Burt Reynolds born in Waycross, Georgia.

MARCH 5, 1936 Dean Stockwell born in Hollywood, California.

MARCH 20, 1936 Ted Bessell born in Flushing, New York.

APRIL 22, 1936 Glen Campbell born in Billstown, Arkansas.

MAY 12, 1936 Tom Snyder born in Milwaukee, Wisconsin.

JUNE 11, 1936 Chad Everett born in South Bend, Indiana.

JULY 24, 1936 Ruth Buzzi born in Westerly, Rhode Island.

SEPTEMBER 24, 1936 Jim Henson born in Greenville, Mississippi.

OCTOBER 24, 1936 David Nelson born in New York City.

NOVEMBER 19, 1936 Dick Cavett born in Gibbon, Nebraska.

DECEMBER 8, 1936 David Carradine born in Hollywood, California.

JANUARY 31, 1937 Suzanne Pleshette born in New York City.

FEBRUARY 2, 1937 Tom Smothers born in New York City.

MAY 1937 Gilbert Seldes writes a critical article, "Errors of Television," for the *Atlantic Monthly* before there is even any television to criticize, thus becoming the first TV critic. Three months later, CBS asked Seldes to start its TV-programming department.

MAY 12, 1937 George Carlin born in the Bronx, New York.

JULY 12, 1937 Bill Cosby born in Philadelphia, Pennsylvania.

SEPTEMBER 5, 1937 William Devane born in Albany, New York.

OCTOBER 15, 1937 Linda Lavin born in Portland, Maine.

NOVEMBER 4, 1937 Loretta Swit born in Passaic, New Jersey.

DECEMBER 8, 1937 James MacArthur born in Los Angeles, California.

DECEMBER 12, 1937 NBC and RCA send the first mobile-TV vans onto the streets of New York City.

DECEMBER 29, 1937 Mary Tyler Moore born in Brooklyn, New York.

FEBRUARY 24, 1938 James Farentino born in Brooklyn, New York.

MAY 22, 1938 Frank Converse born in Saint Louis, Missouri.

JULY 20, 1938 Diana Rigg born in Doncaster, England.

AUGUST 6, 1938 Peter Bonerz born in Portsmouth, New Hampshire.

AUGUST 8, 1938 Connie Stevens born in Brooklyn, New York.

OCTOBER 22, 1938 Derek Jacobi born in Leytonstone, England.

OCTOBER 28, 1938 RCA announces it will start selling TV sets to the public in April 1939.

NOVEMBER 15, 1938 NBC's mobile-TV van, assigned to televise activity at a Ward's Island, New York, swimming pool, spots and televises the first on-location, unscheduled news event: a fire at a nearby barracks.

NOVEMBER 21, 1938 Marlo Thomas born in Detroit, Michigan.

NOVEMBER 26, 1938 Rich Little born in Ottawa, Ontario.

FEBRUARY 6, 1939 Mike Farrell born in Saint Paul, Minnesota.

APRIL 7, 1939 David Frost born in Tenterden, England.

APRIL 9, 1939 Michael Learned born in Washington, D.C.

APRIL 30, 1939 RCA televises the opening of the New York World's Fair, carrying speeches by President Franklin D. Roosevelt, about the end of the Depression, and RCA President David Sarnoff, about the future of broadcasting.

MAY 17, 1939 NBC becomes the first network to televise a baseball game: Columbia versus Princeton, from Baker Field, New York City. Bill Stern called the game, which was won in 10 innings by Princeton, 2–1.

MAY 25, 1939 Dixie Carter born in McLemoresville, Tennessee.

MAY 26, 1939 Brent Musburger born in Portland, Oregon.

JUNE 1, 1939 The first televised American prizefight—Lou Nova versus Max Baer, from Yankee Stadium. Nova won in 11 rounds.

JUNE 20, 1939 An NBC production of the "Pirates of Penzance" becomes the first musical to be shown over regularly scheduled TV.

AUGUST 26, 1939 W2XBS televises the first major-league baseball game: Brooklyn Dodgers versus Cincinnati Reds, from Ebbets Field.

SEPTEMBER 1, 1939 Lily Tomlin born in Detroit.

SEPTEMBER 30, 1939 Fordham takes on Waynesburg (and wins, 34 to 7) at Randall's Island, New York City, in the first televised college football game, over station W2XBS.

OCTOBER 27, 1939 John

Cleese born in Weston super Mare, England.

OCTOBER 28, 1939 Jane Alexander born in Boston, Massachusetts.

NOVEMBER 20, 1939 Dick Smothers born in New York City.

FEBRUARY 1, 1940 NBC transmits the first official network-television broadcast, from New York City to station W2XBS, Schenectady, a distance of about 130 miles.

FEBRUARY 6, 1940 Tom Brokaw born in Webster, South Dakota.

FEBRUARY 8, 1940 Ted Koppel born in Lancashire, England.

FEBRUARY 25, 1940 The Rangers and Canadiens face off in the first televised hockey match, over station W2XBS, from Madison Square Garden. Rangers win, 6–2.

FEBRUARY 27, 1940 Howard Hesseman born in Lebanon, Oregon.

FEBRUARY 28, 1940 First televised basketball game: a doubleheader, Pittsburgh–Fordham and NYU–Georgetown, over station W2XBS from Madison Square Garden. Pitt won, 50–37; NYU took the nightcap, 50–27.

MARCH 2, 1940 First intercollegiate track meet is televised from Madison Square Garden.

MARCH 7, 1940 Daniel J. Travanti born in Kenosha, Wisconsin.

APRIL 23, 1940 Lee Majors born in Wyandotte, Michigan.

MAY 8, 1940 Eric "Ricky"

Nelson born in Teaneck, New Jersey.

JUNE 21, 1940 Mariette Hartley born in New York City.

JUNE 24-29, 1940 The Republican political convention in Philadelphia becomes the first to be televised; Wendell Willkie and Charles Linza McNary become the party presidential and vice-presidential candidates.

JULY 18, 1940 James Brolin born in Los Angeles, California.

AUGUST 19, 1940 Jill St. John born in Los Angeles, California.

AUGUST 22, 1940 Valerie Harper born in Suffern, New York.

AUGUST 29, 1940 Peter Goldmark, CBS chief engineer of television, announces his invention of a workable color-TV system.

SEPTEMBER 12, 1940 Linda Gray born in Santa Monica, California.

1941 TV sets sell at a rate of about 90 a month.

MARCH 12, 1941 Barbara Feldon born in Pittsburgh, Pennsylvania.

APRIL 20, 1941 Ryan O'Neal born in Los Angeles, California.

APRIL 28, 1941 Ann-Margret born in Valsjobyn, Sweden.

MAY 3, 1941 The FCC approves a 525-lines-of-definition, 30-pictures-per-second standard for black-and-white TV broadcast and reception.

JUNE 2, 1941 Stacy Keach born in Savannah, Georgia.

JUNE 22, 1941 Ed Bradley born in Philadelphia, Pennsylvania.

JULY 1, 1941 Commercial television service begins. NBC's WNBT becomes the first licensed commercial station to go on the air. CBS goes on the air at 2:30 P.M. with the first news telecast. The first TV commercial: a 10-second Bulova Watch Time announcement, superimposed over a test pattern at 2:29:10, at a cost to Bulova of $9.

AUGUST 7, 1941 WNBT televises a game of charades, the first audience-participation show.

DECEMBER 7, 1941 CBS televises news of the attack on Pearl Harbor.

DECEMBER 11, 1941 Donna Mills born in Chicago, Illinois.

DECEMBER 13, 1941 John Davidson born in Pittsburgh, Pennsylvania.

DECEMBER 16, 1941 Lesley Stahl born in Swampscott, Massachusetts.

DECEMBER 27, 1941 John Amos born in Newark, New Jersey.

JUNE 18, 1942 Roger Ebert born in Urbana, Illinois.

JUNE 24, 1942 Michele Lee born in Los Angeles, California.

OCTOBER 15, 1942 Penny Marshall born in New York City.

OCTOBER 22, 1942 Annette Funicello born in Utica, New York.

NOVEMBER 2, 1942 Stefanie Powers born in Hollywood, California.

NOVEMBER 18, 1942 Linda Evans born in Hartford, Connecticut.

MARCH 25, 1943 Paul Michael Glaser born in Cambridge, Massachusetts.

APRIL 23, 1943 Herve Villechaize born in Paris, France.

MAY 25, 1943 Leslie Uggams born in New York City.

MAY 31, 1943 Sharon Gless born in Los Angeles, California.

JULY 4, 1943 Geraldo Rivera born in New York City.

JULY 21, 1943 Edward Herrmann born in Washington, D.C.

OCTOBER 8, 1943 Chevy Chase born in New York City.

NOVEMBER 20, 1943 Veronica Hamel born in Philadelphia, Pennsylvania.

JANUARY 6, 1944 Bonnie Franklin born in Santa Monica, California.

JANUARY 19, 1944 Shelley Fabares born in Santa Monica, California.

MARCH 28, 1944 Ken Howard born in El Centro, California.

SEPTEMBER 14, 1944 Joey Heatherton born in Rockville Centre, New York.

SEPTEMBER 25, 1944 Michael Douglas born in New Brunswick, New Jersey.

NOVEMBER 17, 1944 Danny DeVito born in Neptune, New Jersey.

1945 Swiss inventor Hans E. Laube experiments with "Smellovision," in which a "smell pack" was stimulated by television waves to produce an odor appropriate to what was on the screen at the time.

JANUARY 29, 1945 Tom Selleck born in Detroit, Michigan.

FEBRUARY 9, 1945 Mia Farrow born in Los Angeles, California.

FEBRUARY 24, 1945 Barry Bostwick born in San Mateo, California.

MARCH 6, 1945 Rob Reiner born in the Bronx, New York.

MARCH 21, 1945 Nine commercial stations are in operation in the U.S.: three in New York City; two each in Chicago and Hollywood; one each in Philadelphia and Schenectady.

MARCH 31, 1945 Gabe Kaplan born in Brooklyn, New York.

MAY 24, 1945 Priscilla Presley born in Brooklyn, New York.

AUGUST 5, 1945 Loni Anderson born in Saint Paul, Minnesota.

OCTOBER 24–NOVEMBER 14, 1945 More than 25,000 people gawk at an RCA-Victor TV set in the first public demonstration of a television set in a department store, at Gimbel Brothers, Philadelphia.

OCTOBER 30, 1945 Henry Winkler born in New York City.

NOVEMBER 21, 1945 Goldie Hawn born in Washington, D.C.

DECEMBER 22, 1945 Diane Sawyer born in Glasgow, Kentucky.

JANUARY 19, 1946 Dolly Parton born in Sevierville, Tennessee.

FEBRUARY 20, 1946 Sandy Duncan born in Henderson, Texas.

MAY 9, 1946 Candice Bergen born in Beverly Hills, California;

Hour Glass, the first network hour-long musical-variety program, takes to the air over NBC, which at the time consists of three stations: New York City, Schenectady, and Philadelphia.

MAY 20, 1946 Cher born in El Centro, California.

JUNE 19, 1946 First televised heavyweight title fight (Joe Louis vs. Billy Conn, broadcast from Yankee Stadium) seen by largest TV audience ever to see a fight: 141,000. Louis KO'd Conn in the eighth. A year later, the Louis-Wolcott fight attracted a million viewers.

JUNE 28, 1946 Gilda Radner born in Detroit, Michigan.

AUGUST 14, 1946 Susan Saint James born in Los Angeles, California.

OCTOBER 2, 1946 *Faraway Hill* airs on the DuMont Network, becoming the first TV-network soap opera.

OCTOBER 16, 1946 Suzanne Somers born in San Bruno, California.

NOVEMBER 6, 1946 Sally Field born in Pasadena, California.

DECEMBER 14, 1946 Patty Duke born in New York City.

1947 Approximately 44,000 TV sets in America—and more than 40 million radios.

JANUARY 2, 1947 First broadcast of a joint session of Congress.

JANUARY 21, 1947 Jill Eikenberry born in New Haven, Connecticut.

FEBRUARY 2, 1947 Farrah Fawcett born in Corpus Christi, Texas.

FEBRUARY 20, 1947 Peter Strauss born in New York City.

FEBRUARY 21, 1947 Tyne Daly born in Madison, Wisconsin.

MARCH 1, 1947 Alan Thicke born in Kirland Lake, Ontario.

MARCH 14, 1947 Billy Crystal born in Long Beach, New York.

APRIL 12, 1947 David Letterman born in Indianapolis, Indiana.

MAY 7, 1947 *Kraft Television Theatre* becomes the first commercial-TV dramatic series, beginning its distinguished "golden age of television" run on NBC.

JUNE 21, 1947 Meredith Baxter born in Los Angeles, California; Michael Gross born in Chicago, Illinois.

AUGUST 19, 1947 Gerald McRaney born in Collins, Mississippi.

AUGUST 22, 1947 Cindy Williams born in Van Nuys, California.

AUGUST 30, 1947 Peggy Lipton born in Lawrence, New York.

SEPTEMBER 6, 1947 Jane Curtin born in Cambridge, Massachusetts.

SEPTEMBER 13, 1947 The idea of syndicating TV series takes form, as Eastman Kodak and NBC develop a film camera for shooting off the TV screen, permitting the recording and later distribution of live shows for sale or archiving. The films are called "kinescopes."

SEPTEMBER 30, 1947 First telecast of a World Series game, the subway series between the New York Yankees and the Brooklyn Dodgers. The game—sponsored by Gillette and Ford—was seen in New York City, Washington, D.C., Philadelphia, and Schenectady by an audience of around 4 million—3.5 million of them in taverns.

OCTOBER 5, 1947 Harry Truman becomes the first President to make a presidential address to the public on TV from the White House. He spoke about the international food crisis, proposing meatless Tuesdays.

OCTOBER 26, 1947 Jaclyn Smith born in Houston, Texas.

NOVEMBER 6, 1947 *Meet the Press* premieres as a local offering on NBC's Washington, D.C., station. On November 20, it went network.

DECEMBER 19, 1947 Robert Urich born in Toronto, Ontario.

DECEMBER 27, 1947 Say, kids, what time is it? Howdy Doody Time! For the first time, on NBC.

DECEMBER 29, 1947 Ted Danson born in San Diego, California.

1948 An estimated 600,000 TV sets in America, tuned in to 45 stations nationwide.

JANUARY 18, 1948 Ted Mack and *The Original Amateur Hour* begin a 22-year odyssey—it is on all four networks at various times—on the DuMont Network.

MARCH 31, 1948 Rhea Perlman born in Brooklyn.

JUNE 2, 1948 Jerry Mathers born in Sioux City, Iowa.

JUNE 20, 1948 Ladies and jenmin, the first "really big shew":

Ed Sullivan's *Toast of the Town* (changed on September 18, 1955, to *The Ed Sullivan Show*) debuts on CBS with guests Dean Martin and Jerry Lewis.

JULY 1948 Bob Howard's 15-minute show of piano playing and musical entertainment on CBS makes him the first black performer to be sponsored on TV.

JULY 28, 1948 Sally Struthers born in Portland, Oregon.

AUGUST 10, 1948 Smile, for the very first time, someone's on *Candid Camera*, Allen Funt's brazen brainchild, on ABC. Off and on, it found a regular niche on CBS from 1960 to 1967.

AUGUST 15, 1948 CBS inaugurates the first network nightly news broadcast, *CBS-TV News,* with Douglas Edwards as anchor, but is unable to attract any sponsors.

AUGUST 27, 1948 Whitaker Chambers, appearing on *Meet the Press,* accuses Alger Hiss of being a Communist. Hiss sues, and a landmark court case follows.

SEPTEMBER 1948 There are now 36 television stations broadcasting in 19 cities, able to reach one-third of the U.S. population.

SEPTEMBER 17, 1948 John Ritter born in Burbank, California.

SEPTEMBER 21, 1948 "Uncle Milty" takes America by storm: Milton Berle headlines the first *Texaco Star Theater,* and soon captures 92 percent of the viewing audience. Two years later, with more competition, he is still attracting 81 percent of all TV viewers.

SEPTEMBER 26, 1948 Bob

Hope makes his TV debut on Ed Sullivan's *Toast of the Town.*

SEPTEMBER 29, 1948 Bryant Gumbel born in New Orleans, Louisiana.

OCTOBER 17, 1948 George Wendt born in Chicago, Illinois.

OCTOBER 22, 1948 *Break the Bank,* with quizmaster Bert Parks, debuts on ABC.

OCTOBER 29, 1948 Kate Jackson born in Birmingham, Alabama.

NOVEMBER 7, 1948 *Studio One* premieres on CBS.

NOVEMBER 29, 1948 *Kukla, Fran and Ollie* premieres on NBC, after a local run under the title *Junior Jamboree* beginning October 13, 1947, on Chicago TV station WBKB.

DECEMBER 23, 1948 Susan Lucci born in Scarsdale, New York.

1949 An estimated 2,150,000 TV sets in America.

1949 The DuMont Club 20-inch TV set—"With the world's largest direct-view screen—213 square inches"—goes on sale for $995 plus installation.

JANUARY 10, 1949 *The Goldbergs,* starring Gertrude Berg, premieres on CBS.

JANUARY 11, 1949 An all-star cast headed by Milton Berle joins Chicago Mayor Myron Kennely (New York Mayor William O'Dwyer couldn't make it because of strike-arbitration talks with tugboat operators) in a gala two-hour presentation—carried on all networks—celebrating the linking of Eastern and Midwestern networks via coaxial cable. Since only one

channel can use the cable at a time, the networks jockey for the best time slots.

JANUARY 17, 1949 Andy Kaufman born in New York City.

JANUARY 24, 1949 John Belushi born in Chicago, Illinois.

FEBRUARY 1949 Bills are introduced in the New York state legislature to permit tenants in apartment buildings to put antennas on the buildings' roofs. In other states, laws are passed prohibiting the installation of TV sets in automobiles.

FEBRUARY 9, 1949 Judith Light born in Trenton, New Jersey.

MARCH 16, 1949 Erik Estrada born in New York City.

MARCH 17, 1949 Patrick Duffy born in Townsend, Montana.

MARCH 26, 1949 Vicki Lawrence born in Inglewood, California.

MAY 26, 1949 Philip Michael Thomas born in Columbus, Ohio.

APRIL 23, 1949 Joyce DeWitt born in Wheeling, West Virginia.

APRIL 27, 1949 TV's first "women's lib" show—*Leave It to the Girls*—premieres on NBC. A panel of women—led by Maggi McNellis and Eloise ("The Adam-Bomber") McElhone—verbally attack men in general, and the male guest—who is there to defend his gender—in particular.

APRIL 30, 1949 ABC announces it has made "the television development of the year": it has signed *The Lone Ranger* for 52 weekly half-hours, at a cost of $750,000—the largest single show expenditure in TV to date.

MAY 5, 1949 *Stop the Music,* hosted by Bert Parks, premieres on ABC; *Blind Date,* the direct ancestor of *The Dating Game, Love Connection,* and *Studs* among others, also premieres on ABC, hosted by "romance promoter" Arlene Francis.

JUNE 22, 1949 Lindsay Wagner born in Los Angeles; *The Quiz Kids* premieres on NBC.

JUNE 24, 1949 *Hopalong Cassidy,* starring William Boyd, premieres on NBC.

JUNE 27, 1949 Get out your decoder rings: *Captain Video,* starring Richard Coogan, debuts on the DuMont Network. The Captain uses his Scanning Device to keep track of his many agents working for peace around the world—and, suspiciously, they all look very much like cowboy stars in scenes from old Western movies DuMont owns the rights to.

JULY 1, 1949 *Mama,* starring Peggy Wood (who played the role on Broadway in *I Remember Mama*), premieres on CBS.

AUGUST 1949 More than 2 million TV sets around the country; approximately 720,000 of them in New York City alone.

AUGUST 23, 1949 Shelley Long born in Fort Wayne, Indiana.

AUGUST 25, 1949 RCA announces the development of a color-TV system that is compatible with current black-and-white TV sets and would not require owners to purchase adapters to enable their monochrome sets to receive shows televised in color.

SEPTEMBER 5, 1949 *Voice of Firestone* premieres on NBC.

SEPTEMBER 15, 1949 Hiyo, Silver, away: *The Lone Ranger* rides from radio onto ABC.

OCTOBER 6, 1949 *The Ed Wynn Show* becomes the first regularly scheduled network show to broadcast from the West Coast, where it is shown live; the East Coast sees it in kinescope form.

OCTOBER 10, 1949 *Kukla, Fran and Ollie* is broadcast in color over the NBC network—the first regularly scheduled show to be seen by both color and black-and-white sets.

OCTOBER 16, 1949 Perry Como makes his TV debut as host of *Supper Club*—the video version of his radio hit-show—on NBC.

DECEMBER 1949 The number-one household Christmas gift is a TV set—12½-inch screen the most popular size—as sales are 600 percent higher than the previous year and a four-month waiting list exists for some receivers.

DECEMBER 1949 Sales of Howdy Doody–related merchandise for 1949 top $11 million.

DECEMBER 15, 1949 Don Johnson born in Flatt Creek, Missouri.

JANUARY 16, 1950 Debbie Allen born in Houston, Texas.

FEBRUARY 2, 1950 *What's My Line?* begins its long run on CBS.

FEBRUARY 25, 1950 *Your Show of Shows,* starring Sid Caesar, Imogene Coca, Carl Reiner, and Howard Morris, premieres on NBC.

MARCH 23, 1950 *Beat the Clock,* hosted by Bud Collyer, premieres.

APRIL 1950 With a half-million sets sold in March, there are now 5,343,000 TV sets installed in the U.S., according to NBC. There are 103 TV stations in 60 markets.

APRIL 12, 1950 David Cassidy born in New York City.

APRIL 28, 1950 Jay Leno born in New Rochelle, New York.

MAY 1950 The city of Cleveland reports its trolley system is running a deficit of $140,677 instead of last year's surplus of $63,152. It blames TV, saying people are staying home more and not riding the trolleys.

MAY 12, 1950 Bruce Boxleitner born in Elgin, Illinois.

MAY 27, 1950 Frank Sinatra makes his TV debut as a guest on a Bob Hope special.

MAY 29, 1950 *Broadway Open House,* the first late-night talk-and-entertainment show, premieres. Jerry Lester (assisted by "dumb blonde" Dagmar) hosts Tuesdays, Thursdays, and Fridays; Morey Amsterdam is in charge Mondays and Wednesdays.

MAY 31, 1950 Gregory Harrison born in Avalon, Catalina Island, California.

JULY 20, 1950 *Arthur Murray Party Time* premieres on ABC.

JUNE 25, 1950 The Korean conflict ignites; as news footage is sent back to Stateside TV stations for airing on the new network-news shows, it becomes the first living-room war.

JUNE 27, 1950 Julia Duffy born in Minneapolis, Minnesota.

JULY 3, 1950 TV show. Two words. Four syllables. First syllable sounds like . . . : *Pantomime Quiz* begins more than a decade of mostly summer-replacement seasons, first on CBS.

JULY 10, 1950 *Your Hit Parade* premieres on NBC.

JULY 23, 1950 *The Gene Autry Show,* with Pat Buttram and Champion, premieres on CBS.

SEPTEMBER 1, 1950 There are now 7,535,000 TV sets in operation in the U.S., according to NBC; XH-TV, Mexico City, starts broadcasting as Mexico's first commercial-television station, but loses to upstart competitor XEW-TV the rights to *La Hora de Jaudi Dudi* (*Howdy Doody,* dubbed in Spanish).

SEPTEMBER 7, 1950 *Truth or Consequences* premieres on CBS.

SEPTEMBER 14, 1950 Don Ameche makes his TV debut, taking over the role of hotel manager from Edward Everett Horton on ABC's *Holiday Hotel.*

SEPTEMBER 21, 1950 Bill Murray born in Wilmette, Illinois.

OCTOBER 1, 1950 Approximately 8 million TV sets in American homes, tuned in to 107 TV stations; Randy Quaid born in Houston, Texas.

OCTOBER 5, 1950 Say the secret word: Groucho Marx hosts the TV premiere of his successful radio show, *You Bet Your Life,* on NBC.

OCTOBER 7, 1950 Frank Sinatra's debut in his own musical variety program, *The Frank Sinatra Show* on CBS, is a ratings flop, competing against *Your Show of Shows* and, later, Milton Berle on the *Texaco Star Theater.*

OCTOBER 12, 1950 *The George Burns and Gracie Allen Show* debuts on CBS as an every-other-week series.

OCTOBER 28, 1950 *The Jack Benny Show,* 45 minutes long, with guests Ken Murray and Dinah Shore, makes its debut on CBS as a now-and-again series of four specials, then once-monthly broadcasts, then twice-monthly, and finally, starting on October 16, 1960, becoming a weekly series.

OCTOBER 31, 1950 Jane Pauley born in Indianapolis, Indiana; John Candy born in Toronto, Ontario.

DECEMBER 4, 1950 *The First Hundred Years,* TV's first major daytime serial, debuts on CBS.

JANUARY 1, 1951 Zenith begins a 90-day test of Phonevision in Chicago. Three hundred selected TV families will be able to see relatively new feature films by dialing a special number on telephone circuits attached to their TV sets. The sets will then be able to receive an exclusive channel showing the movie for $1; viewers without attachments will only see a scrambled signal. However, major film companies balk at allowing Zenith the rights to first-run films, fearful that Phonevision will destroy movie theaters.

JANUARY 15, 1951 Charo born in Murcia, Spain.

JANUARY 29, 1951 Ann Jillian born in Cambridge, Massachusetts.

FEBRUARY 1951 The DuMont Network establishes the first international TV hookup, supplying Union Radio-Television of Havana with programming, mostly wrestling and boxing matches.

MARCH 3, 1951 *Watch Mr. Wizard* premieres on NBC.

MAY 3, 1951 NBC gives Milton Berle an unprecedented 30-year, $100,000-per-year exclusive contract with the network, requiring that he provide 360 one-hour programs to the network's schedule over the three decades. Berle provides them by June 1956.

JUNE 1951 RCA unveils the first community TV antenna, in Pottsville, Pennsylvania, permitting homes in areas with poor reception to plug into (for a fee) one large, powerful antenna designed to service the entire community. Cost: $135 down payment, $3.75 per month.

JUNE 13, 1951 Richard Thomas born in New York City.

JUNE 17, 1951 Joe Piscopo born in Passaic, New Jersey.

JUNE 28, 1951 *Amos 'n' Andy* premieres on CBS.

JULY 12, 1951 Cheryl Ladd born in Huron, South Dakota.

JULY 14, 1951 There are now close to 13 million TV sets in use in the U.S., and 30 percent of all American homes have at least one television set, according to NBC.

JULY 21, 1951 The National Association for the Advancement of Colored People protests the TV version of *Amos 'n' Andy,* calling it "a gross libel on the Negro and distortion of the truth."

JULY 24, 1951 Lynda Carter born in Phoenix, Arizona.

SEPTEMBER 3, 1951 The plight of the Barron family begins as *Search for Tomorrow* premieres on CBS.

SEPTEMBER 4, 1951 In the first coast-to-coast television program in history (previous transcoastal telecasts involved use of film at one end), President Harry S. Truman

The cast of Amos 'n' Andy.

addresses the opening of the Japanese Peace Treaty Conference in San Francisco. One hundred and seven steel-and-concrete towers spaced 28 miles apart between New York and San Francisco pass the signal via microwave relays. Trendex estimates 14,670,000 viewers are watching.

SEPTEMBER 7, 1951 Julie Kavner born in Los Angeles, California.

SEPTEMBER 9, 1951 Tom Wopat born in Lodi, Wisconsin.

SEPTEMBER 24, 1951 *Love of Life* premieres on CBS.

OCTOBER 15, 1951 Babaloo! *I Love Lucy* premieres on CBS.

OCTOBER 18, 1951 Pam Dawber born in Farmington Hills, Michigan.

OCTOBER 30, 1951 Harry Hamlin born in Pasadena, California.

NOVEMBER 18, 1951 *See It Now* with Edward R. Murrow, a TV version of radio's *Hear It Now,* premieres on CBS, showing live shots of the Statue of Liberty and San Francisco Bay. Says Murrow: "We are impressed by a medium through which a man sitting in his living room has been able for the first time to look at two oceans at once."

DECEMBER 16, 1951 *Dragnet* premieres on NBC.

DECEMBER 24, 1951 *Amahl and the Night Visitors* by Gian Carlo Menotti, the first opera written expressly for TV, premieres on NBC.

DECEMBER 30, 1951 Happy trails on NBC: *The Roy Rogers Show* premieres.

JANUARY 8, 1952 *My Friend Irma,* starring Marie Wilson, premieres on CBS.

JANUARY 14, 1952 *Today* debuts in a 22-by-60-foot studio—"the nerve center of the planet"—built in the RCA Exhibition Hall in Rockefeller Center, with glass walls allowing pedestrians on 49th Street to look in.

FEBRUARY 12, 1952 *Life Is Worth Living,* with Bishop Fulton J. Sheen, debuts on the Dumont Network.

MARCH 14, 1952 Jerry Lewis does his first telethon. He and partner Dean Martin go 18 hours on New York station WNBT and raise $1,148,419.25 for construction of the New York Cardiac Hospital.

APRIL 6, 1952 Marilu Henner born in Chicago.

APRIL 7, 1952 This evening's *I Love Lucy* episode is the first TV show to have been seen in 10 million U.S. homes—10.6 million to be more exact, according to the American Research Bureau.

APRIL 14, 1952 The Federal Communications Commission issues its "Sixth Report and Order," in which it set up the ultra-high frequency (UHF) band of channels 14 through 83, and sets aside certain stations for educational TV.

MAY 16, 1952 Pierce Brosnan born in County Meath, Ireland.

JUNE 16, 1952 *My Little Margie* premieres on CBS as a summer replacement for *I Love Lucy.*

JUNE 19, 1952 *I've Got a Secret* premieres on CBS.

SUMMER 1952 Don Hewitt coins the term "anchorman" for the main news person on-air, using the term applied to the strongest, fastest runner in a relay race, who gets the baton passed to him last.

JULY 1, 1952 Dan Aykroyd born in Ottawa, Ontario.

JULY 3, 1952 *Mr. Peepers* premieres on NBC.

JULY 14, 1952 *Masquerade Party* premieres on NBC. It would later move to CBS, then

ABC, and, in 1960, back to NBC.

JULY 17, 1952 David Hasselhoff born in Baltimore, Maryland.

JULY 21, 1952 Robin Williams born in Chicago, Illinois.

SEPTEMBER 6, 1952 Canadian Broadcasting Company telecasts begin in Montreal and, two days later, in Toronto.

SEPTEMBER 9, 1952 Angela Cartwright born in Cheshire, England.

SEPTEMBER 20, 1952 *The Jackie Gleason Show* premieres on CBS.

SEPTEMBER 23, 1952 Richard Nixon pleads to the nation in the famous "Checkers" speech.

OCTOBER 1, 1952 *This Is Your Life* begins its nearly nine-year life on NBC.

OCTOBER 3, 1952 Two popular radio shows move to TV: *The Adventures of Ozzie and Harriet* premieres on ABC, and *Our Miss Brooks*, starring Eve Arden, premieres on CBS.

OCTOBER 5, 1952 "Good evening, Mr. and Mrs. North and South America and all the ships at sea, let's go to press": *The Walter Winchell Show* premieres on ABC.

OCTOBER 7, 1952 *Death Valley Days* premieres.

OCTOBER 15, 1952 *I Married Joan,* starring Joan Davis and Jim Backus, premieres on NBC.

OCTOBER 20, 1952 Melanie Mayron born in Philadelphia, Pennsylvania.

OCTOBER 26, 1952 *Victory at Sea,* the first network-produced documentary on recent history, debuts on NBC with an original score by Richard Rodgers.

NOVEMBER 1952 RCA demonstrates an experimental TV set that uses transistors instead of vacuum tubes.

NOVEMBER 3, 1952 Roseanne Barr born in Salt Lake City, Utah.

NOVEMBER 4, 1952 CBS and NBC TV coverage of the presidential election becomes a battle of the computers: CBS uses the Univac, an all-electronic, high-speed Remington Rand computer, while NBC uses a computer called Mike Monrobot, made by the Monroe Calculating Machine Co.

NOVEMBER 9, 1952 *Omnibus,* the 90-minute, no-commercials cultural program presented by the Ford Foundation and hosted by Alistair Cooke, debuts on CBS with William Saroyan narrating one of his one-act plays and Rex Harrison and Lilli Palmer starring in *The Trial of Anne Boleyn* by Maxwell Anderson; Lou Ferrigno born in Brooklyn, New York.

DECEMBER 5, 1952 Abbott and Costello's new half-hour filmed comedy series debuts on CBS.

DECEMBER 10, 1952 Susan Dey born in Pekin, Illinois.

JANUARY 19, 1953 Both fictional "Little Ricky" Ricardo and factual Desiderio Alberto Arnaz IV are born to Lucy Ricardo/Lucille Ball.

JANUARY 20, 1953 Dwight Eisenhower's first presidential inauguration is also the first to be broadcast live coast-to-coast.

FEBRUARY 1, 1953 *General Electric Theater* premieres on CBS; Ronald Reagan becomes its host the next season.

FEBRUARY 8, 1953 Walt Disney makes his TV debut, on *The Ed Sullivan Show* on CBS, appearing with a group of his artists and reconstructing Disney's invention of "The Big Bad Wolf."

FEBRUARY 12, 1953 Joanna Kerns born in San Francisco.

APRIL 3, 1953 *TV Guide* premiere issue published, with 10 editions and a circulation of 1,562,000 copies.

MAY 24, 1953 Paddy Chayefsky's "Marty," starring Rod Steiger, airs as an episode of *Goodyear TV Playhouse.*

MAY 25, 1953 The first educational-TV station, KUHT-TV, Houston, begins telecasting from 5:00 to 9:00 P.M. daily.

JUNE 2, 1953 American TV-news operations, in one of the first big efforts to "scoop" each other, jockey to telecast the first films of Queen Elizabeth II's coronation. The networks rent airplanes and equip them with photo labs to develop the film on the flight from England to the U.S. According to Nielsen, 18,744,000 sets tune in.

JUNE 29, 1953 *Name That Tune* premieres on NBC.

AUGUST 1953 According to a survey taken by the Admiral Corporation, there are more television sets in the Cleveland-Akron-Canton, Ohio, area than there are telephones or bathtubs.

SEPTEMBER 1, 1953 There are now 25,233,000 TV sets in the U.S., according to NBC. That means that 55 percent of all U.S.

homes have a television receiver.

SEPTEMBER 6, 1953 Walter Winchell goes on the air to hint that "a top television actress" will soon be confronted with her Communist Party affiliation, starting a flurry of rumor-mongering and Red Peril panic. A week later, Winchell gives that "actress"—Lucille Ball, who had registered to vote for the Communist Party in the 1936 election—a clean bill of political health.

SEPTEMBER 18, 1953 *TV Guide*'s first Fall Preview Issue is published, in part to boost sagging circulation caused by a hot summer, few homes with air conditioning, and people staying outdoors instead of watching TV.

SEPTEMBER 20, 1953 *The Loretta Young Show* (first called *A Letter to Loretta*) sweeps onto the NBC Sunday-night schedule.

SEPTEMBER 29, 1953 *Make Room for Daddy* (later *The Danny Thomas Show*) premieres.

OCTOBER 2, 1953 *Person to Person* premieres on CBS.

OCTOBER 19, 1953 The TV-viewing nation is stunned when Arthur Godfrey, accusing popular singer and Godfrey regular Julius La Rosa of having "a lack of humility," fires him on the air.

NOVEMBER 20, 1953 For the first time in months, *I Love Lucy* slips from the top spot in the ratings, falling to second, behind *Dragnet*. The new popularity of the *Dragnet* theme is considered responsible.

NOVEMBER 22, 1953 RCA tests its new compatible color system on the air for the first

time with a telecast of the *Colgate Comedy Hour*.

JANUARY 3, 1954 Bing Crosby hosts his own show for the first time, rating third behind *I Love Lucy* and *Arthur Godfrey's Talent Scouts*. He beats out *Dragnet*.

JANUARY 4, 1954 *The Pinky Lee Show* premieres.

JANUARY 10, 1954 *The Mask* premieres on ABC, becoming the first hour-long mystery/detective series with a continuing cast of characters.

JANUARY 29, 1954 Oprah Winfrey born in Kosciusko, Mississippi.

FEBRUARY 18, 1954 John Travolta born in Englewood, New Jersey.

FEBRUARY 21, 1954 Señor Wences makes his first appearance on Ed Sullivan's *Toast of the Town*.

MARCH 1954 There are 370 TV stations on the air, with another 202 licensed and ready to get the go-ahead.

MARCH 1954 The first commercial in color is produced for Pall Mall cigarettes, to be shown on the first Pall Mall–sponsored show to be color-cast; a black-and-white version is also made and shown immediately.

MARCH 1, 1954 Ron Howard born in Duncan, Oklahoma.

MARCH 9, 1954 Edward R. Murrow on *See It Now* narrates a 30-minute program denouncing the Communist witch-hunt tactics of Senator Joseph R. McCarthy of Wisconsin. Though McCarthy is given a half-hour rebuttal, the Murrow

show contributes significantly to McCarthy's decline and fall, and is considered one of the great, courageous moments of TV journalism.

APRIL 1954 The nation is transfixed—and glued to TV sets anywhere—as, starting this month and continuing on into June, TV shows the army-McCarthy hearings.

APRIL 1, 1954 An H-bomb explosion is televised for the first time.

JUNE 15, 1954 Jim Belushi born in Chicago, Illinois.

JULY 17, 1954 *TV Guide* goes from listing TV shows Friday through Thursday to listing them Saturday through Friday.

AUGUST 7, 1954 The British Empire Games, from Canada, becomes the first international sports TV broadcast.

AUGUST 26, 1954 *Lux Video Theatre* becomes the first regular hour-long dramatic show to originate from Hollywood; its new tack is to redo successful old movies within those 60 minutes: Dorothy McGuire plays the Olivia De Havilland role in "To Each His Own" in the opener.

SEPTEMBER 11, 1954 Miss America Pageant televised nationally for the first time, on ABC, with John Daly emceeing.

SEPTEMBER 12, 1954 *Lassie* premieres on CBS.

SEPTEMBER 19, 1954 *People Are Funny,* hosted by Art Linkletter, premieres on NBC.

SEPTEMBER 20, 1954 *Studio One* presents what will come to be considered a masterwork of television's Golden Age: Reginald Rose's "Twelve Angry Men."

SEPTEMBER 27, 1954 The Steve Allen–hosted *Tonight Show* premieres; two years later, Ernie Kovacs becomes host two nights a week.

OCTOBER 3, 1954 *Father Knows Best,* starring Robert Young and Jane Wyatt, premieres on CBS.

OCTOBER 4, 1954 *December Bride,* starring Spring Byington and Harry Morgan, premieres on CBS.

OCTOBER 15, 1954 *The Adventures of Rin Tin Tin* premieres on ABC.

OCTOBER 27, 1954 *Disneyland,* the first of the several Walt Disney TV-show titles and configurations through the years, premieres on ABC, and soon beats *Arthur Godfrey and His Friends* in the ratings, knocking it out of the top 10.

NOVEMBER 7, 1954 *Face the Nation* debuts on CBS.

DECEMBER 15, 1954 "Davy Crockett, Indian Fighter," first of three parts of a *Disneyland* series starring Fess Parker in the title role, airs and starts a coonskin craze.

JANUARY 2, 1955 *The Bob Cummings Show* develops into a series on NBC.

JANUARY 12, 1955 *Kraft TV Theatre* presents an original hour-long TV drama about big business, "Patterns," thus launching the successful writing career of its author, Rod Serling; Kirstie Alley born in Wichita, Kansas.

JANUARY 19, 1955 President Eisenhower conducts the first televised (though filmed) presidential news conference; later, Michael Anthony gets the first check from John Beresford Tipton and goes in search of *The Millionaire.*

MARCH 7, 1955 Mary Martin stars on NBC in the TV production of *Peter Pan;* for the first time, a hit play forgoes the customary road tour after its Broadway run in favor of a one-time TV production. (Martin performs it again live on January 9, 1956.)

JUNE 7, 1955 CBS debuts *The $64,000 Question,* hosted by Hal March, which becomes one of the most-watched, fastest-growing (and cheapest to produce) cult hits of early television.

JULY 2, 1955 An' a one, an' a two: *The Lawrence Welk Show,* a longtime top-rated Los Angeles show, bubbles onto the ABC-network schedule.

JULY 4, 1955 *The Soupy Sales Show,* replacing *Kukla, Fran and Ollie* for the summer, premieres on ABC as a Monday-through-Friday early-evening network show from Detroit.

SEPTEMBER 6, 1955 ". . . and long may his story be told": *The Life and Legend of Wyatt Earp* premieres on ABC.

SEPTEMBER 10, 1955 *Gunsmoke,* which *TV Guide* describes as "a western *Dragnet*"—begins its 20-year occupation of Dodge City and the Longbranch Saloon, on CBS. A special filmed insert has John Wayne introduce James Arness to the public as the show's lead.

SEPTEMBER 20, 1955 Atten-hut! *The Phil Silvers Show* ("You'll Never Get Rich"), known familiarly as just plain "Bilko," begins its run on CBS; *Cheyenne,* starring Clint Walker, premieres on ABC.

OCTOBER 1, 1955 "Baby, you're the greatest." *The Honeymooners,* previously a segment of Jackie Gleason's variety show, premieres on CBS in its new half-hour film version.

OCTOBER 2, 1955 Good evening! *Alfred Hitchcock Presents* premieres on CBS.

OCTOBER 3, 1955 A great day for children's TV: *The Mickey*

Shooting an intro for The Alfred Hitchcock Hour, *1964.*

Mouse Club on ABC debuts, and so does *Captain Kangaroo* on CBS.

DECEMBER 24, 1955 The Lennon Sisters make their first appearance on *The Lawrence Welk Show.*

FEBRUARY 10, 1956 *My Friend Flicka* premieres on CBS.

MARCH 13, 1956 Edward R. Murrow and the *See It Now* crew go to the Middle East for a special 90-minute examination of the Arab-Israeli conflict.

APRIL 2, 1956 *The Edge of Night* and *As the World Turns,* both CBS daytime serials, go on the air.

APRIL 18, 1956 Grace Kelly marries Prince Rainier of Monaco in a civil ceremony at the royal palace, then next day in a religious ceremony in the cathedral, as TV cameras roll and send the images back to the United States on film, since there is no live television relay link between the U.S. and Europe.

JUNE 1, 1956 Lisa Hartman born in Houston, Texas.

JUNE 24, 1956 *The Steve Allen Show* becomes Ed Sullivan's competition on NBC.

JULY 9, 1956 Dick Clark becomes the host of *Bandstand,* then a local Philadelphia afternoon dance show. It went national over ABC on August 5, 1957, and on prime time on October 7, 1957.

JULY 25, 1956 Dean Martin and Jerry Lewis break up as a comedy team, exactly ten years from the day they formed their act in Atlantic City.

JULY 30, 1956 Delta Burke born in Orlando, Florida.

AUGUST 13, 1956 Televised coverage by all three networks of the Democratic national convention, in Chicago, involves the tiniest TV cameras yet devised: CBS's 5-inch, 1½-pounders that fit into vest pockets; NBC's "creepie-peepies" (portable one-man cameras with their own power packs) and "hidden ears" (wristwatch microphones attached to hip-pocket recorders).

SEPTEMBER 9, 1956 Elvis Presley's appearance on *The Ed Sullivan Show* gives it the highest rating in the show's eight-year history: a 43.7, translating into 60,710,000 people watching—the highest ever scored by a regularly scheduled show.

SEPTEMBER 12, 1956 *Twenty-One,* a game show hosted by Jack Barry, premieres on NBC. Two years later, on October 18, 1958, it is taken off the air after its producers acknowledge many of the shows were rigged, with some contestants receiving answers ahead of time.

OCTOBER 4, 1956 The first *Playhouse 90* airs on CBS.

OCTOBER 11, 1956 Rod Serling's "Requiem for a Heavyweight," soon to be considered among the greatest of golden age dramas, is presented on CBS's *Playhouse 90.* Ed Wynn, in his first dramatic role, and son, Keenan Wynn, appear together professionally for the first time.

NOVEMBER 5, 1956 *The Nat "King" Cole Show* premieres on NBC, making Cole the first black man to top a network variety show.

NOVEMBER 30, 1956 The kinescope is dead: CBS becomes the first commercial network to use videotape in a broadcast.

DECEMBER 18, 1956 Will the real *To Tell the Truth* please stand up and premiere on CBS.

JANUARY 1957 There are now more than 40 million TV sets in the U.S., and 467 TV stations. By comparison, Britain has 6,139,773 TV sets; France, 393,550; West Germany, 538,857; Italy, 301,728; and Turkey, 1,000.

FEBRUARY 16, 1957 LeVar Burton born in Landsthul, West Germany.

FEBRUARY 18, 1957 Vanna White born in Conway, South Carolina.

MARCH 11, 1957 NBC begins a TV experiment in teaching and learning—feeding five half-hour series of educational programs at 6:30 A.M. Mondays to Fridays to 18 noncommercial educational stations and to NBC stations and affiliates in cities without educational stations.

JUNE 1957 41,000,000 homes have TV sets and 39,000,000 homes are getting daily newspapers; TV becomes a major source of news for the American public.

JULY 29, 1957 *The Jack Paar Show* becomes the latest *Tonight Show* incarnation on NBC.

SEPTEMBER 14, 1957 *Have Gun, Will Travel* premieres on CBS.

SEPTEMBER 15, 1957 *Bachelor Father* premieres on CBS.

SEPTEMBER 18, 1957 *Wagon*

Train begins its trek across the West on NBC; Jon Provost, playing Timmy, debuts as Lassie's new friend, a replacement for aging Tommy Rettig.

SEPTEMBER 21, 1957 *Perry Mason* premieres on CBS.

SEPTEMBER 22, 1957 *Maverick* deals itself onto ABC's Sunday schedule.

OCTOBER 3, 1957 *The Real McCoys* premieres on ABC.

OCTOBER 4, 1957 *Leave It to Beaver* premieres on CBS; the Soviet Union launches *Sputnik I,* the first man-made satellite, sending sponsors and TV producers scurrying for science-fiction projects.

OCTOBER 5, 1957 *Gumby* canceled by NBC. He and Pokey ride into the sunset.

Barbara Hale (Della Street) of Perry Mason.

OCTOBER 10, 1957 *Zorro* premieres on ABC.

DECEMBER 9, 1957 Donny Osmond born in Ogden, Utah.

JANUARY 1958 Movie attendance is at 30 million admissions a week, down from a one-time peak of 90 million. TV, which now reaches 41.2 million homes, is blamed.

JANUARY 18, 1958 Leonard Bernstein conducts the first of his *Young People's Concerts* on CBS.

JANUARY 20, 1958 Lorenzo Lamas born in Los Angeles, California.

APRIL 1, 1958 After nearly three years on the air, Hugh O'Brian as Wyatt Earp kills his first man. The real Earp apparently killed only four in his career.

JUNE 1958 Trigger retires at age 25. Trigger, Jr., steps in.

JULY 9, 1958 Jimmy Smits born in New York City.

SEPTEMBER 6, 1958 *Wanted—Dead or Alive,* starring Steve McQueen, debuts on CBS.

SEPTEMBER 22, 1958 *Peter Gunn* premieres on NBC; on CBS, David Susskind produces a special TV version of Mary Chase's *Harvey,* starring Art Carney.

SEPTEMBER 23, 1958 Clint Walker—who has been on strike at Warner Brothers for higher residuals, more time off, the right to make personal appearances without giving Warner's half the money, and the OK to make records on labels of his own choice—is replaced on *Cheyenne* by Ty Hardin in the role of Bronco Layne.

SEPTEMBER 24, 1958 *The Donna Reed Show* debuts on ABC.

SEPTEMBER 25, 1958 CBS's *Playhouse 90* presents a play called "The Plot to Kill Stalin."

CBS News is subsequently barred from the U.S.S.R.

SEPTEMBER 27, 1958 Shaun Cassidy born in Los Angeles, California.

SEPTEMBER 30, 1958 Carol Burnett, John Byner, Jackie Vernon, and Dorothy Loudon become household names during the run of *The Garry Moore Show,* which premieres this night on CBS. On ABC, a five-year run of trying to tell as many of the 8 million stories as possible begins for *Naked City;* and *The Rifleman* premieres on ABC.

OCTOBER 8, 1958 *Bat Masterson,* starring Gene Barry, debuts on NBC.

OCTOBER 17, 1958 *An Evening with Fred Astaire,* the first TV special for the fifty-nine-year-old dancer, airs on NBC. It will later win nine Emmys, among them Outstanding Single Program of the season.

NOVEMBER 22, 1958 Jamie Lee Curtis born in Los Angeles, California.

JANUARY 4, 1959 Host Allen Ludden launches the first toss-up as *The G.E. College Bowl* takes to the air on CBS.

JANUARY 9, 1959 "Head 'em up, move 'em on": *Rawhide* begins its seven-year cattle drive on CBS.

FEBRUARY 1959 There are now an estimated 50,000,000 TV sets in 42,400,000 homes in the U.S. (67 percent of the world's total) tuned in to 463 VHF and 84 UHF stations.

MAY 16, 1959 Mare Winningham born in Phoenix, Arizona.

JULY 25, 1959 Nikita Khrushchev verbally attacks visiting U.S. Vice-President Richard Nixon, who forcefully replies, in a Cold War impromptu debate at the American Color Television Exhibition in Moscow—and the American public sees it that same day on TV: a videotape of the so-called "kitchen debate," smuggled out of Russia, is flown back to the U.S. in time for the news.

AUGUST 1959 NBC announces that *Today* will stop broadcasting live from 7:00 to 9:00 A.M. (ET), and will instead be videotaped the previous afternoon for airing in the morning, with only Frank Blair live in the studio to do news.

SEPTEMBER 12, 1959 *Bonanza,* the first Western to be broadcast in color, premieres on NBC.

SEPTEMBER 29, 1959 *Rocky and His Friends,* costarring Bullwinkle J. Moose, premieres on ABC; *The Many Loves of Dobie Gillis* premieres on CBS.

OCTOBER 2, 1959 Next stop: *The Twilight Zone* premieres on CBS; Charles Collingwood replaces Edward R. Murrow on CBS's *Person to Person,* does taped segments, and actually goes to the homes of those interviewed.

OCTOBER 13, 1959 Marie Osmond born in Ogden, Utah.

OCTOBER 15, 1959 *The Untouchables* premieres on ABC.

OCTOBER 27, 1959 *CBS Reports* premieres.

OCTOBER 30, 1959 Sir Laurence Olivier (in his first dramatic appearance in an American television production), Judith Anderson, Hume Cronyn,

Hair-bleaching for Dobie Gillis's *Dwayne Hickman.*

Jessica Tandy, Denholm Elliott and Jean Marsh star in W. Somerset Maugham's "The Moon and Sixpence" on NBC.

DECEMBER 1959 For the first time, annual TV commercial time sales ($1,240,000,000) exceed motion picture box-office receipts ($1,235,000,000) for the past twelve months.

JANUARY 1, 1960 A blimp is used for the first time on TV by CBS, to capture aerial shots of the Orange Bowl Regatta in Miami.

FEBRUARY 1960 CBS becomes the first network to insist that all of its owned stations present frequent editorials in order to "serve the public interest by stimulating thinking and decision-making about important public issues."

APRIL 23, 1960 Valerie Bertinelli born in Wilmington, Delaware.

MAY 4, 1960 Lucille Ball and Desi Arnaz are divorced.

MAY 12, 1960 Two heart-throb musical idols of succeeding generations meet: Elvis (the Pelvis) Presley is greeted on his return from military service by Frank (the Voice) Sinatra on the latter's TV show.

MAY 24, 1960 Mitch Miller, as a one-time fill-in on the *Ford Startime* series, puts on a show introducing his *Sing Along* format. It is an instant sensation, and soon NBC finds a spot on its regular lineup for it.

SEPTEMBER 24, 1960 *The Howdy Doody Show* goes off the air after 13 years and 2,343 shows.

SEPTEMBER 26, 1960 Presidential candidates John F. Kennedy and Richard M. Nixon meet for what is scheduled to be the first of several televised *Great Debates.*

SEPTEMBER 29, 1960 *My Three Sons* begins its 12-year run, premiering on ABC, then moving to CBS in 1965.

SEPTEMBER 30, 1960 *The Flintstones,* the first all-new cartoon series ever scheduled on the networks in prime time, premieres on ABC.

OCTOBER 3, 1960 *The Andy Griffith Show* premieres on CBS.

OCTOBER 7, 1960 *Route 66* premieres on CBS.

NOVEMBER 25, 1960 Edward R. Murrow spotlights the plight of migrant farm workers in Belle Glade, Florida, in "Harvest of Shame," a CBS documentary.

APRIL 1961 There are now approximately 600,000 color-TV sets in the 47 million American TV homes, but still only one network doing any regular color broadcasting: NBC, owned by RCA, the dominant manufac-

The guys behind the Route 66 *guys.*

turer of color-TV sets.

APRIL 3, 1961 Eddie Murphy born in Brooklyn, New York.

APRIL 29, 1961 "Spanning the globe to bring you the constant variety of sport . . . the thrill of victory, the agony of defeat," *ABC's Wide World of Sports* debuts.

MAY 5, 1961 Televisions all across America are tuned in as astronaut Alan B. Shepard, Jr., lifts off in the first U.S. manned suborbital space flight at Cape Canaveral.

MAY 8, 1961 Mickey Rooney makes a guest appearance on Jackie Cooper's *Hennesey* series—25 years after the last time they worked together, as child stars, in *The Devil Is a Sissy.*

MAY 9, 1961 In a speech to 2,000 delegates attending the National Association of Broadcasters convention in Washington, D.C., FCC Chairman Newton Minow calls television "a vast wasteland."

MAY 29, 1961 One month

after his wife's suicide, Dave Garroway announces that he will be leaving *The Dave Garroway Today Show* on or before October 31.

JUNE 9, 1961 Michael J. Fox born in Edmonton, Alberta, Canada.

SEPTEMBER 16, 1961 *The Defenders* premieres on CBS.

SEPTEMBER 17, 1961 *Car 54, Where Are You?* debuts on NBC.

SEPTEMBER 23, 1961 NBC debuts the first regular, major, prime-time motion-picture showcase on TV: *Saturday Night at the Movies,* the first feature of which is *How to Marry a Millionaire.*

SEPTEMBER 28, 1961 *Dr. Kildare* premieres on NBC; so does *Hazel.*

OCTOBER 1, 1961 *Mister Ed* premieres on CBS.

OCTOBER 2, 1961 *Password,* hosted by Allen Ludden and destined to be one of TV's most enduring game shows, premieres on CBS's morning schedule; later, *Ben Casey,* starring Vince Edwards and Sam Jaffe, premieres on ABC.

OCTOBER 3, 1961 *The Dick Van Dyke Show* premieres on CBS.

NOVEMBER 19, 1961 Lucille Ball marries nightclub comedian Gary Morton.

JANUARY 13, 1962 A car accident on an early-morning rain-slicked Los Angeles street takes the life of Ernie Kovacs.

FEBRUARY 14, 1962 First Lady Jacqueline Kennedy takes CBS's Charles Collingwood—and the American public—on a

televised tour of the White House. The show, directed by Franklin Schaffner, is broadcast on both CBS and NBC tonight at 10, and on ABC two nights later.

APRIL 4, 1962 The hitherto unseen Alan Brady on *The Dick Van Dyke Show* is seen—and is series creator Carl Reiner. In a two-part episode starting tonight, Rob Petrie's brother also makes a two-episode appearance—and is Van Dyke's real-life brother, Jerry.

APRIL 9, 1962 Ann-Margret becomes the hit of the Oscars telecast—and a household word—when she gives a sizzling performance of the nominated song "Bachelor in Paradise."

APRIL 16, 1962 Walter Cronkite replaces Douglas Edwards to become CBS News anchorman.

SEPTEMBER 11, 1962 Kristy McNichol born in Los Angeles, California.

SEPTEMBER 19, 1962 *The Virginian,* the first 90-minute Western series, rides onto the NBC Wednesday schedule, where it will stay for eight seasons.

SEPTEMBER 23, 1962 *The Jetsons* premieres on ABC.

SEPTEMBER 26, 1962 *The Beverly Hillbillies* premieres on CBS.

OCTOBER 1, 1962 Johnny Carson takes over as host of *The Tonight Show; The Lucille Ball Show* (later renamed *The Lucy Show,* then *Here's Lucy*) settles into CBS's Monday-night schedule.

OCTOBER 11, 1962 *McHale's Navy* sails onto ABC's schedule.

NOVEMBER 8, 1962 Lucille Ball Arnaz Morton pays $2,552,975 to buy out Desi Arnaz's 300,350 shares of stock in Desilu Studios, the former RKO. Lucy thus becomes president and chief stockholder of Desilu, and the highest-ranking woman TV executive in the world.

JANUARY 6, 1963 *Mutual of Omaha's Wild Kingdom,* starring Marlin Perkins and animal friends, premieres on NBC.

FEBRUARY 22, 1963 Pebbles Flintstone is born to Wilma and Fred Flintstone at the Bedrock Rockapedic Hospital. The Ideal Toy Corporation celebrates by manufacturing 250,000 Pebbles dolls.

MARCH 1963 CBS announces that Mike Wallace will be joining CBS News as a special staff correspondent with roving assignments in the news-and-features area.

MARCH 4, 1963 Lucie Arnaz, age 11, makes her TV debut in "Lucy Is a Soda Jerk," an episode of her mother's program, *The Lucy Show.*

APRIL 1, 1963 *General Hospital* debuts on ABC.

JUNE 11, 1963 TV finds a symbol for the civil rights struggle as news cameras capture Governor George Wallace standing in a doorway of the University of Alabama to block court-ordered desegregation of the university by two black students.

SEPTEMBER 16, 1963 "There is nothing wrong with your TV set": ABC premieres "a drama which reaches from the inner mind to . . . *The Outer Limits.*"

SEPTEMBER 17, 1963 Dr. Richard Kimble climbs out of a train and hits the road for four years of one-armed-man searching as *The Fugitive* premieres on ABC.

SEPTEMBER 18, 1963 "They're cousins, identical cousins . . . ": *The Patty Duke Show* joins the ABC Wednesday schedule.

SEPTEMBER 24, 1963 *Petticoat Junction* premieres on CBS.

SEPTEMBER 25, 1963 *The Danny Kaye Show* starts its four-season run on CBS.

SEPTEMBER 29, 1963 *My Favorite Martian* premieres on CBS, after which the much-awaited *The Judy Garland Show* debuts on the same network.

NOVEMBER 7, 1963 Charles O. Finley, owner of the Oakland A's baseball team, sends a letter to the commissioner of baseball, proposing the idea that World Series games be played on weekday nights and weekend days, to capture the maximum TV audience. Eight years later, the commissioner acted.

NOVEMBER 22-25, 1963 The assassination of President John F. Kennedy is one of the nation's darkest moments, and one of TV's most shining—TV news comes of age, as a soothing messenger.

JANUARY 4, 1964 ABC replaces *The Jerry Lewis Show* with *The Hollywood Palace,* a variety show whose first host is Bing Crosby. Where Lewis's show lasted just several months, this will be on the air for six years.

JANUARY 10, 1964 *That Was the Week That Was* has its premiere on NBC.

FEBRUARY 9, 1964 The Beatles turn up on *The Ed Sullivan Show*—and turn the world of entertainment upside down.

MARCH 20, 1964 The *Jeopardy!* answer is: This show premiered on this date on NBC, with Art Fleming as host.

APRIL 22, 1964 The New York World's Fair opens and becomes the most "TV-ized" fair ever, from closed-circuit-TV announcement-and-information boards throughout the fairgrounds to network coverage of the event, including an NBC 90-minute color special this night, hosted by Henry Fonda; regular *Today*-show coverage; and the East Coast portion of the Emmy awards telecast from the fairgrounds.

APRIL 30, 1964 After this date, by act of Congress, all TV sets manufactured for home use must be capable of receiving ultra-high-frequency (UHF) stations—Channels 14–83—as well as stations 2–13 on the very-high-frequency (VHF) band.

MAY 4, 1964 *Another World*—the daytime serial that starts with "the death of William, and will trace the effect of this sad event on his widow and two grown children, and on his brother James and his family"—premieres on NBC.

MAY 8, 1964 Melissa Gilbert born in Los Angeles, California.

SEPTEMBER 14, 1964 *Voyage to the Bottom of the Sea* dives onto the ABC Monday-night schedule.

SEPTEMBER 15, 1964 *Peyton Place* premieres on ABC.

SEPTEMBER 16, 1964 *Shindig* premieres on ABC.

SEPTEMBER 17, 1964 *Bewitched,* starring Elizabeth Montgomery, premieres on ABC.

SEPTEMBER 18, 1964 *The Addams Family,* starring John Astin and Carolyn Jones, premieres on ABC.

SEPTEMBER 22, 1964 *The Man from U.N.C.L.E.* premieres on NBC.

SEPTEMBER 24, 1964 *The Munsters,* starring Fred Gwynne and Yvonne De Carlo, premieres on CBS. And, on NBC, Fess Parker hands in his Davy Crockett coonskin cap for one worn by his new character, *Daniel Boone.*

SEPTEMBER 25, 1964 *Gomer Pyle, U.S.M.C.* premieres on CBS.

SEPTEMBER 26, 1964 *Gilligan's Island* premieres on CBS.

NOVEMBER 9, 1964 ABC pits Les Crane against Johnny Carson in the late-night talk-show arena. Carson wins.

DECEMBER 19, 1964 During the Liberty Bowl football game, played inside Atlantic City's Convention Hall, ABC devises a TV camera first: an overhead camera shooting straight down on the playing field.

JANUARY 1, 1965 On WNEW-TV, New York, Soupy Sales tells his kiddie viewers to go into their daddies' wallets and remove "those little green pieces of paper with pictures of George Washington, Benjamin Franklin, Lincoln, and Jefferson on them, send them to me, and I'll send *you* a postcard from Puerto Rico." After a deluge of paper money, Sales is suspended by the station, but viewer outrage reinstates him.

JANUARY 12, 1965 *Hullabaloo* makes its groovy debut as a rock-and-roll showcase on NBC.

APRIL 28, 1965 *My Name Is Barbra,* Barbra Streisand's first TV special, is broadcast on CBS.

MAY 24, 1965 CBS airs the *National Drivers' Test,* a viewer-participation show that tests viewers' auto knowledge and safety; it is a ratings success, and acts as a model for other, similar viewer-self-examination quizzes concerning citizenship, health, income tax, and honesty, on CBS and other networks.

AUGUST 1965 There are now 51 million TV sets in the U.S., 3.6 million of which are color TVs.

SEPTEMBER 13, 1965 Paul Bryan (Ben Gazzara) gets the bad news, health-wise, and begins to *Run for Your Life* on NBC.

SEPTEMBER 14, 1965 *My Mother, the Car,* starring Jerry Van Dyke, Avery Schreiber, and the voice of Ann Sothern, debuts on NBC . . . and sets a standard that comics and critics will joke about for years.

SEPTEMBER 15, 1965 *Green Acres,* starring Eddie Albert and Eva Gabor, premieres on CBS; Barbara Stanwyck in *The Big Valley* debuts on ABC; *Lost in Space* blasts off on CBS; and, on NBC, *I Spy,* with Robert Culp and Bill Cosby—the first black actor to star in a regularly scheduled drama series—premieres.

SEPTEMBER 16, 1965 *The Dean Martin Show*—the kind of show, according to its star, "where a man can take his wife and kids, his father and mother, and sit around a bar and watch," debuts on NBC.

SEPTEMBER 17, 1965 *Hogan's Heroes* premieres on CBS, as does *The Wild, Wild West.*

SEPTEMBER 18, 1965 Would you believe . . . *Get Smart,* starring Don Adams, premieres on NBC. And so does *I Dream of Jeannie.*

SEPTEMBER 19, 1965 *The F.B.I.* premieres on ABC.

NOVEMBER 8, 1965 *Days of Our Lives,* starring Macdonald Carey, premieres on NBC's daytime schedule, replacing *Moment of Truth.*

NOVEMBER 25, 1965 *A Visit to Washington with Mrs. Lyndon B. Johnson on Behalf of a More Beautiful America* is aired on ABC.

DECEMBER 9, 1965 *A Charlie Brown Christmas,* the first television version of Charles Schulz's popular comic strip *Peanuts,* airs on CBS.

JANUARY 12, 1966 *Batman* premieres—POW!—on ABC.

JANUARY 13, 1966 Tabitha is born to Samantha and Darrin Stephens on *Bewitched.*

FEBRUARY 1966 There are now an estimated 189,837,950 TV sets in the world, with the U.S. having the most, followed by Japan and the Soviet Union.

FEBRUARY 15, 1966 Fred Friendly—president of the CBS News Division, a 16-year network veteran, and one of "Murrow's boys"—resigns suddenly after his superior, John Schneider, turns down his request to broadcast a Senate Foreign Relations Committee hearing on Vietnam.

FEBRUARY 19, 1966 Justine Bateman born in Rye, New York.

MARCH 28, 1966 *The Avengers* premieres on ABC, replacing *Ben Casey* after its five-year run.

MAY 8, 1966 Lee J. Cobb and Mildred Dunnock re-create their 1949 Broadway stage roles in a superb CBS production of Arthur Miller's "Death of a Salesman."

JULY 4, 1966 Arnold the Pig born on a farm in Alabama.

JULY 11, 1966 *The Newlywed Game,* which tests how well or poorly recently married couples know each other, premieres on ABC.

SEPTEMBER 8, 1966 "To seek out new life and new civilizations. To boldly go where no man has gone before . . . " *Star Trek* beams up to NBC's schedule for its not-quite-five-year mission; and Ann Marie (Marlo Thomas) starts her own five-year mission on ABC's *That Girl.*

SEPTEMBER 12, 1966 *Family Affair,* starring Brian Keith and Sebastian Cabot, premieres on CBS. On NBC, hey-hey, it's *The Monkees.*

SEPTEMBER 17, 1966 CBS decides to accept *Mission: Impossible* for its Saturday schedule.

OCTOBER 17, 1966 *Hollywood Squares* premieres on NBC; as of this date, all of NBC's newscasts are in color.

DECEMBER 15, 1966 Walt Disney dies.

DECEMBER 18, 1966 The first showing of what will become a TV Christmas classic: the animated version of Dr. Seuss' *How the Grinch Stole Christmas,* narrated by Boris Karloff, on CBS.

JANUARY 12, 1967 *Dragnet* returns to the air in a new series with all-new episodes on NBC, seven years after it was canceled.

JANUARY 15, 1967 A television viewing audience of 51,180,000—the biggest football audience of that time—watches the Green Bay Packers defeat the Kansas City Chiefs in the first Super Bowl.

FEBRUARY 5, 1967 *The Smothers Brothers Comedy Hour* premieres on CBS.

MARCH 6, 1967 Hal Holbrook performs his much-acclaimed one-man theatrical show, *Mark Twain Tonight!,* on CBS.

APRIL 17, 1967 ABC pits Joey Bishop against Johnny Carson in the late-night talk-show arena. Carson wins.

JUNE 25, 1967 National Educational Television participates in a two-hour, all-live show, *Our World,* that originates in 19 nations on five continents, and is seen simultaneously in 30 countries via four satellites—the first global television hookup in history. The show includes views of Japanese shrimp-farming, a Rachmaninoff concerto, and the Beatles.

AUGUST 29, 1967 *The Fugitive* stops running. Dr. Richard Kimble finds the one-armed man, and 72 percent of all TVs in America are tuned in to this final episode.

SEPTEMBER 7, 1967 *The Flying Nun,* starring Sally Field, debuts on ABC.

SEPTEMBER 9, 1967 NBC gives a moderately well-known comedy team a slot for a special this night, and Rowan and Martin return the favor by presenting the first-ever *Laugh-In.*

SEPTEMBER 11, 1967 *The Carol Burnett Show* premieres on CBS.

SEPTEMBER 14, 1967 *Ironside,* starring Raymond Burr, premieres on NBC.

SEPTEMBER 16, 1967 *Mannix* slugs its ways onto the CBS schedule.

NOVEMBER 5, 1967 Date public television from this day: over a network of 119 of the nation's educational stations, the Ford Foundation–financed Public Broadcast Laboratory—a news-and-opinion magazine of the air shaped by Fred W. Friendly, headed by Av Westin, hosted by Edward P. Morgan—takes to the air.

NOVEMBER 16, 1967 Lisa Bonet born in San Francisco, California.

JANUARY 22, 1968 Sock it to me: *Rowan & Martin's Laugh-In* premieres as a regular series on NBC, replacing *The Man from U.N.C.L.E..*

FEBRUARY 8, 1968 Gary Coleman born in Zion, Illinois.

FEBRUARY 21, 1968 At exactly 4:31 P.M. on Stage 1 at the Desilu Studios, with Andy Griffith saying the line "Are you gonna see her again?," *The Andy Griffith Show* shoots its final scene and ends its eight-season run.

MARCH 20, 1968 Mrs. Peel's long-lost husband is found, and she leaves John Steed and secret agentry on *The Avengers.*

JUNE 1, 1968 Patrick McGoohan is not a number, he is a person—and the star of *The Prisoner,* debuting on CBS as a summer replacement for *The Jackie Gleason Show.*

AUGUST 25-29, 1968 Shouting "The whole world is watching"—and, in the U.S., perhaps 80 million people were—self-styled "Yippies" are beaten and routed by the Chicago police during the Democratic convention.

SEPTEMBER 1968 The 1968–69 television season becomes the first to have a network feature film in prime time every single night of the week.

SEPTEMBER 17, 1968 *Julia* premieres on NBC, becoming the first TV comedy series to have a black woman (Diahann Carroll) in a starring role other than a domestic, and the first black character living in a mostly white environment.

SEPTEMBER 20, 1968 *The Name of the Game,* a movie-length series about the publishing/reporting business with a trio of stars (Gene Barry, Robert Stack, Anthony Franciosa) who trade off leads each week, premieres on NBC.

SEPTEMBER 21, 1968 *Adam-12* premieres on NBC.

SEPTEMBER 22, 1968 With a one-hour program of Chopin, Scarlatti, Schumann, and Scriabin, Vladimir Horowitz makes his first appearance on TV in a CBS concert taped at Carnegie Hall.

SEPTEMBER 24, 1968 Tick, tick, tick . . . : *60 Minutes* premieres on CBS, as does *The Doris Day Show.* And, on ABC, so does *The Mod Squad.*

SEPTEMBER 26, 1968 "Book 'em, Dano. Murder One": *Hawaii Five-O* premieres on CBS.

NOVEMBER 17, 1968 With 50 seconds to go in a tight New York Jets–Oakland Raiders football game, the score 32–29 Jets, NBC ends transmission of the game and cuts away to begin showing the regularly scheduled movie, *Heidi.* The Raiders score two touchdowns in nine seconds. They win. NBC loses.

DECEMBER 1, 1968 TV turns sexy: Ann-Margret revs up a motorcycle—and some male viewers—in her CBS special, *The Ann-Margret Show.* Two days later, on December 3, Brigitte Bardot asks, "How would you like to spend an evening with me?," on her own special on NBC.

JANUARY 12, 1969 The Joe Namath–led New York Jets defeat the Baltimore Colts, 16–7, in the Super Bowl.

FEBRUARY 5, 1969 *Turn-On,* an ABC comedy-variety series from the producers of *Laugh-In,* with guest star Tim Conway, debuts and is almost immediately canceled after affiliates—having been deluged with thousands of angry calls from incensed and insulted viewers—refuse to carry it after just one show.

FEBRUARY 9, 1969 CBS presents the Royal Shakespeare Company's version of *A Midsummer Night's Dream,* starring Diana Rigg, David Warner, and Helen Mirren.

MARCH 29, 1969 The funeral ceremonies following the death of Dwight D. Eisenhower are accorded five days of television coverage.

APRIL 4, 1969 CBS axes *The Smothers Brothers Comedy Hour* after a long battle over the show's controversial content.

APRIL 11, 1969 Rome as only he could see it is presented in *Fellini, a Director's Notebook,* an NBC special.

APRIL 13, 1969 Eight years after they first worked together, and three years after the demise of their classic sitcom, Dick Van Dyke and Mary Tyler Moore get together again for a special, *Dick Van Dyke and the Other Woman* on CBS.

JUNE 15, 1969 *Hee Haw* premieres on CBS.

JULY 1, 1969 Prince Charles formally becomes Prince of Wales in ceremonies seen in the U.S. in a morning-long telecast, via satellite.

JULY 20, 1969 Approximately 700 million people on earth watch their TV screens to view another heavenly body, and the first men to visit it: Apollo 11 lands on the moon. Soon after, TV shows Neil Armstrong taking "one small step for man, one giant leap for mankind."

JULY 25, 1969 Senator Edward Kennedy goes on TV to talk about the incident at Chappaquiddick.

AUGUST 18, 1969 CBS pits Merv Griffin against Johnny Carson in the late-night talk-show arena. Carson wins.

SEPTEMBER 14, 1969 *The Bill Cosby Show,* with the star portraying high-school coach Chet Kincaid, premieres on NBC.

SEPTEMBER 17, 1969 *Room 222* premieres on ABC; *Then Came Bronson* debuts on NBC.

SEPTEMBER 23, 1969 *Marcus Welby, M.D.* premieres on ABC.

SEPTEMBER 24, 1969 *Medical Center,* starring James Daly and Chad Everett, premieres on CBS.

SEPTEMBER 26, 1969 *The Brady Bunch* premieres on ABC.

SEPTEMBER 29, 1969 *Love, American Style* premieres on ABC.

OCTOBER 5, 1969 John Galsworthy's *The Forsyte Saga* airs the first of its 26 chapters on Public Television; later, PBS presents the first in a series of courtroom-style debates on burning public issues, *The Advocates.*

NOVEMBER 10, 1969 "D" is for "debut," which is what *Sesame Street* does on U.S. noncommercial stations, informing and shaping an entire generation of three-to-five-year-olds.

NOVEMBER 13, 1969 Vice-President Spiro Agnew, in a televised speech from Des Moines, stirs up a national controversy by attacking the network news commentaries.

DECEMBER 17, 1969 Tiny Tim marries Miss Vicki on *The Tonight Show Starring Johnny Carson.*

JANUARY 5, 1970 Agnes Nixon does it again. After shepherding *Search for Tomorrow, As the World Turns, Guiding Light,* and *One Life to Live,* she premieres her latest this day on ABC—*All My Children.*

JANUARY 11, 1970 The Kansas City Chiefs upset the Minnesota Vikings, 23–7, in the final Super Bowl game before the American and National Football Leagues merge.

FEBRUARY 14, 1970 Buffalo Bob Smith, his cowboy suit fresh out from mothballs, appears on the stage of the University of Pennsylvania's Irvine Auditorium, asks the capacity audience, "Hey, kids, what time is it?"—and thus not only a Howdy Doody revival but a general TV nostalgia movement is launched nationwide.

MARCH 7, 1970 Most people watch "the eclipse of the century" at home on their TV screens, as covered by all three networks.

APRIL 13, 1970 Ricky Schroder born in Staten Island, New York.

APRIL 30, 1970 President Richard Nixon stands up and points to a map—a visual-aid first for a presidential speech—as he informs the American public that he has authorized a military incursion into Cambodia.

MAY 4, 1970 TV news footage shows, and commentators explore, the shocking events at Kent State University in Ohio, where four students are killed by National Guardsmen during an anti–Vietnam War protest.

SEPTEMBER 16, 1970 *McCloud* premieres on NBC, one of the quartet of separate dramas, *Four-in-One,* sharing the same Wednesday-night time slot. The others are Rod Serling's *Night Gallery, San Fran-* *cisco International,* and *The Psychiatrist.*

SEPTEMBER 17, 1970 *The Flip Wilson Show* debuts on NBC.

SEPTEMBER 19, 1970 She turns the world on with her smile: *The Mary Tyler Moore Show* premieres on CBS.

SEPTEMBER 21, 1970 *NFL Monday Night Football* premieres on ABC, with the New York Jets versus the Cleveland Browns.

SEPTEMBER 24, 1970 Two Neil Simon concepts premiere on ABC: *The Odd Couple,* starring Tony Randall and Jack Klugman, and an all-black-cast version of *Barefoot in the Park.*

SEPTEMBER 25, 1970 *The Partridge Family* premieres on ABC.

OCTOBER 5, 1970 Alistair Cooke is hired by WGBH, Boston's PBS station, to be the introducer of its soon-to-air series of British imports: *Masterpiece Theatre.*

OCTOBER 7, 1970 *Civilisation,* a 13-week series hosted by Sir Kenneth Clark, premieres on public-television stations around the U.S.

NOVEMBER 20, 1970 *Wall Street Week: with Louis Rukeyser* debuts on 30 Eastern public-TV stations.

JANUARY 12, 1971 *All in the Family* premieres on CBS.

FEBRUARY 5, 1971 Apollo 14 lands on the moon with Alan Shepard in command. TV pictures are transmitted back to earth in color.

FEBRUARY 8, 1971 Captain Kangaroo visits Mister Rogers on his show; on February 22, Mister Rogers returns the favor. The guest spots are intended to enhance children's emotional security by letting them know that their two heroes are friends.

FEBRUARY 14, 1971 The multi-Academy-Award-winning 1959 movie "Ben-Hur" is shown in fours hours on CBS, becoming the first Top 10 movie box-office champ to be telecast.

FEBRUARY 23, 1971 CBS airs the most controversial news show of the year: *The Selling of the Pentagon,* which examines and exposes the Department of Defense's propaganda activities. It becomes a subject of debate in Congress.

MARCH 17, 1971 CBS cancels *The Ed Sullivan Show* after 23 years. Sullivan will do specials; his slot is taken by *CBS Sunday Night Movies.*

JUNE 7, 1971 After having stated that "I am so healthy that I expect to live on and on," J. I. Rodale, publisher of the health-oriented magazine *Prevention,* has a heart attack and dies on-air during *The Dick Cavett Show* on ABC.

AUGUST 1, 1971 The much-praised BBC production of *The Six Wives of Henry VIII,* starring Keith Michell, is shown over six consecutive Sundays (one wife shed each week) on CBS; in a bizarre bit of programming *The Sonny and Cher Comedy Hour* debuts the same evening as its lead-in.

SEPTEMBER 15, 1971 Peter Falk dons his beat-up raincoat and becomes *Columbo* for the first time, on NBC.

SEPTEMBER 29, 1971 *McMillan and Wife* premieres on NBC.

OCTOBER 11, 1971 Hugh Downs turns over the *Today* show reins to TV news veteran Frank McGee.

OCTOBER 18, 1971 *The Electric Company,* the *Sesame Street* follow-up for second-through-fourth-graders, begins this week on more than 200 PBS stations.

NOVEMBER 30, 1971 *Brian's Song,* the story of the friendship of Chicago Bears football players Brian Piccolo (James Caan) and Gale Sayers (Billy Dee Williams), airs on ABC.

DECEMBER 19, 1971 *The Homecoming: A Christmas Story,* a made-for-TV movie that becomes the pilot for one of TV's most popular series, *The Waltons,* airs on CBS.

JANUARY 14, 1972 *Sanford and Son* premieres on NBC.

FEBRUARY 17, 1972 TV goes along with President Nixon on his historic visit to Communist China and, in May, to the Soviet Union, where he spoke to the Russian people on live TV.

APRIL 16, 1972 The Apollo 16 voyage to the moon tries to win back a public that has become slightly bored with moonshots by scheduling the astronauts' lunar rovings during prime time.

MAY 15, 1972 As TV news cameras roll, Arthur Bremer takes a gun and shoots George Wallace, who is campaigning for the Democratic presidential nomination.

SEPTEMBER 5, 1972 As world-wide TV viewers of the Olympics watch in horror, Arab terrorists calling themselves the Black September group take hostage, then kill Israeli athletes at the Munich games.

SEPTEMBER 12, 1972 *Maude,* starring Bea Arthur, premieres on CBS.

SEPTEMBER 14, 1972 *The Waltons* say goodnight to each other for the first time, on CBS.

SEPTEMBER 16, 1972 *The Bob Newhart Show* premieres on CBS; *The Streets of San Francisco,* with Karl Malden and Michael Douglas, begins its run on ABC.

SEPTEMBER 17, 1972 *M*A*S*H* premieres on CBS.

OCTOBER 14, 1972 His friends call him "Grasshopper," but to the cowboys who try to beat him up he is "that Chinaman" Caine: *Kung Fu,* starring David Carradine, premieres on ABC.

OCTOBER 27, 1972 *Captain Kangaroo* presents its 5,000th show.

NOVEMBER 1, 1972 Television edges another step toward (or back to) adult drama with *That Certain Summer,* an ABC TV-movie about homosexuality starring Hal Holbrook, Martin Sheen, and Scott Jacoby.

NOVEMBER 8, 1972 Home Box Office (HBO) goes on the air, with a test group of 365 subscribers in Wilkes-Barre, Pennsylvania. In slightly more than five years, its subscriber base swells to more than a million on 500 cable systems in 46 states and Puerto Rico—and the age of cable TV has begun.

JANUARY 11, 1973 *An American Family,* a stunning and probing 12-part documentary about the lives of the William C. Loud family of Santa Barbara,

California, from May 1971, to January 1972, premieres on PBS.

FEBRUARY 14, 1973 TV captures the real-life drama of the first of 566 American POWs—some captive as long as eight years—returning home from Southeast Asia.

FEBRUARY 27, 1973 TV news crews descend on South Dakota, where Native American activists occupy Wounded Knee, symbol and site of a massacre of Sioux men, women, and children a century before.

MAY 17, 1973 The televised Senate hearings into the Watergate affair begin.

OCTOBER 2, 1973 *Police Story,* an anthology series created by Joseph Wambaugh, debuts on NBC.

OCTOBER 16, 1973 NBC's late-late talk/interview program, *The Tomorrow Show,* with host Tom Snyder, premieres at 1:00 A.M.

OCTOBER 24, 1973 *Kojak* premieres on CBS.

DECEMBER 6, 1973 Live TV captures House Minority Leader Gerald R. Ford being sworn in as Vice-President of the United States, replacing Spiro T. Agnew, who pleaded no-contest to charges of income-tax evasion.

DECEMBER 16, 1973 Katharine Hepburn, appearing in her first television role, stars with Sam Waterston and Michael Moriarty in Tennessee Williams's play "The Glass Menagerie" on ABC.

DECEMBER 19, 1973 After reading a news item that said the federal government had fallen behind in getting bids to supply toilet tissue, Johnny Carson on that night's *Tonight Show* said, "You know what else is disappearing from the supermarket shelves? Toilet paper. There's an acute shortage of toilet paper in the United States"—thus setting off unprecedented, rumor-fueled, three-week panic buying of toilet paper all over America. There was no shortage—until Carson's statement.

JANUARY 15, 1974 *Happy Days* premieres on ABC.

JANUARY 18, 1974 *The Six Million Dollar Man,* which has been seen as a now-and-again 90-minute movie special, premieres as a regular series on ABC.

JANUARY 31, 1974 Cicely Tyson portrays the life of a 110-year-old black woman, spanning the history of America from slavery to the civil-rights movement, in the multi-Emmy-winning adaptation of Ernest J. Gaines' novel *The Autobiography of Miss Jane Pittman* on CBS.

FEBRUARY 13, 1974 Dick Van Dyke, a recently acknowledged alcoholic, stars in *The Morning After,* an ABC TV-movie about the disastrous effects of out-of-control drinking on a family.

FEBRUARY 22, 1974 The final *Sonny & Cher Comedy Hour* is taped, 58 hours after Sonny Bono files legal-separation papers to dissolve their marriage.

MARCH 3, 1974 PBS's new science series, *Nova,* debuts.

MARCH 13, 1974 NBC airs the powerful and controversial TV-movie *The Execution of Private Slovik,* about the only American soldier executed for desertion since the Civil War, with Martin Sheen starring.

MARCH 21, 1974 An era ends: *Here's Lucy* on CBS airs its last original episode—and signals the end of series television for Lucille Ball; later this night, the entire Loud family—now split, divorced, and scattered since becoming nationally known from the PBS documentary series *An American Family*—appears on a special edition of *The Dick Cavett Show* on ABC.

JULY 4, 1974 Beginning this night, and continuing with new installments every night for the next two years, CBS presents 912 little flashbacks to events in American history that occurred on the same date two centuries before, aimed at reminding viewers of the nation's 200th birthday. They are all hosted by well-known celebrities and are called "Bicentennial Minutes."

JULY 29, 1974 Jim Hartz becomes the new top man on the *Today* show, replacing the late Frank McGee as Barbara Walters' early-morning partner on NBC.

AUGUST 8, 1974 Richard Nixon resigns as President of the United States in a live TV broadcast.

SEPTEMBER 11, 1974 *Little House on the Prairie* premieres on NBC.

SEPTEMBER 13, 1974 *The Rockford Files* premieres on NBC.

NOVEMBER 16, 1974 *The Godfather* has its TV premiere in two parts (tonight and November 18) on NBC, which is reputed to have paid a record-setting $10 million for one showing.

DECEMBER 5, 1974 Documentary filmmaker Frederick Wiseman sets off a storm of controversy with his examination of life and death at the Yerkes Primate Research Center in *Primate,* on PBS.

JANUARY 5, 1975 Jacob Bronowski's *The Ascent of Man*—a 13-part BBC series that does for science what Kenneth Clark's *Civilisation* did for art—premieres this week on PBS stations.

JANUARY 6, 1975 NBC's *Another World* becomes the first daily half-hour soap opera to expand to hour length.

JANUARY 18, 1975 *The Jeffersons,* an *All in the Family* spin-off, premieres on CBS.

JANUARY 23, 1975 *Barney Miller* premieres on ABC.

MARCH 4, 1975 After A. C. Nielsen pollsters call up thousands of TV viewers to find out their TV favorites, the results lead to the first "People's Choice Awards," a two-hour special on CBS.

SEPTEMBER 9, 1975 *Welcome Back, Kotter* premieres on ABC.

SEPTEMBER 10, 1975 *Starsky and Hutch* premieres on ABC.

SEPTEMBER 20, 1975 Howard Cosell tries to become the next generation's Ed Sullivan as host of *Saturday Night Live with Howard Cosell* on ABC.

SEPTEMBER 29, 1975 WGPR-TV, Channel 62 in Detroit, becomes the first station in the continental United States to be owned and operated by blacks.

SEPTEMBER 30, 1975 The Muhammad Ali–Joe Frazier title fight from the Philippines—the "Thrilla in Manila"—is sent by satellite to the U.S. and shown on HBO. This single event sold HBO to hundreds of thousands of cable customers, and possibly made cable TV a going proposition.

OCTOBER 11, 1975 Live from New York, it's *Saturday Night Live,* with guest host George Carlin and the Muppets.

NOVEMBER 3, 1975 *Good Morning America,* ABC's answer to NBC's dominant early-morning *Today* show, debuts with hosts David Hartman and Nancy Dussault.

DECEMBER 1975 NBC begins phasing out the peacock symbol and the short animated bit of its colorful plumage that the network has used for years to denote the airing of a color presentation. By early 1976, it is gone for good.

DECEMBER 16, 1975 The Norman Lear–produced *One Day at a Time,* starring Bonnie Franklin, Valerie Bertinelli, and Mackenzie Phillips, begins its nine-season run on CBS.

JANUARY 11, 1976 Jane Alexander and Edward Herrmann are *Eleanor and Franklin* tonight and January 12 on an ABC special.

JANUARY 14, 1976 *The Bionic Woman* bounces onto the ABC schedule.

JANUARY 20, 1976 *The Adams Chronicles,* a 13-week history of the great American family, premieres on PBS.

JANUARY 21, 1976 *Dance in America* debuts on PBS.

JANUARY 27, 1976 *Laverne and Shirley* spins off from *Happy Days* and premieres on ABC.

FEBRUARY 1, 1976 The first installment of the 12-hour-long *Rich Man, Poor Man* premieres on ABC, making Nick Nolte a star.

FEBRUARY 2, 1976 Jackie Gleason, Art Carney, and Audrey Meadows are reunited in an ABC special, *The Honeymooners—The Second Honeymoon.*

MARCH 9, 1976 *Family* premieres on ABC.

JUNE 7, 1976 David Brinkley joins John Chancellor as co-anchor of the *NBC Nightly News,* an attempt by the network to bolster ratings against Walter Cronkite and to hark back to the good old days of Huntley-Brinkley.

SEPTEMBER 6, 1976 In an experiment, New York station WOR-TV replaces its usual schedule for five nights with exclusively British TV programming from Thames Television.

SEPTEMBER 22, 1976 *Charlie's Angels* jiggles onto the ABC Wednesday-night schedule.

SEPTEMBER 29, 1976 *Alice,* based loosely on the movie "Alice Doesn't Live Here Anymore," and starring Linda Lavin, Polly Holliday, Vic Tayback and Beth Howland, debuts on CBS.

OCTOBER 3, 1976 *Quincy,* starring Jack Klugman as a medical examiner/detective, premieres as part of the *NBC Sunday Mystery Movie.*

OCTOBER 4, 1976 Barbara Walters joins Harry Reasoner as co-anchor of ABC's evening newscast; the two do not get along, and ratings do not improve.

OCTOBER 11, 1976 Jane Pauley shows up for her first day of work on the *Today* show.

DECEMBER 17, 1976 At 1:00 P.M. (ET), WTCG-TV, Atlanta, begins satellite transmissions of its regular scheduling to four cable systems, thus becoming the first superstation. Three years later, WTCG, which stands for Turner Communications Group, changes its call letters to WTBS.

JANUARY 23, 1977 *Roots* debuts, with 12 hours over eight consecutive nights, and becomes the most-watched dramatic show in TV history. Its final two hours, on January 30, are viewed by an estimated 80 million people.

JANUARY 29, 1977 Freddie Prinze, star of the NBC hit sitcom *Chico and the Man* (which premiered September 13, 1974), commits suicide at age 22.

FEBRUARY 27, 1977 Fed up with "the excessive violence and distorted image of sex" on TV, the Reverend Donald Wildmon declares "Turn the Television Off Week." Ratings show few people do.

MARCH 15, 1977 Renata Scotto and Luciano Pavarotti are seen in *La Bohème* on PBS and heard in stereo on local stations, the first live "simulcast" from the Metropolitan Opera House at Lincoln Center; *Eight Is Enough* premieres on ABC, as does *Three's Company.*

APRIL 1977 There are now 71 million homes in the U.S. (97 percent of all homes) with at least one television set; nearly

half of those have two sets, and of those with two sets nearly 75 percent own a color set, according to an A. C. Nielsen survey. There are also now 710 commercial-TV stations and 252 public stations.

APRIL 3, 1977 Amid loud protests from some clergymen—who have not even seen it—NBC presents Part One of Franco Zeffirelli's six-hour *Jesus of Nazareth,* with the second part to be aired on April 10. Fifty percent of the viewing audience watch Part One, making it the second-most popular show of the week—just behind *Laverne and Shirley.*

SEPTEMBER 13, 1977 *Soap* premieres on ABC, with thousands of protests even before its first airing.

SEPTEMBER 20, 1977 *Lou Grant,* a sort of spin-off of *The Mary Tyler Moore Show,* premieres on CBS.

SEPTEMBER 24, 1977 *The Love Boat* smoothly sails onto the ABC Saturday-night schedule.

OCTOBER 3, 1977 Dick Cavett, highly regarded but low-rated talk-show host, moves onto public television with a new half-hour, five-day-a-week *Dick Cavett Show.*

NOVEMBER 6, 1977 *I, Claudius* starring Derek Jacobi and John Hurt, begins its saga on PBS.

NOVEMBER 12, 1977 Francis Ford Coppola combines his two Oscar-winning films—plus never-before-seen footage—into one continuous narrative, and *The Godfather* and *The Godfather, Part II* become the nine-hour, four-night *Mario Puzo's The Godfather: The Complete*

Novel for Television, beginning this night, on NBC.

JANUARY 15, 1978 The Super Bowl is played—and televised—at night for the first time, and becomes the second-most-watched TV show in history, topped only by the final episode of *Roots.*

JANUARY 23, 1978 An ABC special, *Roots—One Year Later,* examines the influence and impact of the miniseries *Roots.*

JANUARY 28, 1978 "De plane, Boss, de plane!" arrives for the first time on the premiere of *Fantasy Island* on ABC.

APRIL 2, 1978 *Dallas* premieres on CBS.

APRIL 16, 1978 For nine and a half hours over four consecutive nights, NBC presents *Holocaust,* with a large all-star cast headed by Fritz Weaver, Michael Moriarty, Meryl Streep, and James Woods.

JUNE 6, 1978 *20/20* premieres on ABC, but its first hosts—Harold Hayes and Robert Hughes—are fired after the first show, and replaced by Hugh Downs.

AUGUST 1, 1978 Harry Reasoner returns to CBS after taking advantage of an oral escape-clause in his contract with ABC. He is almost immediately put back on *60 Minutes,* which he had started in 1968 with Mike Wallace.

SEPTEMBER 12, 1978 *Taxi* gets off to a better-than-fare start on ABC.

SEPTEMBER 14, 1978 *Mork & Mindy,* a *Happy Days* spin-off, premieres on ABC.

SEPTEMBER 17, 1978 The ceremony formalizing the success of the peace talks between Menachem Begin and Anwar Sadat—the Camp David accords between Israel and Egypt—is televised live from the White House East Room.

SEPTEMBER 18, 1978 *WKRP in Cincinnati* premieres on CBS.

SEPTEMBER 19, 1978 The chairs on which Archie and Edith Bunker sat through eight seasons of *All in the Family* are presented to the Smithsonian Institution; *The Paper Chase,* starring John Houseman and James Stephens, premieres on CBS.

OCTOBER 1, 1978 The most ambitious project ever attempted by television—the 25-hour, $25-million dramatization of James Michener's *Centennial*—begins this night on NBC, starring Richard Chamberlain, Robert Conrad, Raymond Burr, and Clint Walker.

OCTOBER 14, 1978 Just when you thought it was safe to go back in the water again: NBC presents Part One of the two-part, two-hour *Rescue from Gilligan's Island*, with the original cast members minus Tina Louise.

NOVEMBER 3, 1978 *Diff'rent Strokes* premieres on NBC.

JANUARY 28, 1979 Bringing class, calm, and Americana to the air, CBS premieres *Sunday Morning with Charles Kuralt.*

FEBRUARY 14, 1979 On PBS, *Julius Caesar* is the first work to be televised as part of a huge, ambitious project by the BBC to present all of Shakespeare's 37 plays over a six-year period. *As You Like It, Romeo and Juliet,*

Richard II, Measure for Measure, and *Henry VIII* will follow in the 1979 season, at roughly two-week intervals.

FEBRUARY 18, 1979 *Roots: The Next Generations,* a continuation of the story of the Afro-American experience as seen through the lives of author Alex Haley's family, begins its 12-hour run on ABC.

MARCH 28, 1979 The big story for weeks to come happens today: the breakdown and near-meltdown of the Three Mile Island nuclear-power plant near Harrisburg, Pennsylvania.

APRIL 22, 1979 Carol Burnett gives a strong dramatic performance as a mother who wants to know how her son died in Vietnam in the TV-movie *Friendly Fire* on ABC.

AUGUST 24, 1979 *The Facts of Life,* a spin-off of *Diff'rent Strokes,* debuts on NBC.

SEPTEMBER 13, 1979 *Benson,* starring Robert Guillaume, debuts on ABC.

OCTOBER 2, 1979 Bob Vila, Norm Abram, and PBS hit the nail on the head as *This Old House* debuts.

OCTOBER 8, 1979 James Earl Jones gives a one-man performance as Paul Robeson on PBS.

NOVEMBER 29, 1979 ABC Washington anchorman Frank Reynolds takes the night off; the man picked to fill in for him on the network's three-week-old late-night news special, *The Iran Crisis: America Held Hostage,* is ABC's diplomatic correspondent: Ted Koppel. Although it isn't called that yet, *Nightline* is born.

DECEMBER 20, 1979 *Knots Landing,* which spun Gary Ewing off of *Dallas* and out to the West Coast, debuts on CBS.

JANUARY 4, 1980 President Jimmy Carter in a nationally televised address declares that, if the Soviet Union does not get out of Afghanistan, the U.S. will boycott the 1980 Summer Olympics in Moscow. NBC, which has acquired the rights to televise the Olympics for $87 million, is stunned, and in May publicly announces that it won't be airing the Games, at a loss of millions of dollars in ad revenues.

JANUARY 25, 1980 Black Entertainment Television (BET), a cable-TV programming service geared to an African American viewership, begins operation.

FEBRUARY 3, 1980 A six-hour retrospective of Bob Hope's more than 30 years of entertaining at military bases and hospitals in the U.S. and overseas begins tonight and concludes on February 10 on NBC.

FEBRUARY 12, 1980 *Mystery!,* a new series on PBS, begins a four-part dramatization of *Rumpole of the Bailey.*

FEBRUARY 22, 1980 Al Michaels yells, "DO YOU BELIEVE IN MIRACLES? YES!," and American-TV sports watchers go crazy as the United States Olympic hockey team beats the invulnerable Soviet Union team, 4–3, to win the Gold Medal at the Winter Games in Lake Placid.

MARCH 16, 1980 The Tele-Caption decoder, permitting deaf TV viewers to see and read closed-captioning on favorite shows, is introduced throughout the U.S. Sixteen hours a week of network programming begin on ABC, NBC, and PBS—CBS rejects the system to back one of its own.

MARCH 21, 1980 A prominent oilman is shot by an unknown assailant in *Dallas* tonight, setting off a national hysteria and placing a question on everybody's lips: Who Shot J.R.?

MARCH 24, 1980 ABC's nightly updates of the U.S. hostage crisis in Iran, going on since November, are officially converted, on Day 142, into a regular nighttime news show, *Nightline,* with anchor Ted Koppel.

JUNE 1, 1980 Ted Turner's Cable News Network—television's first 24-hour all-news service—begins.

SEPTEMBER 15, 1980 *Shogun,* a 12-hours-over-five-consecutive-nights miniseries based on the best-selling novel by James Clavell and starring Richard Chamberlain, begins on NBC.

SEPTEMBER 28, 1980 Astronomer Carl Sagan points us toward billions and billions of stars on *Cosmos,* a 13-part science-and-space-exploration series beginning on PBS.

SEPTEMBER 30, 1980 Vanessa Redgrave stars in the harrowing tale of concentration-camp prisoners who survive by playing in a camp orchestra, in Arthur Miller's *Playing for Time,* on CBS.

OCTOBER 26, 1980 Sophia Loren plays a dual role—her mother and herself—in the autobiographical TV-movie, *Sophia Loren: Her Own Story,* on NBC.

DECEMBER 8, 1980 At approximately 11:00 P.M., news bulletins break into regularly scheduled programs and lead the late-night news: John Lennon has been shot and has died at New York's Roosevelt Hospital. The next day, *Good Morning America* spends its entire two hours on the story.

DECEMBER 11, 1980 *Magnum, P.I.* premieres on CBS.

JANUARY 12, 1981 *Dynasty* premieres on ABC.

JANUARY 15, 1981 *Hill Street Blues* premieres on NBC.

JANUARY 20, 1981 As millions watch on TV, two big news events occur simultaneously: Ronald Reagan is sworn in as the 40th President of the United States, and Iran frees the 52 American hostages.

MARCH 9, 1981 Dan Rather takes over for Walter Cronkite on *CBS Evening News.*

MARCH 30, 1981 As TV news cameras roll, John W. Hinckley, Jr., tries to assassinate President Ronald Reagan outside a hotel in Washington, D.C.

JUNE 30, 1981 Fred Silverman, whose canny programming skills boosted ratings first at CBS and then at ABC, is fired as president of NBC after failing to improve that network's third-place standing.

JULY 4, 1981 Showtime, the premium cable movies-and-entertainment service, ends its part-time status and inaugurates a round-the-clock schedule.

JULY 29, 1981 Before an international TV audience (and U.S. networks, which start their coverage at 5:00 A.M.), Charles, Prince of Wales and heir to the British throne, and Lady Diana Spencer are married at Saint Paul's Cathedral in London.

AUGUST 1, 1981 MTV is launched. The music video becomes big business and the major form of music promotion, and the fast-cut, graphically vivid look and feel of it all is immediately and far-reachingly influential in TV and movies.

NOVEMBER 15, 1981 *This Week with David Brinkley* debuts on ABC.

NOVEMBER 16, 1981 Sixteen million breathless viewers watch as Luke Spencer and Laura Baldwin are married on *General Hospital.*

JANUARY 12, 1982 PBS's *American Playhouse* premieres with the presentation of "The Shady Hill Kidnapping," a one-hour original by John Cheever.

JANUARY 18, 1982 Jeremy Irons and Anthony Andrews—along with able assistance from Sir Laurence Olivier, Sir John Gielgud, and Claire Bloom—star in *Brideshead Revisited,* an 11-part *Great Performances* series adapted from Evelyn Waugh's novel, on PBS.

JANUARY 23, 1982 *CBS Reports* presents a documentary, "The Uncounted Enemy: A Vietnam Deception," that causes General William Westmoreland to sue the network for libel; his suit was later withdrawn.

FEBRUARY 1, 1982 *Late Night with David Letterman* premieres on NBC, replacing Tom Snyder's *Tomorrow Coast to Coast.*

APRIL 5, 1982 *NBC Nightly News* anchor John Chancellor is replaced by the co-anchor team of Tom Brokaw and Roger Mudd.

APRIL 24, 1982 Ingrid Bergman is *A Woman Called Golda,* a film based on the life of Golda Meir and filmed in Israel, and shown at various times this week on Operation Prime Time, a "network" of approximately 120 TV stations across the country.

JULY 6, 1982 *NBC News Overnight,* with news hosts Linda Ellerbee and Lloyd Dobyns (soon after replaced by Bill Schechner), premieres.

SEPTEMBER 22, 1982 *Family Ties* premieres on NBC.

SEPTEMBER 30, 1982 *Cheers* premieres on NBC.

OCTOBER 25, 1982 *Newhart* premieres on CBS.

OCTOBER 26, 1982 *St. Elsewhere* begins its rounds on NBC.

NOVEMBER 28, 1982 Norman Mailer's *The Executioner's Song,* the story of killer Gary Gilmore, begins its two-night, four-hour telecast on NBC. Tommy Lee Jones and Rosanna Arquette star.

JANUARY 10, 1983 *The Life and Adventures of Nicholas Nickleby,* an astounding dramatization of the Dickens novel transferred from its acclaimed theatrical production to TV by the Royal Shakespeare Company, plays over nine hours on four consecutive nights on PBS.

FEBRUARY 28, 1983 After 11 years, 251 episodes, and 14 Emmys (out of 99 nominations), *M*A*S*H* says goodbye in a two-and-a-half-hour final episode on CBS, watched by 107 million viewers, the biggest U.S. audience ever to watch a single TV program.

MARCH 7, 1983 The Nashville Network, owned by the same people who own the Grand Ole Opry, begins service.

MARCH 19, 1983 The producers just say yes, and First Lady Nancy Reagan appears as a special guest on NBC's *Diff'rent Strokes* to promote her antidrug message.

MARCH 27, 1983 Richard Chamberlain and Rachel Ward star in the ten-hour, four-night ABC presentation of Colleen McCullough's *The Thorn Birds.*

APRIL 18, 1983 The Disney Channel begins operation.

MAY 1, 1983 Giant lizards in people costumes are the villains in *V,* a two-night, four-hour TV-movie (later to become a series) on NBC.

MAY 16, 1983 Diana Ross, Stevie Wonder, Lionel Richie, Marvin Gaye, the Temptations, the Four Tops, Smokey Robinson and the Miracles, and others appear to celebrate *Motown 25: Yesterday, Today, Forever,* on NBC.

MAY 31, 1983 *Buffalo Bill,* a dark comedy with a thoroughly unlikable talk-show-host hero played by Dabney Coleman, begins its near-legendary but brief run on NBC.

AUGUST 4, 1983 Over the weekend of July 23, the tapes for this day's *Search for Tomorrow* show were stolen. Thus, for the first time since 1968, the thirty-two-year-old daytime serial is performed live.

AUGUST 9, 1983 *American Family Revisited—the Louds Ten Years Later* is an HBO special that looks at the family that made TV history; but this time the interviews are controlled, the areas of discussion were agreed to in advance, and the participants receive a fee.

SEPTEMBER 17, 1983 As more than 17 million TV homes watch, Vanessa Williams is crowned the first black Miss America.

OCTOBER 4, 1983 *Vietnam: A Television History,* a landmark 13-part documentary that attempts to give an overall picture of the war, including what

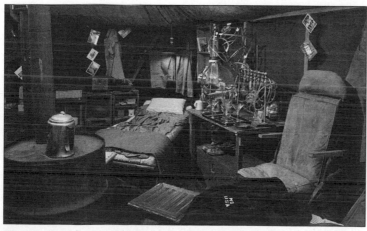

The "Swamp" from M*A*S*H, *now in the Smithsonian.*

it was like for the other side, begins on PBS.

OCTOBER 10, 1983 *Adam,* a TV-movie about the abduction of Adam Walsh, airs on NBC.

NOVEMBER 13, 1983 Charlton Heston stars in *Chiefs,* a six-hour CBS miniseries which follows the case of an unsolved murder through 40 years and three police administrations.

NOVEMBER 20, 1983 Jason Robards heads a big-name star cast in what becomes the most-watched TV-movie in history, ABC's *The Day After,* about the effects of a nuclear war on Lawrence, Kansas.

JANUARY 4, 1984 *Night Court* debuts on NBC.

JANUARY 9, 1984 Glenn Close, Ted Danson, and Roxana Zal star in a powerful, sensitive look at incest in *Something About Amelia* on ABC.

JANUARY 19, 1984 *Reilly: Ace of Spies,* a 12-part series starring Sam Neill, begins on PBS.

FEBRUARY 1, 1984 The Arts and Entertainment Network (A&E), built from the ashes of the ARTS and The Entertainment Channel cultural services, goes into operation.

MARCH 10, 1984 The first meeting of RALPH—the Royal Association for the Longevity and Preservation of *The Honeymooners*—with more than 2,100 members, holds its first convention, showing rare episodes of the show, and ogling such relics as Ralph's original bus-driver uniform and Alice's apron.

MARCH 19, 1984 *Kate & Allie* premieres on CBS.

MAY 13, 1984 Jane Fonda stars in the Depression-era drama *The Dollmaker,* an ABC TV-movie.

MAY 18, 1984 Keeping it in the family, Bobby Ewing is shot in the season-ending *Dallas* cliffhanger.

MAY 24, 1984 Viewers of *Guiding Light* get to choose the name of the newborn son of Quint and Nola—should he be Henry, Thomas, or Quinton, Jr.?—by calling a special 900 phone number and voting. Scenes have been taped with all three names; the most popular name's scene will be inserted on the show of May 25.

JULY 13, 1984 *Brothers,* a situation comedy which deals with homosexuality, begins its controversial run on Showtime.

SEPTEMBER 16, 1984 "MTV cops" is what NBC wanted; what it got was the debut of *Miami Vice.*

SEPTEMBER 20, 1984 *The Cosby Show* premieres on NBC.

SEPTEMBER 30, 1984 *Murder, She Wrote,* starring Angela Lansbury, premieres on CBS.

OCTOBER 10, 1984 *The Brain,* an eight-part series that explores the workings of that vital organ, begins on PBS.

DECEMBER 16, 1984 PBS's *Masterpiece Theatre* airs the first of 14 episodes of *The Jewel in the Crown,* based on British author Paul Scott's tetralogy, *The Raj Quartet.*

DECEMBER 28, 1984 *The Edge of Night* telecasts its final episode, ending its 28-year run on network TV.

JANUARY 1, 1985 VH-1, MTV's more mainstream sister station, debuts.

MARCH 3, 1985 *Moonlighting,* with Cybill Shepherd and Bruce Willis, debuts as ABC's hip romantic-comedy/detective-show of the season.

MAY 6, 1985 Australian media baron Rupert Murdoch buys Metromedia TV stations for $2 billion, not long after his purchase of Twentieth Century–Fox, thus setting the stage for the Fox Television Network, which would become the first truly strong, profitable and lasting attempt at a fourth commercial network.

JULY 1, 1985 *Alive from Off Center,* a showcase for new-wave music, dance, and theater, premieres on PBS.

JULY 13, 1985 TV hookups between concerts in London and Philadelphia beam Live Aid to televisions all over the world, raising money for African famine relief.

SEPTEMBER 14, 1985 *The Golden Girls,* starring Bea Arthur, Betty White, Rue McClanahan, and Estelle Getty, premieres on NBC.

NOVEMBER 5, 1985 Lucille Ball returns to TV as a bag lady in the CBS made-for-TV movie *Stone Pillow.*

NOVEMBER 11, 1985 Aidan Quinn, Gena Rowlands, and Ben Gazzara star in the first significant made-for-TV movie to tackle the subject of AIDS, *An Early Frost,* on NBC.

DECEMBER 10, 1985 Raven-Symone is born in Atlanta, Georgia.

JANUARY 28, 1986 The space shuttle Challenger explodes over Cape Canaveral, 73 seconds after lift-off, as millions watch in horror on TV.

MARCH 25, 1986 When Balki met Larry: *Perfect Strangers* debuts on ABC.

MARCH 29, 1986 Following on the heels of Live Aid and Farm Aid—concerts to raise money for famine victims, and the suffering American farmer—Robin Williams, Whoopi Goldberg, and Billy Crystal present *Comic Relief,* a live, three-hour benefit comedy show, on HBO.

APRIL 21, 1986 Geraldo Rivera opens Al Capone's vaults and—with much attendant publicity, and in what was to become the most-watched syndicated program ever—he finds nothing but dirt.

MAY 16, 1986 Pam Ewing awakens, goes to the bathroom, and, in a season-ending cliffhanger, has her dead husband, Bobby, say "Good morning" to her from the shower— and, after a summer hiatus, we discover that Pam had dreamed the entire 1985–86 season of *Dallas.*

JUNE 1, 1986 The U.S. Senate allows TV cameras into its chambers for the first time, on a six-week trial basis. The House of Representatives has had TV coverage for years.

AUGUST 9, 1986 Eight years and three networks after they began, the law students on *The Paper Chase* finally get their diplomas, in a special two-hour movie on Showtime.

SEPTEMBER 8, 1986 *The Oprah Winfrey Show,* a local

smash success, goes national via syndication.

SEPTEMBER 15, 1986 Robert MacNeil acts as host/writer for a nine-week series about *The Story of English,* on PBS.

SEPTEMBER 29, 1986 *Designing Women* premieres on CBS.

OCTOBER 3, 1986 For McKenzie, Brackman, Chaney and Kuzak, everything is admissible, including their briefs, as *L.A. Law* debuts on NBC.

JANUARY 18, 1987 Shirley MacLaine plays herself in five-hour, two-night TV-movie, *Out on a Limb,* based on her 1983 best-selling autobiography.

FEBRUARY 15, 1987 Amid political controversy, and seen as a way to smooth ruffled conservative feathers after the perceived-liberal *The Day After,* ABC airs *Amerika,* a seven-part, 14½-hour miniseries, beginning this night, dealing with what would happen if the United States were to live under Soviet domination.

MARCH 27, 1987 With today's show, CBS's *The Price Is Right* becomes the longest-running daytime game show ever seen continually on the same network. This 3,112th show breaks the mark established by NBC's *Concentration* in 1973.

APRIL 5, 1987 Tracey Ullman, the English comedienne and pop singer, makes her U.S. TV debut in *The Tracey Ullman Show* on the new Fox Broadcasting Network. Same night, same network, the Bundys become the TV sitcom Family from Hell as *Married . . . with Children* premieres.

SUMMER 1987 Congress's

Iran-contra hearings, especially the July testimony of Marine Lieutenant Colonel Oliver North, mesmerize the TV-viewing nation.

SEPTEMBER 11, 1987 Dan Rather walks off *The CBS Evening News,* and there is dead air over the network for nearly seven minutes, after the anchor is angered when the U.S. Open tennis tournament runs over and causes a delay in the start of his newscast.

SEPTEMBER 25, 1987 *Beauty and the Beast,* a romance-novel-cum-fantasy drama with a gallant, lionlike mutant as the hero, debuts on CBS and becomes a cult hit.

SEPTEMBER 28, 1987 *Star Trek: The Next Generation* premieres in syndication at various times this week.

SEPTEMBER 29, 1987 *thirtysomething* premieres on ABC.

OCTOBER 16, 1987 After a 58-hour ordeal, 18-month-old Jessica McClure is rescued from an abandoned well in Midland, Texas, as millions watch and pray—and TV producers line up for the TV-movie rights to the ordeal.

JANUARY 31, 1988 *The Wonder Years* debuts on ABC.

FEBRUARY 7, 1988 *America's Most Wanted,* a show that re-creates and publicizes crimes and enlists viewers in finding the victimizers—and hosted by John Walsh, whose son Adam was kidnapped and killed in a highly publicized 1971 case— premieres on the Fox network.

FEBRUARY 21, 1988 Television preacher Jimmy Swaggart stands before his public, sobbing, and admits "I have sinned," after reports of his involvement with pornography and prostitutes. Electronic evangelism is dealt a heavy blow.

APRIL 26, 1988 *China Beach* premieres on ABC.

MAY 22, 1988 Ripped from the headlines, a two-part TV-movie about the most sensational child-custody case of the century, *Baby M,* starring JoBeth Williams, John Shea, and Robin Strasser, begins tonight on ABC.

SEPTEMBER 1988 A strike begun in February by the Writers Guild of America shuts down production of shows, delaying the start of the 1988–89 season.

OCTOBER 18, 1988 *Roseanne* debuts on ABC.

NOVEMBER 1, 1988 *TV Guide* is purchased by Rupert Murdoch.

NOVEMBER 13, 1988 ABC presents the first 18 hours of the 30-hour miniseries *War and Remembrance* (the follow-up to *Winds of War*) in seven parts over an 11-day period beginning this night, with the remainder to air later in the season.

NOVEMBER 14, 1988 *Murphy Brown* premieres on CBS.

FEBRUARY 5, 1989 *Lonesome Dove,* an adaptation of Larry McMurtry's Pulitzer Prize–winning novel about an epic 2,500-mile cattle drive—starring Robert Duvall, Tommy Lee Jones, Robert Urich, Danny Glover, Anjelica Huston, and Diane Lane—begins its four-night run on CBS.

MAY 21, 1989 A media

dramatization of a real-life media event: *Everybody's Baby: The Rescue of Jessica McClure,* is aired as a TV-movie starring Patty Duke and Roxana Zal, on ABC.

JULY 23, 1989 Fox Broadcasting Company's *America's Most Wanted* and *Totally Hidden Video* win their time slots, and for the first time the upstart "fourth network" beats ABC, CBS, and NBC.

AUGUST 3, 1989 Diane Sawyer, wooed away from CBS's *60 Minutes,* teams up with hard-nosed reporter Sam Donaldson (she will characterize it as "Emily Dickinson meets The Terminator") in ABC's TV news-magazine *PrimeTime Live.* Despite denials of personality differences, they will soon be co-anchoring from different cities.

AUGUST 26, 1989 *TV Guide* finds itself in a mini-controversy when its cover illustration of Oprah Winfrey looking sleek and sexy is discovered to be a composite made up of Oprah's head and Ann-Margret's body, appropriated from another photo.

OCTOBER 12, 1989 *This Old House* on PBS introduces its Bob Vila replacement—Steve Thomas, on somewhat equal footing with master carpenter Norm Abram—as it hammers away at its 11th season.

OCTOBER 17, 1989 At 5:04 P.M., Al Michaels is in the middle of a pregame show for the third game of the World Series at San Francisco's Candlestick Park when a major earthquake hits, knocking the show off the air, and turning the night into a television-news event.

OCTOBER 21, 1989 Billy

Crystal sees if *perestroika* has a funny bone in his comedy special from the Soviet Union, *Midnight Train to Moscow,* on HBO.

NOVEMBER 9, 1989 TV witnesses an event that only weeks before seemed impossible: the opening of the Berlin Wall, and the end of the Cold War era.

DECEMBER 18, 1989 A CBS airing of a "lost" episode from 1956 that had never been reshown becomes the "*I Love Lucy*" Christmas Special—and is the highest-rated Christmas special of 1989.

JANUARY 14, 1990 *America's Funniest Home Videos* premieres on ABC; *The Simpsons* premieres on the Fox network.

APRIL 8, 1990 A damn fine piece of pie, a cup of java, and thou—and Laura Palmer dead and wrapped in plastic: David Lynch's bizarrely humorous *Twin Peaks* premieres with a two-hour TV-movie episode on ABC.

APRIL 15, 1990 *In Living Color,* a show of social humor with a multi-ethnic cast, premieres on the Fox network.

APRIL 21, 1990 In a significant first, the antidrug special *Cartoon All-Stars to the Rescue* is shown at the same Saturday-morning time on ABC, CBS, NBC, and Fox Broadcasting, as well as Black Entertainment Television, Nickelodeon, and the USA Network. Featuring ALF, Bugs Bunny, the Chipmunks, Daffy Duck, the Smurfs, Winnie the Pooh, and one of the Teenage Mutant Ninja Turtles, the show aims its message at the 20 million 5-to-11-year-olds who watch Saturday-morning cartoon shows.

MAY 16, 1990 The bright lights of imagination flicker and dim as Jim Henson, creator of the Muppets, dies in New York City of pneumonia at the age of 54.

MAY 21, 1990 In one of television's most memorable farewells, *Newhart*'s final episode has Dick Loudon hit on the head with a golf ball—only to prove to be a figment of the imagination of Bob Hartley, the character of Bob Newhart's previous show.

MAY 31, 1990 *Seinfeld*, starring stand-up comedian Jerry Seinfeld in a format-bending sitcom, debuts on NBC.

JUNE 18, 1990 Fulfilling composer Richard Wagner's dream of having audiences see his four operas in the *Der Ring des Nibelungen* performed on four consecutive nights, PBS begins the 17-hour, English-subtitled Metropolitan Opera production of *The Ring* with *Das Rheingold* tonight, followed by *Die Walküre, Siegfried,* and *Götterdämmerung.*

JULY 12, 1990 *Northern Exposure,* starring Rob Morrow as a doctor bound by contract to practice medicine for five years in the tiny town of Cicely, Alaska, debuts this night, becomes the surprise hit of the summer, and is renewed for fall.

AUGUST 5, 1990 Madonna ends her global "Blond Ambition" tour in Nice, France, and HBO shows that concert on a tape-delayed basis.

SEPTEMBER 15, 1990 *TV Guide* breaks tradition and issues four Fall Preview issues over as many consecutive weeks.

SEPTEMBER 21, 1990 Burt Reynolds returns to TV in *Evening Shade* on CBS.

SEPTEMBER 23, 1990 *The Civil War,* an 11-hour miniseries that was five years in the making and which includes the voice-overs of Jason Robards, Jr., Julie Harris, Morgan Freeman, and Sam Waterston, begins on PBS.

NOVEMBER 11, 1990 Patty Duke plays herself in *Call Me Anna,* an ABC TV-movie based on her best-selling book about the traumas she experienced growing up as a child star and her subsequent battle against manic-depression.

DECEMBER 1, 1990 Some of the biggest names in pop music, including David Byrne, U2, and the Neville Brothers, contribute music videos of Cole Porter songs in a 90-minute special, *Red Hot & Blue,* geared to raising money for AIDS research.

JANUARY 1, 1991 There are now 93.1 million homes with TV sets in the U.S., of which 98 percent have a color TV, 64 percent have two or more sets, and 60.3 percent have cable, according to a Nielsen survey.

JANUARY 13, 1991 NBC revives *Dark Shadows,* which ran on ABC from 1966 to 1971, first as a four-hour, two-part movie premiering this night, and then as a short-lived series, with Ben Cross as Barnabas Collins (played in the original by Jonathan Frid) and Jean Simmons.

JANUARY 16, 1991 After a months-long buildup and the passing of a United Nations deadline for it to leave Kuwait, Iraq is attacked by allied forces

in Operation Desert Storm— and the networks eliminate all regular programming to provide continuous news coverage of the event, with CNN's Bernard Shaw, Peter Arnett, and John Holliman reporting from right in the middle in Baghdad.

FEBRUARY 12, 1991 Nancy Weston survives her ovarian cancer, but Gary Shepherd is killed in a car accident on the way to the hospital, in *thirtysomething.*

FEBRUARY 17, 1991 A "r-r-really big" (and surprising) "shew": a CBS retrospective of clips from the old *Ed Sullivan Show* is watched by more than one-third of all people with TV sets, and is the season's second-highest-rated special (only the Academy Awards telecast attracts more viewers).

MARCH 3, 1991 One of America's least funny—but most seen—Home Videos is made: George Holliday looks from his terrace to see Los Angeles police beating a black suspect named Rodney King. Holliday's home-video footage of the incident was seen nationally on network newscasts and led to the indictment of four officers and an investigation of police-brutality allegations across the U.S.

APRIL 8, 1991 The entire U.S. TV-viewing population—and every supermarket tabloid in America—seems to go on a Michael Landon vigil, after the star of *Bonanza, Little House on the Prairie,* and *Highway to Heaven* announces to the press that he has incurable pancreatic cancer. He dies July 1, 1991.

MAY 3, 1991 What would life have been like at Southfork had J. R. Ewing never lived? That's the concept in the two-hour series finale after 13 seasons of *Dallas,* on CBS.

JULY 1, 1991 The Courtroom Television Network, a cable channel that offers televised real trials 24 hours a day, begins operation.

JULY 27, 1991 *TV Guide* publishes its 2,000th issue.

AUGUST 18, 1991 American TV is witness to something no one ever thought they would see: an attempted coup to depose Soviet President Mikhail Gorbachev, the dramatic rise of anticoup resistance leader and hero Boris Yeltsin, and the beginning of the end of the Soviet Union.

SEPTEMBER 20, 1991 *Brooklyn Bridge* premieres on CBS.

OCTOBER 11, 1991 America stands transfixed in front of TV screens everywhere as the Senate hearings on the confirmation of Clarence Thomas to the Supreme Court turn to the sexual-harassment charges of law professor Anita Hill and Thomas's defense.

DECEMBER 2, 1991 Network news dives to the supermarket-tabloid level as it begins its breathless, media-circus coverage of the William Kennedy Smith rape trial.

MAY 22, 1992 Johnny Carson ends his hosting stint on *The Tonight Show,* leaving Jay Leno to defend the supremacy of the late-night show on NBC.

INDEX